HISTORY OF
THE UNITED STATES

VOLUME III

THE PONY EXPRESS, 1860

Painted by Maynard Dixon for the Wells Fargo Bank,
San Francisco

THE MARCH OF DEMOCRACY

A
HISTORY OF THE UNITED STATES

By

James Truslow Adams

Volume III

CIVIL WAR AND RECONSTRUCTION

NEW YORK

CHARLES SCRIBNER'S SONS

CONTENTS

ILLUSTRATIONS

ILLUSTRATIONS

x

ILLUSTRATIONS

ILLUSTRATIONS

ILLUSTRATIONS

xiii

ILLUSTRATIONS

ILLUSTRATIONS

END OF VOLUME

GREAT SCENES AND PERSONAGES
OF OUR HISTORY

XV

ILLUSTRATIONS

VOLUME III

CIVIL WAR AND RECONSTRUCTION

CHAPTER I

WAR COMES AT LAST

THE tension of the nation could be felt clearly in the Congress which sat through the winter and spring months of 1860. Not only did its members go armed but it is said that armed supporters of the two parties often crowded the galleries. Almost any move precipitated a crisis. For example, debate over a bill the purpose of which was to grant land free of charge to settlers in the West brought out all the antagonism of the South to the increasing of population outside of its own borders, and clearly showed the difficulty in which the Democratic Party found itself when trying to please both the South and the West. In February, Jefferson Davis gave warning to the head of that party, Douglas, by introducing a resolution demanding a slave code for all of the Territories. In spite of straddling, it was evident that the Illinois senator, who was also a Presidential aspirant, would find it difficult indeed to keep his party a national one.

In April the Democrats held their convention at Charleston, South Carolina—the first time they had gone south of Mason and Dixon's line. Caleb Cushing, of Massachusetts, was chairman, and although there was scarcely a man of national reputation in the meeting, the Douglas wing was in the majority. A platform embodying Davis's demand for a Territorial slave code was voted down, and one more consonant with Douglas's stand was adopted, the change resulting in the withdrawal of al-

DEMOCRATIC
STATE CENTRAL COMMITTEE.

IN VIEW OF THE RESOLUTION ADOPTED IN Convention of Delegates of the Several States, who withdrew from the Charleston Convention, and at the request of members of the South Carolina Delegation, a meeting of the Central Committee of the Democratic party in South Carolina, will be held in Columbia, on *Wednesday*, the 9th May, for consideration of important business.

THEODORE G. BARKER,

May 5   o 2   Chairman of State Central Committee.

ANNOUNCEMENT OF A POLITICAL MEETING FOLLOWING SOUTH CAROLINA'S WITHDRAWAL FROM THE DEMOCRATIC CONVENTION

From "The Charleston Courier" of May 5, 1860, in the Confederate Museum, Richmond.

most all of the delegates from South Carolina, Georgia, Florida, Alabama, Mississippi, Louisiana, Texas, and Arkansas. The seceders held a convention of their own later at Richmond, but even the regular Democrats who remained in Charleston could not agree on a candidate after 57 ballots, and adjourned to meet at Baltimore on

June 18. Douglas had not been able to poll more than 152½ votes of the necessary 202.

Meanwhile, the Republicans met at Chicago on May 16. No delegates to this convention appeared from the Carolinas, Tennessee, Georgia, or any of the Gulf States except Texas, and it was a question whether some of the delegates from the slave States really represented anybody, as has been said, but themselves, although they were allowed to be seated. The party generally expected the nomination of Senator William H. Seward of New York, but as the result of only three ballots it became evident that he could not win and Abraham Lincoln received the unanimous vote of the convention. Although the nation had watched him as he had swung around Illinois in his debate with Douglas, his future greatness was wholly unsurmised, and it was with dire forebodings, difficult for us to appreciate now, that great numbers in the new Republican Party saw this rather uncouth Westerner, who had never held high office and whose abilities as an executive were greatly mistrusted, chosen to lead instead of the noted Seward, who as Governor of New York and senator in Washington had long been before the public in responsible and notable offices.

The Republicans were confident of victory against the divided and demoralized Democrats, although they knew that they themselves would have no strength except in the North and West. The Republican Party of 1860 was distinctly a sectional one, and in spite of many

3

of the Abolitionists having joined it, it was a very practical one. To succeed it must carry not only States like New York and Pennsylvania, on account of their heavy votes in the Electoral College, but also the newer West, where it undertook to enlist the support of the settlers, notably of the substantial Germans and Scandinavians under the influence of men like the young immigrant, Carl Schurz of Wisconsin.

There was no difficulty about choosing a Vice-President to run with Lincoln in the person of Hannibal Hamlin of Maine, and the platform was skilfully constructed to please as many of the discordant elements, not yet welded, as possible. Quoting the Declaration of Independence it deduced that "the normal condition of all the territory of the United States is that of freedom"; rebuked talk of disunion; stood for States' Rights and freedom in the Territories; branded the slave trade as a "crime against humanity"; and demanded the immediate admission of Kansas. To catch the West, it advocated free homestead lands and a railway to the Pacific, whereas for the East it suggested a tariff for the encouragement of industry. When the South heard of the proceedings at Chicago it muttered secession, but the Republicans did not even yet believe that their own success would really bring about disruption.

Meanwhile, the Democrats had been trying to arrange matters for their adjourned meeting at Baltimore, where the delegates arrived on the appointed 18th of June.

With a good deal of difficulty over the question of delegates, organization was effected in three days, but only
after most of the Southern members and a few from the
North had bolted a second time. Those who were left
nominated Douglas for the Presidency, but the seceders,
who included delegates from twenty-one of the then
thirty-three States, meeting in a near-by hall, nominated
John C. Breckenridge of Kentucky, on a pro-slavery
platform which included a demand for the annexation
of Cuba.

A fourth party, called the Constitutional Union, had
also come into being, which had existence only in this
campaign, and which nominated John Bell of Tennessee
for President, writing a platform which insisted chiefly
upon maintaining the Union and obeying the Constitution and the laws.

The Republicans were regarded as unquestionably the
strongest, and realized that neither of the other three
candidates could possibly be elected, though in a four-
cornered fight it might be possible to throw the election
into the House of Representatives, as in 1824. The chief
danger for the Republicans was the fear of the public
that if they elected Lincoln they might be bringing on
the dissolution of the Union. This fear the Republicans
laughed at and soothed, but in doing so showed either
a greater desire to win or a lesser political prescience
than the public.

THE ELECTION OF LINCOLN

When the votes were counted, the result revealed more clearly perhaps than in any other election the peculiar workings of our electoral system. It had originally been intended, of course, that the people at large should have little or nothing to do with the election of a President. The Presidential electors, chosen for the most part in early days by the State legislatures, were expected to meet in their respective States and,—by exercising a knowledge of public men and a wisdom and experience in affairs which the people could not possess,—to vote for a suitable person for President. With the development of democracy, this system, though retained as machinery, had really come to be discarded in principle, the people voting direct for electors who were pledged to vote for certain candidates for President. Owing, however, to the fact that the number of electors from each State has to be the same as the number of the State's senators and representatives in Congress, a majority of *popular* votes under our system does not mean a majority of *electoral* votes.

To over-simplify the example in order to make it clear, we may say that four States with 1,000,000 population each might have one electoral vote each, and another with 5,000,000 population might have five. If all the people in the four States and 2,000,000 in the fifth State

6

voted for Jones, Jones would have 6,000,000 popular
votes out of 9,000,000, but only four electoral votes. His
opponent, Brown, who polled not a single vote in four
States and only 3,000,000 in the fifth State, would have
won the five electoral votes of that State, and so be
elected President.

In 1860, Lincoln polled 1,866,452 popular votes,
Douglas 1,376,957, Breckenridge 859,781, and Bell 588,-
879, but the electoral votes were respectively 180, 12, 72,
and 39. Thus not only was Lincoln elected President,
although he polled well on to a million less votes than
his combined opponents, but Douglas, who polled about
1,377,000 popular votes to Breckenridge's 850,000, received only 12 electoral votes to the latter's 72! The
original system, devised to keep the election out of the
hands of the people, has wholly broken down, without,
however, placing the election in the hands of the people
but rather in those of chance, for it has occurred several
times that even when there have been only two parties
in the field, the candidate who received the lesser number of popular votes has been elected to office. A reasonable reorganization of what is now a senseless system
would require an amendment to the Constitution, and
that would not be easy to bring about as the political
parties are accustomed, in all their machinery and planning, to the present method.

In 1860, although the Republicans had entirely mis-
read the signs of the times, and their success at the polls

7

☛ THE QUESTION

IF LINCOLN

will be elected or not, is one which interests all parties, North and South.   Whether he

IS ELECTED

or not, the people of

SOUTH CAROLINA

(whose rights have been for a number of years trampled upon) have the advantage of supplying themselves with CLOTHING, at the well-known CAROLINA CLOTHING DEPOT, 261 King-street, at such prices as

WILL LEAD

them to be satisfied that the reputation of this Establishment has been

BOLDLY

and fearlessly maintained

FOR A

number of years, supplying its

SOUTHERN

Customers with all the Latest Styles, and at as low prices as any Clothing House *in the present*

CONFEDERACY

of all the States.
   Thankful for the liberal patronage extended, the Proprietors desire merely to inform their customers and the public generally, that their present STOCK OF CLOTHING IS COMPLETE in all its departments, and are now prepared to offer Goods on the most reasonable and satisfactory terms.   A call is therefore solicited by
   OTTOLENGUIS, WILLIS & BARRETT,
November 5   261 King-street.

THE "CAROLINA CLOTHING DEPOT" MADE GOOD USE OF DAILY EVENTS
IN ADVERTISING, AS THE SMALL PRINT ABOVE WILL SHOW
From "*The Charleston Courier*" *of November* 7, 1860, *in the
Confederate Museum, Richmond.*

was to spell secession in spite of their denials, it was fortunate that chance had given us Lincoln to occupy the

8

White House. Whatever might have been possible under happier conditions, passions had been aroused too deeply and for too long to permit of peaceful compromise. We had at last come to the inevitable turning which led to the field of blood. Whatever Republicans in the North might have said in the campaign, secession at once became the leading issue in the South, when the result of the election became known.

The Charleston Courier struck the popular Southern note when it estimated that the immediate drop in the price of slaves would amount to $430,000,000 for the whole South, and asserted that "slave property is the foundation of all property in the South. When security in this is shaken, all other property partakes of its instability. Banks, stocks, bonds, must be influenced. . . . The ruin of the South, by the emancipation of her slaves, is not like the ruin of any other people. . . . It is the loss of liberty, property, home, country—everything that makes life worth having."

There were approximately 4,000,000 slaves in the Southern and border States. A prime field hand in the cotton belt was worth $1500 to $2000, but if we take the average of all as somewhat under $400 each, the Southerners had $1,500,000,000 invested in this form of property. Had emancipation come about as in the British Empire by freeing the slave and compensating the owner, the South would still have had to face a great economic and social problem in training the negro to rise from the status and characteristics of a slave to those of a free laborer. This, indeed, might not have been an insuperable difficulty. One can only surmise what might have been the results of a sudden or even a comparatively gradual substitution in the South for the $1,500,000,000 of capital locked up in slaves of a similar amount from compensation which would have been liquid. With free labor and adequate liquid capital, the South might have solved the social problem and entered upon a new economic and industrial phase. There is little use, however, in considering such vague possibilities.

In the first place, the South knew it would *not* be compensated. For several decades the Abolitionists had been shouting for emancipation or dissolution of the Union. It was true that the government had never claimed to interfere with slavery in the States where it had been legal, but that was not the view of the increasing anti-slavery party in the North. Even Lincoln had said that eventually the Union must become all one thing or the other. As it would obviously never become all slave, the inference was clear.

The discussion had for long centred about slavery, and, as *The Courier* had rightly pointed out, all Southern property was dependent upon that in the last analysis. The Southerners had watched the rising tide of Abolitionism, and had feared that eventually it must spell ruin for their property almost precisely in the same way as, many decades later, the brewers and distillers watched

the rising tide of Prohibitionism and the threatened ruin
of their property, except that the situation was infinitely
more serious for the South, where emancipation meant
confiscation of most of the working capital of the richer
element in an entire section.

Although there are no accurate statistics, it is probable
that the great majority of Southern whites owned no
slaves at all, the estimates placing slave-owning families
as one in five, but this had little influence on the general
situation. Not only did the slaveless white hope to own
one some day, as the Northern poor man hoped to ac-
cumulate property, but if the crash occurred in all forms
of investments,—lands, banks, and so on,—the slaveless
Southerner would suffer with the slave-owners. In addition, there were the strong racial feeling, and the social
and economic complications that might ensue from turning loose 4,000,000 blacks to compete as freemen with
the poorer whites.

This brings us to the point that although slavery was
the topic foremost in the discussions, there were in the
background all sorts of intangibles. The whole way of
life and the outlook on it in the South had become
entirely different from those in the North, and each section naturally prized its own and, unfortunately, despised
those of the other. The South had had a great history, and
had given a great heritage to the Union. The first successful settlement had been within its borders and not in those
of New England. Virginia had for long been the most

important colony, and throughout the colonial period the part which the South had played had been as brilliant

CHARLESTON

MERCURY

EXTRA:

Passed unanimously at 1.15 o'clock, P. M. December 20th, 1860.

AN ORDINANCE

To dissolve the Union between the State of South Carolina and other States united with her under the compact entitled "The Constitution of the United States of America."

We, the People of the State of South Carolina, in Convention assembled, do declare and ordain, and it is hereby declared and ordained,

That the Ordinance adopted by us in Convention, on the twenty-third day of May, in the year of our Lord one thousand seven hundred and eighty-eight, whereby the Constitution of the United States of America was ratified, and also, all Acts and parts of Acts of the General Assembly of this State, ratifying amendments of the said Constitution, are hereby repealed; and that the union now subsisting between South Carolina and other States, under the name of "The United States of America," is hereby dissolved.

ABBEVILLE

BANNER

EXTRA.

Passed unanimously at 1.15 o'clock, P. M. December 20th, 1860.

AN ORDINANCE

To dissolve the Union between the State of South Carolina and other States united with her under the compact entitled "The Constitution of the United States of America."

We, the People of the State of South Carolina, in Convention assembled, do declare and ordain, and it is hereby declared and ordained,

That the Ordinance adopted by us in Convention, on the twenty-third day of May, in the year of our Lord one thousand seven hundred and eighty-eight, whereby the Constitution of the United States of America was ratified, and also, all Acts and parts of Acts of the General Assembly of this State, ratifying amendments of the said Constitution, are hereby repealed; and that the union now subsisting between South Carolina and other States, under the name of "The United States of America," is hereby dissolved.

THE

UNION

IS

DISSOLVED!

THE

UNION

IS

DISSOLVED!

EXTRAS OF *THE CHARLESTON MERCURY* AND *THE ABBEVILLE BANNER* ANNOUNCING SECESSION

From the originals in the Confederate Museum, Richmond.

as that of the North. In the Revolution and the early years of the Republic the North had no such list of leaders to give to the common cause as the South had furnished in Washington, Jefferson, Madison, Monroe, John Marshall, and others.

Both sections had started with slavery, but economic conditions in the North had made it unprofitable and its passing had been painless. In the South, on the other hand, economic conditions had fastened it on the people with such apparent inevitability that even Lincoln had said he would not know how to get rid of it if he were a Southerner. It had been a huge misfortune for the South. It had developed its social life on a false basis; forced it to justify itself by opposing the strong moral currents of the day; sapped its intellectual life; made it intensely sectional in its complete preoccupation with trying to save what was in truth a lost cause; and bred that unhealthy romanticism and super-sensitiveness which are the concomitants of such conditions.

On the other hand, the Northern anti-slavery men, without sympathy for the plight of the other section of our nation, and with no statesmanlike plan to offer, cruelly and bitterly assailed the South in every aspect of its life,—economic, intellectual and moral. The South, feeling itself in no way inferior to the North, returned the scorn and disdain with interest, and believed itself wantonly singled out for attack by a portion of the Union bent insanely upon its destruction. The Southerners' hopes of keeping the balance at least even by the extension of slave territory had failed, and, to many, Southern civilization seemed to be standing at bay when the Republicans elected a sectional and Northern administration. The November election was the signal for action but Lincoln would not be inaugurated until March, and meanwhile Buchanan, the honest but weak and incapable signer of the Ostend Manifesto, was President for another four months.

SOUTHERN STATES SECEDE

South Carolina at once called a convention to consider the situation. This met first at Columbia, and then, on account of small-pox, adjourned to Charleston. In the convention, assertions were made that the Constitutional guarantees had been destroyed, that for its own industrial benefit the North had persisted in burdening the South with heavy tariffs, that it had bought men to go to Kansas and armed them to prevent that State from becoming slave, that it was intent on abolition, and that, finally, there was no possibility of safe compromise or of continuing the bonds of union. On December 20, 1860, the convention repealed the Act which had bound the State to the Constitution in 1788 and declared that the union of South Carolina with the United States of America was at an end.

Even yet throughout the South there were conservative men, like Alexander H. Stephens and Jefferson Davis himself, who advised caution and delay, but the secessionist elements rapidly gained control in the cotton States, and by February 1, Georgia, Florida, Alabama,

Mississippi, and Louisiana had seceded, to be followed by Texas on the 23d. In the same month in which Texas seceded, delegates from each of these other States met at Montgomery, Alabama, to draw up a provisional constitution for the "Confederate States of America," and to elect officials of the new government.

In main outline the new constitution followed the now discarded Federal one of the United States, but there were a few notable alterations, and, probably owing to the haste necessary, there were no definite relations established between the sovereignties of the individual States and that of the Confederation. In most respects rather inferior to the old Constitution, in at least two the new one contained marked improvements. One of these was the provision that the President, instead of having to veto an appropriation bill as a whole or not at all, was enabled to veto specific sections in it,—a device that could prevent an enormous amount of ill-advised expenditure of public funds. The other point provided that members of the President's Cabinet might be given seats in Congress and take part in the debates, thus grafting one of the most valuable portions of the British Parliamentary system on to our Congressional one. No provision was made for a Supreme Court, and the slave trade was prohibited, but slavery was protected and guaranteed extension in any new territory which the Confederacy might acquire.

Although it was to have been expected that one of the

"fire-eaters" and ardent Secessionists would have been elected to head the new government, such men as W. L. Yancey, Barnwell Rhett, and Robert Toombs were discarded and Jefferson Davis was elected President, with Alexander H. Stephens as Vice-President. The passing over of the claims of South Carolinians to high office, for Rhett got none at all, roused that State, foremost always in threatened and actual secession, to wrath. Moreover, Davis, from the standpoint of conciliating all Southern interests, was not wise in the selection of his Cabinet, which contained scarcely any of the "aristocracy" and only one man, Judah P. Benjamin, who was nationally well-known, a distinguished New Orleans lawyer who had also been United States senator.

Benjamin, however, who was an English Jew, had not been popular among the planter aristocrats, and President Davis himself, who had been born of a rather shiftless father on the Kentucky frontier, did not get on well with them, which perhaps helped to draw him closer to Benjamin. Davis, delicate in health, was sensitive, sincere and honest, with an unfortunate flair for trusting the judgment of the wrong people, including himself. He was a West Point graduate, and in his career as a colonel in the army, as a member of Congress, as Secretary of War in Pierce's Cabinet, and as United States senator, he had acquired above all a supreme self-confidence in his abilities as a soldier, a confidence that unhappily his ability did not warrant.

While all this was happening in the South, the position of the weak and amiable Buchanan in the White House was one of extreme delicacy and difficulty. Seven States of the Union of which he was President had seceded and formed a separate government, defying that of the United States. His difficulties had, indeed, thickened from the day his successor was elected. Even had the President been a man of great strength and ability it would have been almost impossible to strike out a policy of his own, when he had only four months to serve and knew nothing of the policy of the man who would soon have to take up the reins.

There were eight Federal forts with garrisons in such States as would probably, and soon did, secede, including Fort Sumter at Charleston. Major Anderson, a devoted Union officer, was in command there, and in January, 1861, an effort was made to reinforce and victual him by sea. A small merchant ship, *Star of the West,* was despatched from New York, but on her arrival at Charleston she was fired on by Confederate batteries, which Anderson did not feel justified in silencing by his own fire, and she was forced to return. There was yet hope in the North that permanent secession might be avoided, and, wisely, Buchanan procrastinated.

Congress was debating another compromise measure, suggested this time by Crittenden, the successor in the Kentucky senatorship to the great compromiser Clay. The plan included the re-establishment of the old Missouri Compromise line of 36° 30′ for Territories only, a hands-off policy by Congress in States and in the District of Columbia, and a provision for indemnifying fugitive-slave owners if the slaves were not returned. This was the best of a number of measures proposed, and might have been accepted by the cotton senators had the Republicans agreed, but they absolutely refused to do so, and in this they were firmly backed by the President-elect, Lincoln, who believed that it would only result in a vigorous Southern insistence upon further territorial expansion to the south of us. Crittenden, having been defeated in his measure in the Senate, suggested a referendum to the people at large, and while this was being debated, the seven Southern States seceded, and the situation became greatly altered.

A "Peace Conference," held in February at the suggestion of Virginia, failed to provide any practical suggestions, and the only plans brought forward were clearly unsatisfactory to both sections. While all these efforts to avert catastrophe were being made, the 4th of March was drawing near. When it came, the supreme responsibility rested upon Lincoln.

LINCOLN'S INAUGURATION

In his inaugural address the incoming President dwelt on the fact that there was no intention of interfering with slavery in the slave States. He asserted the validity and necessity of enforcing the Fugitive Slave

LITTLE BO-PEEP'S FEARS FOR HER FOOLISH SHEEP AS SHE SEES EUROPEAN POWERS
READY TO DEVOUR THE SECEDING STATES

From "Strong's Dime Caricature," 1861, in the Library of Congress, Washington.

Law, and discussed calmly the nature of the Federal Union. That Union, he believed, could not be broken without the consent of all the States, and he declared that to the extent of his ability, in spite of resolutions, he would see that the Federal laws were everywhere enforced, adding that in his opinion no State was outside of the Union. Why, he continued, should that Union be destroyed? "One section of our country believes slavery is *right* and ought to be extended, while the other believes it is *wrong* and ought not to be extended. This is the only substantial dispute. . . . Physically speaking, we cannot separate. We cannot remove our respective sections from each other, nor build an impassable wall between them." The country, he asserted, belonged to all the people who inhabited it, and if they grew weary of their institutions they could amend them constitutionally or attempt to overthrow them by revolution. "Nothing valuable can be lost by taking time."

Closing, he spoke to both North and South. "In *your* hands, my dissatisfied fellow-countrymen, and not in *mine,* is the momentous issue of civil war. The government will not assail *you.* You can have no conflict without yourselves being the aggressors. *You* have no oath registered in heaven to destroy the government, while *I* shall have the most solemn one to 'preserve, protect, and defend' it. I am loath to close. We are not enemies, but friends. We must not be enemies. Though passion may have strained, it must not break our bonds of affection.

20

The mystic chords of memory, stretching from every battle-field and patriot grave to every living heart and hearthstone all over this broad land, will yet swell the chorus of the Union, when again touched, as surely they will be, by the better angels of our nature."

There had been much prejudice against Lincoln, whose character was not yet understood, and, indeed, had not fully developed, and whose appearance and inveterate habit of seeming flippant and careless when most serious always did him harm. The Inaugural, now one of our famous State Papers, was regarded when it was delivered with almost universal disappointment, and was generally considered to be vacillating and weak. The Southerners failed to see the determination behind it, and in the North, James Gordon Bennett, the influential owner of *The New York Herald,* wrote in an editorial that the address would have been "as instructive if President Lincoln had contented himself with telling his audience a funny story and let them go." With all the services which Greeley had rendered to the nation as editor, and they had been great, he was now to enter upon a stage of his career in which sound judgment seemed to have abandoned him on most occasions, and throughout Lincoln's term the President was to be fiercely and unfairly opposed by one of the most influential of New York journals.

Although only seven States had actually seceded when Lincoln entered upon office, it was impossible to induce any Southerner to serve in his Cabinet, which was thus entirely sectional. For Secretary of State the choice natu-

THE INAUGURAL ADDRESS.

The Inaugural Address of the new President does not require of us the usual synopsis of such documents made for the benefit of indolent readers; for apart from the interest with which it is universally looked for, its brevity will bring it within the compass of the efforts of the most reluctant readers Of Messages, while its plainness and directness of speech will make its meaning clear to the lowest capacity. It is marked by no useless words and no feeble expression; "he who runs may read" it, and to twenty millions of people it will carry the tidings, glad or not, as the case may be, that the Federal Government of the United States is still in existence, with a Man at the head of it.

The Address can not fail to exercise a happy influence upon the country. The tone of almost tenderness with which the South is called upon to return to her allegiance, can not fail to convince even those who differ from Mr. Lincoln that he earnestly and seriously desires to avoid all difficulty and disturbance, while the firmness with which he avows his determination to obey the simple letter of his duty, must command the respect of the whole country, while it carries conviction of his earnestness of purpose, and of his courage to enforce it.

EXCERPTS FROM HORACE GREELEY'S EDITORIAL COMMENTS ON PRESIDENT LINCOLN'S INAUGURAL ADDRESS
From "The New York Tribune," March 5, 1861.

rally fell upon Seward, Lincoln's chief opponent for the Presidential nomination and one of the ablest men in the party. Salmon P. Chase of Ohio went to the Treasury, and, in fulfillment of a bargain made at the nominating convention, of which Lincoln did not know at the time but which he felt he could not repudiate afterward, the notorious political boss of Pennsylvania, Simon Cameron, became Secretary of War. It was the price Cameron had demanded for swinging the delegates from Pennsylvania, with its heavy electoral vote, into the Lincoln column. Gideon Welles of Connecticut was appointed to the Navy Department, and, approaching the South, Montgomery Blair of Maryland and Edward Bates of Missouri were made Postmaster General and Attorney General. It was a much abler group of men than Davis had been able to gather around him in the Confederate Cabinet, but was, nevertheless, to give the President ample trouble.

Whatever irresponsible hot-heads among the people on either side might demand, both Davis and Lincoln, on whom supreme responsibility rested, wisely decided to move slowly. This was particularly necessary in Lincoln's case, as he was hoping to save as many States as possible, especially those on the border, from seceding, and therefore wished to refrain from any use of force until the Secessionists had themselves started armed rebellion by an overt act of war. Toward the end of March, he did order supplies to be forwarded by the navy to Fort Sumter, but Seward was chafing at what he considered the President's senseless and dangerous delay, which he misinterpreted as due to complete lack of policy. It must be remembered that at this time Lincoln was still regarded as a backwoods politician whom chance had put into the White House, and an inexperienced man who, the Secretary of State thought, would have to be guided and used by himself and other statesmen.

Mulling the situation over, the secretary, who really did possess ability but on this occasion lost all sense of realities, had formulated an inconceivably fantastic plan, which he presented to Lincoln on April 1. The two important points in it were, first, that Lincoln, in Seward's opinion, being apparently incapable of formulating policies, should place himself in the secretary's hands, abdicating all real power and retaining only the shadow; and, second, that in order to reunite the North and South the best policy would be to force a foreign war, preferably with France and Spain, and perhaps also with Russia and England! When confronted with this extraordinary paper by his chief officer of state, the President merely remarked that if this "must be done, I must do it," and mercifully kept the document concealed for the rest of his life, so it was not until years later that the discovery was made of how complete an ass Seward had made of himself.

The egoistic secretary had also been negotiating with three agents of the Confederate Government, very much apparently on his own responsibility, for he promised them that no effort would be made to relieve Sumter when, in truth, Lincoln had already ordered the vessels from New York. This fact having been discovered by the

Southern agents, the Confederate Cabinet decided, after much hesitation, to capture the position before relief arrived, and on April 12 the bombardment from the shore batteries began against the fort, which was on an island.

Major Anderson and his force replied as well as they could, but after a continuous bombardment of nearly thirty-six hours, it seemed evident to Anderson that the situation was hopeless, and he surrendered. Meanwhile the relief ships had arrived but without the most important one in the small fleet, which Seward, although he had nothing to do with the navy, had detached and sent to Florida by special order. In any case, the eventual result would have been no different, and after marching out with the honors of war, the Federal troops from Fort Sumter were embarked on the ships and carried back to the North.

THE WAR BEGINS

The war so long dreaded had at last begun. The South had fired the first shot, had captured a Federal fort by force, and when the Stars and Stripes were hauled down there could no longer be any ignoring of the stark fact of rebellion. If in spite of what Webster and other Northern Unionists had declared, the South had really believed there might be peaceful secession, that section was now undeceived. A wave of patriotic emotion for the Union swept like a great tide over the hearts of men in the Northern States. Even among many in the South, who honestly felt that they must place allegiance to their State above that to the Union, there was sorrow at the breaking of the old ties. Two days after Sumter had surrendered, Lincoln issued a call for 75,000 volunteers, and immediately militia regiments were on their way to Washington from the North.

The call to war on April 15 meant that a final decision must be reached by those States which had been wavering. They must either fight for the Union or join the Confederacy. So far it had been only South Carolina and the Gulf States which had taken the plunge, while the upper South, in somewhat closer touch with Northern civilization and less irrevocably tied to the belief in slavery as a fundamental economic necessity, had been willing to try for a while longer to work out some compromise within the Union.

North Carolina had actually voted against secession, but had to reverse its decision when Virginia made its position impossible by joining the Confederacy. Perhaps no State which seceded did so more reluctantly than the Old Dominion, oldest and in many respects greatest of the original thirteen. Opinion was bitterly divided but on April 17 the State Convention, by a vote of 103 to 46, resolved to submit the question to the people, and on the 17th of May the verdict was for the South. Arkansas had seceded on the 6th and Tennessee on the 7th, North Carolina following on the 20th, making in all eleven States in the Confederate Union.

Flag of Fort Sumter. FORT SUMPTER.

A SOUTHERN SONG.

AIR—"Star Spangled Banner."

O say, have you heard how the Flag of our sires
Was insulted by traitors, in boastful alliance,
When for Union's dear cause, over Sumter's red fires,
In the front of Rebellion it waved its defiance?
Over Sumter it flew,
Over patriots true,
And through all that fierce conflict still dearer it grew.
'Twas the Flag of Fort Sumter! we saw it still wave
O'er the heads of the Free and the hearts of the Brave!

That banner so bright, it was nailed to its mast,
As a sign that for Freedom there's still no surrender!
And the staff that up-bore it, in battle's dread blast,
Yet remains to be raised by its gallant defender!
Over Sumter it flew,
Over ANDERSON true,
And through all the dark conflict still dearer it grew,
'Twas the flag of Fort Sumter! O long may it wave
O'er the heads of the Free and the hearts o! the Brave!

Come now and gather round me,
A story I'll relate,
It happened near a city
Of South Carolina state.

CHORUS.

And now Old Uncle Abe,
If you'll take good advice!
You'll ne'er invade our Southern soil.
Think o'er the matter twice

There was in Charleston harbor,
A fortress strong and great,
Commanded by Bob Anderson,
Which caused much debate.
And now Old Uncle Abe, &c.

Now Beauregard did loudly swear,
He would Fort Sumpter take,
And for to carry out his threat,
Did many batteries make.
And now Old Uncle Abe, &c.

PARTS OF A NORTHERN AND A SOUTHERN SONG ON THE FALL OF SUMTER

From the Collection of Union and Confederate Songs in the Library of Congress, Washington.

27

The influence of slavery, the natural drag of the other Southern States which were more akin to these border States in mode of life and thought, a political philosophy of extreme States' Rights, and other mixed motives and sentiments, determined the result in the upper South, but not without far more division of opinion than in the cotton country. Partly from long hostility to its eastern section, the Virginians in the far-western part of that State refused to secede, and from this refusal was born the State of West Virginia, later admitted to the Union in 1863.

The important border States of Maryland, Kentucky, and Missouri were still uncertain, and it was largely to win them for the Union during anxious weeks that Lincoln insisted the war was not for the abolition of slavery but solely to preserve the Union. Unfortunately this statement of facts alienated to some extent the extreme anti-slavery opinion in the North, and also, as we shall see later, public opinion in England. The policy, however, bore important fruit, for Kentucky voted against secession, and although Missouri was in constant internal turmoil throughout the war it also remained in the Union. That Maryland should remain in it was essential, but the secessionist movement there was strong, and Southern sympathizers had mobbed the regiments from the North as they moved toward Washington through Baltimore, and had destroyed bridges and railroads. Although the State was to remain divided in sentiment throughout the struggle, it also was saved to the Union, and with it the small slave State of Delaware.

Thus eleven seceded States faced the twenty-three, of which four were slave, which still formed the original Union which they were determined to preserve by force. Now that peaceful secession was proved to have been a fallacy, it might seem at first glance as though the South had staked her all on a desperate throw. The North had a white population of approximately 21,000,000 to the South's 5,500,000, or if we divide the population of the border States of hesitating allegiance, the figures might have stood 20,000,000 to 6,500,000. Moreover, the transportation system of the North was far superior to that of the South, as were its cash resources, banking facilities, ships of war and commerce, and factories for producing every sort of necessary article for war or trade. Comparatively, the South was destitute of the means of providing by large-scale production almost all the things it would need, except food, and if the North blockaded her ports, she would be unable to import necessities or export her cotton.

THE ADVANTAGES OF THE SOUTH

On the other hand she had advantages, some real and some fancied, which at first disguised the hopelessness of her struggle. If the disparity in the numbers of troops was bound to be heavily in her disfavor, she had her 3,500,000 slaves who could be kept at work back of the lines, releasing an unusually high percentage of her white population for actual fighting. The Southerner, used to an outdoor life, was also considered to be a better fighter than the Northerner from shop and office and factory and, at least in the beginning, the Southerners were better led.

To a great extent they had been brought up in the old English tradition, and had never been attracted by a business career. Managing their plantations, or going into law, politics, and the army, it happened that a large number of our leading West Point graduates were from below Mason and Dixon's line. The decision that all had to make when war came, a decision which broke up families both North and South and arrayed parent against child and brother against brother, was a peculiarly difficult one for the officers in our army. Those from the South were among the finest men in that section, and it was only, for the most part, after a long agony of self-questioning as to their duty, that many of them felt compelled to resign their commissions and to fight against the Union for their homes, families, and States. Thus it happened that whatever other resources the North had at the beginning it had no officers to compare with J. E. Johnston, Braxton Bragg, P. G. T. Beauregard, James Longstreet, A. S. Johnston, T. J. Jackson, and, above all, with Robert E. Lee, who remained possibly the ablest soldier of all throughout the war.

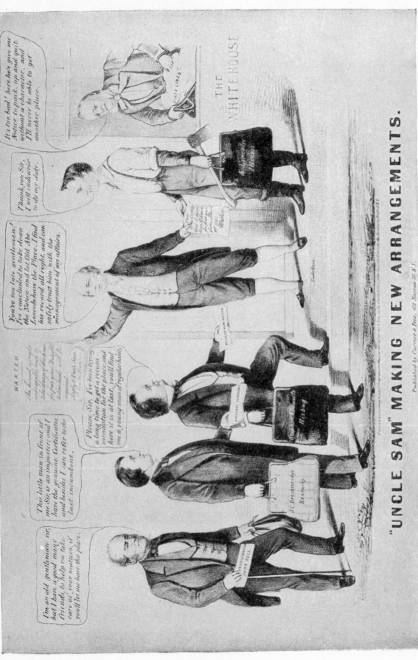

AFTER THE 1860 ELECTION

Uncle Sam announces to Douglas, Breckenridge, and Bell that he has decided to let "Old Abe Lincoln" take charge of his affairs for the next four years.

From a cartoon by Currier and Ives, in the Library of Congress.

FORD WITH PONTOON BRIDGE, BULL RUN, VIRGINIA

PART OF THE 6TH MAINE INFANTRY AFTER THE BATTLE OF FREDERICKSBURG
From photographs in the collection of the War Department.

The South also had the advantage of operating on interior lines, whereas the North would have to attack from the outside, and completely overwhelm the South if it were to be conquered. This situation neutralized to a considerable extent the disparity in numbers. Moreover, from the standpoint of being conquered, the very lack of a highly organized industrial economy, which was a disadvantage from other points of view, was an advantage from this one. In an agricultural country there is no one vital point at which an army can strike, and a war of conquest against it must to some extent be a war of attrition.

The card, however, in the hand of the South which she firmly believed would be the trump one in the war, was the need of the world for cotton. In view of the huge industrial development in the previous decades and the part that cotton was playing in it, the South was certain, as one of her senators said, that if cotton were not raised and shipped, England "would topple headlong, and carry the whole civilized world with her. . . . Cotton is king." From a combination of circumstances this was to prove false prophecy, and Northern wheat was to be crowned in place of Southern cotton, but this could not be foreseen when the South seceded with the belief that she held the key to the world's industry, and that the world therefore would have to support her.

Lastly, we may note that the South felt it had a better moral basis for the war than the North. Whatever might be thought of fine-spun interpretation of States' Rights and the original nature of the compact of Union, the fact remained that here were about 6,000,000 of people with their 3,500,000 of slaves, legally held, who only asked to be allowed to secede in peace from a Union they believed

LEE'S RESIGNATION OF HIS U. S. ARMY COMMISSION
From the original letter in the War Department, Washington.

had become inimical to their own welfare and threatening to the foundations of their whole social and economic life. As opposed to this, the slavery issue being deliberately set aside as a motive for the war, the North could only advance that of its insistence upon maintaining the Union at any cost, even by the coercion of 6,000,000 unwilling citizens in a contiguous group of States.

Not only in Europe but even in the North, there were many who felt that this was both unjust and impossible. The Union might win a decision by arms but what would become of it, if it were to have to maintain itself permanently by force? As Lee and many other Southerners who were devoted to the Union as well as to their own States felt, a Union based on bayonets instead of hearts would cease to have any value and would bring in its train a demoralization of private and public life.

For a while, this view prevailed also among our best friends in England. Slavery was the root cause of the war, it is true, but Lincoln, who with far-sighted wisdom from the beginning had made the assumption that none of the States was in reality out of the Union even if it had seceded, and who, moreover, had had to keep slavery in the background in order to win the border States, asserted that he was simply defending the Constitution, and that the Constitution defended slavery. The most liberal opinion in England, which would have been whole-heartedly with us in a war for human freedom, could not follow us in a war simply to compel a Union which was no longer desired. In general the so-called English upper classes were in favor of the South, which had in the old days been in closer personal contact with England and whose ways of life, barring the existence of slavery, the English upper class much preferred to those of the mercantile North.

In addition, the waves of revolution which only a few

years before had swept over Europe had alarmed the conservative elements, and as in Europe conservatism and monarchy were allied, as were radicalism and de-

> Can they drive the Southerners like a flock of sheep, smoke them out of their own nests like wasps, ferret them out like rabbits, and bag them like game? Let them just look forward a little, and con-sider the probable state of things next year, and the year after, and twenty years hence. Even we who sang such songs of triumph in 1814 and 1815, felt that we and all Europe would have done much bet-ter to think what we were about in 1793. If a clear foresight shows, and must show, that there must be two Federations, and that on no other footing will peace ever be made, it will be much better that it should come to pass after one year's war, than after ten or twenty. It is not as if the Union or two Unions were the only alternative. As the war proceeds, no man can tell what new, powers and combinations may arise, and particularly how far the Western States will endure the taxes and financial obligations necessary for the war. The advice we offer is only what the Americans have given to all the world. It is a hank of their own cotton—a pipe of their own tobacco. Let them

PART OF A *LONDON TIMES* EDITORIAL REFLECTING ENGLISH SYMPATHY WITH THE SOUTH AS REPRINTED IN *THE CHARLESTON COURIER* OF SEPTEMBER 30, 1861

In the Confederate Museum, Richmond.

mocracy, the English conservatives were ready to look with complacency on the break-up of the greatest ex-ample of successful democracy which the world had yet had placed before it. On the other hand, the English working class, and particularly the cotton spinners of the industrial north of England, were in favor of the great republic, and before the war was over were courageously and gladly to suffer hardship and unemployment for the cause of the Union. Throughout the war, on the whole, the British Government, as distinct from the public opinion of any one class, steered not only an impartial,

WHAT THE TYRANTS OF THE OLD WORLD THINK OF SECESSION.
"Oh! ain't we Sorry!!!"

THE JOY OF EUROPE AT SECESSION
From a cartoon in "Harper's Weekly," December 1, 1860.

but even at times a friendly, course toward the United States.

When the war broke, however, it was clear that it was to be a great struggle, and although here in America, Lincoln's assumption that there had been no legal secession might simplify matters when it might come eventually to bringing the Southern States back into the Union if the North won, the assumption also unfortunately

35

implied, as developed in the case of the Confederate schooner *Savannah*, that the men of the Southern navy, preying on our commerce, were legally mere pirates. This was a complication consequent upon the President's working theory. We ourselves might smooth such difficulties over by occasionally not letting our right hand know what our left was doing, but such a situation was impossible for foreign nations. A great maritime power like England could not treat the naval officers and crews of a newly formed nation of 6,000,000 fighting for their independence as mere pirates without transgressing the dictates of humanity.

Consequently, although the British Government never recognized the Confederacy as an independent power, it did recognize its status as a belligerent on May 13, 1861, the very day on which our new minister, Charles Francis Adams, arrived at his post in London. Although many in our North, little versed in international law, construed this as a hasty and unfriendly action, it was the only one which England could take, and Mr. Adams's position was in fact much simplified by its having been taken before he had entered upon his duties.

In general, Europe believed that the North could not conquer the South, and could not hold her permanently in subjection if it did do so. The first battle strengthened this opinion. The extra session of Congress which assembled on July 4 had authorized Lincoln to borrow $200,-000,000, issue $50,000,000 in notes, and raise the army to

500,000 men. Meanwhile we had two small armies, one of about 22,000 troops under General Patterson facing a much smaller Confederate force under General Johnston at Winchester in the Shenandoah Valley; and another of 30,000 under General McDowell, the opposing Confederate force to which was that of 23,000 men under Beauregard which was lying at Manassas. The Confederacy had made Richmond its capital, and the people of the North, demanding, as the public always does in war, immediate and tangible victories, insisted upon an instant capture of the rebel centre which it was naïvely hoped might end the struggle almost as soon as begun. On both sides there was the usual belief entertained at the beginning of all great wars, that it would be "short."

DISASTERS OF THE NORTH

Neither side as yet had a trained or properly equipped army. For the most part the troops were raw civilians, without even uniforms; and the officers, even the few from the old regular army, had had no experience in the actual handling of large bodies of men in the field. To meet the popular demand, however, in spite of the protests of old General Winfield Scott, the head of the Union army, it was decided in Washington to bring on an engagement in a thrust toward Richmond.

Patterson was ordered to keep Johnston's forces occupied while McDowell marched against Beauregard, who by July 20 had taken a position behind the small stream called Bull Run near Manassas. On that day he was joined by about 6000 men from the force of Johnston who had outplayed Patterson. McDowell's plan of attack, which he launched that morning, was not bad, and for the earlier part of the day the battle, although with increasing confusion, was on the whole favorable to the Federals. The Southerners stood their ground with

An Appeal for Peace
SENT TO LIEUT. GEN. SCOTT,
JULY 4, 1861.

A PETITION FROM THE WOMEN OF MARYLAND, JULY 4, 1861
From the original broadside in the Rare Book Room, New York Public Library.

granite firmness, General Jackson there gaining his sobriquet of "Stonewall," and when another detachment of over 2000 men from the force that Patterson had been supposed to be engaging arrived, the Union army became demoralized. The retreat became a rout, and, throwing away their muskets, the soldiers fled toward Washington as a disorderly mob, with not the slightest semblance of discipline left, one of the generals on horseback making even better time than the most panic-stricken of his men. Nearly ten per cent of the Federal troops had been killed, wounded or captured, and approximately 2000 of the Confederates.

The trouble had come from attempting a major operation with an utterly untrained and unprepared army, and the enemy, which was fortunately unable to pursue, had been as demoralized by victory as McDowell's forces by defeat. Although the battle was considered a disgraceful disaster for the Union, the Northerners pulled themselves together with a grim determination which they had not felt before, whereas the Southerners were misled into believing that they could relax their efforts, and that the war was practically won.

Immediately after the disaster, Lincoln appointed General George B. McClellan, a business man who was also a West Point graduate, in command of the military forces of the Eastern department, and later, when his long refusal to move against the enemy had aroused feeling against him both in the public and the War Department, the President stood by him by raising him to the rank of General-in-Chief of all the Union forces. This was in spite of the fact that Lincoln himself had also urged action and had become impatient. Persistently, however, McClellan refused to budge, treating all critics, even the President himself, with scant courtesy or consideration, and creating a strong public prejudice against himself.

Nevertheless, during the nine months of summer, autumn, and winter when McClellan was training his men and organizing his forces, he was becoming immensely popular among the troops, and forging a magnificent weapon of offense out of the "Army of the

Potomac." But until the spring of 1862 nothing further took place in that section, except occasional raids by the unopposed rebels, who would probably have taken a much more important offensive had it not been for Jefferson Davis, who, with his unfortunate delusion as to his own military abilities, was to hamper his generals throughout the war.

There is nothing more disliked by newspapers than lack of news, and by the late spring of 1862 *The Examiner* in Richmond was shouting the cry to the South of "On to Washington," while by June Greeley was using screaming type in *The Tribune* for his slogan of "Forward to Richmond." In the middle of February, McClellan had boastfully announced that he would take that city within ten days, but except for some foolish marching he had done nothing, and before we come to the real attempt at a forward movement in June, we must consider what had been happening in other quarters.

The autumn of 1861 had brought about a serious complication in our relations with England, made more dangerous by the inconsiderate haste which some of our high officials made to put their necks in the noose of an untenable contention. One of the first moves of the Confederate Government had naturally been to despatch agents to England to seek formal recognition of the independence of the new Confederation. The commission, headed by the capable William L. Yancey, had been unable to induce the British Government to make any move in their favor but were still in England when two more

Headquarters Department of Fairfax, Virginia,
ARLINGTON HOUSE, May 25, 1861.

A PROCLAMATION

By *Major General SANDFORD, New York State Militia, in the Service of the United States.*

———

Fairfax county being occupied by the troops under my command, I deem it proper to repeat publicly the assurances I have personally given to many of the good citizens about me, that all its inhabitants may return to, or remain in their homes and usual pacific occupations in peace and confidence, and with assured protection to their persons and property; as the United States forces in Virginia will be employed for no other purpose than that of suppressing unlawful combinations against the constituted authorities of the Union, and of causing the Laws thereof to be duly respected and executed.

By order of Major General Charles W. Sandford:

GEORGE W. MORELL,
Division Inspector.

TO THE
Citizens of the State,
AND THE
PEOPLE of RICHMOND

THE ENEMY UNDOUBTEDLY
ARE APPROACHING THE CITY!

And may be expected at any hour, with a view to its capture, its pillage, and its destruction. The strongest considerations of self and of duty to the country,

CALL EVERY MAN TO ARMS!

A duty which none can refuse without dishonor. All persons, therefore, able to wield a musket, will immediately

Assemble upon the Public Square

Where a regiment will be found in arms, and around which all can rally, and where the requisite directions will be given for arming and equipping those who respond to this call.

☞ The Governor confidently relies that this appeal will not be made in vain.

WM. SMITH,
GOVERNOR OF VIRGINIA.

(*Left*) A PROCLAMATION ISSUED BY MAJOR–GENERAL SANDFORD OF THE UNION FORCES IN VIRGINIA, MAY 25, 1861
(*Right*) A PROCLAMATION ISSUED BY GOVERNOR SMITH OF VIRGINIA, PROBABLY IN 1861
From the original broadsides in the Rare Book Room of the New York Public Library and in the Confederate Museum, Richmond.

agents, John Slidell of Louisiana and James M. Mason of Virginia, were also despatched by the government at Richmond, the former to negotiate in London and the latter in Paris.

41

At Havana they had boarded the British mail steamer *Trent*, and their plans having been published in a newspaper which happened to come under the eye of Captain

DRAFT OF THE FIRST PAGE OF A LETTER FROM MASON AND SLIDELL
TO CAPTAIN WILKES, NOV. 8, 1861, AFTER THEIR CAPTURE, GIVING
DETAILS OF THAT EVENT FOR FUTURE RECORD
From the Manuscript Division, Library of Congress.

Wilkes of the U. S. S. *Jacinto,* stopping in the West Indies on the way home from Africa, that over-zealous naval officer determined to intercept the *Trent*, and capture the Confederate agents. This he promptly did.

42

Unfortunately his knowledge of international law was not equal to his zeal, and instead of taking the *Trent* into a port where the matter could be handled by a Court of Admiralty, he at once, on the high seas, transferred Slidell and Mason to his own vessel. When news reached England that an American naval officer had illegally seized and carried off passengers from the deck of a British mail boat, the British lion roared with rage. Unfortunately the American eagle, when it had received the same news, had screamed with delight. Congress publicly thanked Wilkes, who became a popular hero over-night, and although Lincoln and one or two members of the Cabinet realized that the action was illegal, the enthusiasm of the populace had to be reckoned with for the moment.

Public opinion in England had to be taken into consideration also, and the government despatched 8000 troops to Canada, while Lord Russell drew up a demand for apology which was happily much improved in tone by the blue pencil of the Prince Consort. Eventually we had to release the two Southerners, who were returned to a British vessel, and the affair was smoothed over, but not without leaving unjustly a good deal of sore feeling in the North against England, which even such a man as James Russell Lowell, who should have known better, did not hesitate to fan into fury in popular verse.

Meanwhile, the North had for some months before the close of 1861 been maintaining a fairly complete blockade of all Southern ports. At least it was reducing the tonnage entering them by between 80 and 90 per cent; and although a good many vessels slipped through, and it was impossible to patrol the entire Atlantic and Gulf coasts, the South was beginning to feel the pinch. In the West, General Pope had cleared Missouri of Confederate forces, and Grant, under Frémont, had seized Paducah and Cairo. Frémont was displaying his incapacity with unconscious abandon, and had had to be handled rather severely by Lincoln when the inconsiderate general issued a proclamation freeing, on his own responsibility, the slaves of Missourians in arms against the Union, to the great embarrassment of the President, who was then trying to keep slave-holding Kentucky in the Union. Frémont's rather stubborn attitude toward Lincoln in this matter, a few minor defeats and proved lack of ability, ensured his removal, and Hunter was commissioned in his stead.

The next year's campaign in the West, however, was to be the work of Grant. On the whole, the year ended with little to encourage either North or South, and all that it handed on to the next was the knowledge that the war would not be "short."

CHAPTER II

THE TRIAL BY COMBAT

THE year 1861 had ended, as we have seen, with no decisive progress made by either North or South. We Americans have never prepared in advance for war, and in any case it would have been impossible to have prepared for one between two sections of the country. Neither side had any adequate plans for military operations, and in the North a succession of generals, the newspapers, the Secretary of War, and even Lincoln himself, all took a hand in planning military operations. For a long time this had only the usual effect on the broth when there are too many cooks, especially when they know none too much of the art of cooking.

But from the beginning of 1862 onward the strategy of the struggle takes on simpler outlines, and it is those broad outlines which interest most of us who are not military experts. In the first place, as all the South had asked for was to be allowed to leave the Union in peace, and as the North had declined to consent, it was clear that the North would have to take the offensive while the South remained on the defensive. One line of policy would call for the strangling of the South by closing all avenues to the outside world. On land, this would be the work of the Union armies, and on sea of the blockading squadron. We shall comment later on the efforts of the South to retaliate against Northern commerce, efforts which had some important repercussions but did not affect the course of the struggle.

THE THREE MAJOR OPERATIONS

From the beginning of 1862 to the end of the war, there were three major operations of chief importance. One of these was the gaining of control by the North of the Mississippi River from source to mouth, thus cutting the Confederacy in two from east to west. The second was Sherman's march to the sea, more or less cutting it in twain again from north to south, with enormous destruction of property and effect on morale. The third and last was the forcing of the largest Confederate army, under its ablest leader, to surrender before Richmond. In the course of the four years after 1861 there were to be side issues, and many battles, but for a proper understanding of events we should keep these three main objectives in mind, though they were far from being initiated or carried on simultaneously.

At the beginning of 1862 plans had been made to open the Mississippi, hold Tennessee and Kentucky, and to press in on Richmond, the last operation to be carried on not only from Washington as before, but also with troops moving northward by way of Albemarle Sound in

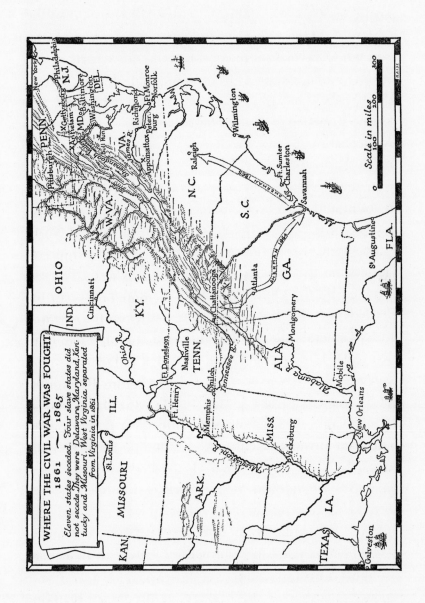

WHERE THE CIVIL WAR WAS FOUGHT
1861 — 1865

Eleven states seceded. Four slave states did not secede. They were Delaware, Maryland, Kentucky and Missouri. West Virginia separated from Virginia in 1861

Scale in miles
0   100   200   300

47

North Carolina. In January a new Secretary of War, Edwin M. Stanton, had been appointed to succeed Cameron whose favoritism in contracts and other matters had become so scandalous as to necessitate his removal. Stanton was about as agreeable to handle as a porcupine, and had no knowledge of military affairs, but he brought to his department both the honesty and driving power it had hitherto totally lacked.

In the West, Major-General Henry W. Halleck was in command with headquarters at St. Louis, and Grant, now become a brigadier-general, with a force of about 15,000 men, was stationed at Cairo, some distance below Halleck on the Mississippi at the point where that river is joined by the Ohio. Although the major force of the Confederates in this district was gathered at Nashville under General Albert Johnston, smaller bodies had built two forts, Henry and Donelson, on the Tennessee and Cumberland Rivers near the Tennessee-Kentucky line. Johnston's troops had posted themselves on the Mississippi at Columbus, about twenty miles below Grant, and had even invaded Kentucky. Columbus itself was too strong to warrant an attack by the Federals but would have to be abandoned by the rebels if the much weaker forts in its rear on the two tributary rivers should fall.

Up to this time, Grant had been anything but a success. His four years spent unwillingly at West Point had brought him no distinction, although he was subsequently mentioned for bravery in the Mexican War.

Without any interest in military life, moved about from one army post to another after peace with Mexico in 1848, finally stuck in miserable places in California and Oregon, far from his wife and child, whom he was unable to support, he had unhappily taken to drink and had had to resign his commission, Jefferson Davis being the Secretary of War who accepted it. The years after that until the Civil War were filled with merely a dreary and unsuccessful succession of small jobs, ending with a clerkship in his father's leather store in Galena, Illinois. When the Civil War broke, however, he seemed to become a changed man. Volunteering for service again, he secured the colonelcy of a regiment, and to every one's surprise, including his own, had been made brigadier in August, 1861.

In January, 1862, Grant urged Halleck to let him attack Forts Henry and Donelson, which a reconnaissance had indicated to him might be taken. The permission finally given, Grant, supported by Commodore A. H. Foote with small gun-boats, proceeded up the Tennessee River with 17,000 men. Fort Henry proved easy of capture, and Grant then moved his force twelve miles overland to take the fort on the Cumberland River, the plan being for Foote to go round by water and join him in the attack. The fire from the fort was so heavy, however, that Foote was forced to withdraw, and while Grant was in consultation with him, the land forces were suddenly attacked and almost defeated by the Confederates, Grant arriving in haste only just in time, by a magnificent counter attack, to force the Confederates back into the fort.

It was mid-February, and sleet and cold made that night a terrible one for the Union soldiers, entirely without protection and partially without food. Inside the fort, however, its commander, General S. B. Buckner, realized the impossibility of holding it against assault the following day. In the morning of the 16th, he asked for terms, and Grant's reply, which was to make him famous, was immediately given: "No terms except unconditional and immediate surrender can be accepted. I propose to move immediately upon your works." Without further argument, Fort Donelson fell with 14,000 men; the North went wild with joy over the first victory of the year; and Grant was named a major-general by the President, and "Unconditional Surrender Grant" by the public, a play on his initials of U. S.

Another Union force, of about 37,000 men, operating under General D. C. Buell, had advanced as far South as Nashville, which had been evacuated by the Confederates, about 40,000 of whom had been massed at Corinth with the object of attacking and destroying Grant before Buell could join him. A misunderstanding with Halleck had resulted in the temporary suspension of Grant but he had soon been reinstated, and by the middle of March was in command at Savannah, Tennessee, nine miles from Pittsburgh Landing, where he

Galena, Ill.
May 24th 1861

Col. L. Thomas,
Adjt. Gen. U.S.A.
Washington D.C.

Sir:

Having served for fifteen years in the regular army, including four years at West Point, and feeling it the duty of every one who has been educated at the Government expense to offer their services for the support of that Government, I have the honor, very respectfully, to tender my services, until the close of the War, in such capacity as may be offered. I would say that in view of my present age and length of service, I feel myself competent to command a Regiment if the President, in his judgement, should see fit to entrust one to me.

Since the first call of the President I have been serving on the Staff of the Governer of this State rendering such aid as I could in the organization of our State Militia, and am still engaged in that capacity. A letter addressed to me at Springfield Ill. will reach me.

I am very Respectfully
Your Obt. Svt.
U. S. Grant

GRANT'S LETTER OF MAY 24, 1861, TENDERING HIS SERVICES TO
THE FEDERAL GOVERNMENT

From the original in the War Department, Washington.

was concentrating his whole body of about 38,000. Grant appears to have been wholly ignorant of the fact that while he was making preparations for an advance on Corinth, General Johnston had decided to attack him at Pittsburgh Landing. Early on the morning of April 6, the unexpected attack was launched while Grant was breakfasting in perfect confidence at Savannah. Hastening to the rescue of his forces, which had not yet been joined by Buell's, he sent entreaties for haste to that commander, and also to General Lew Wallace, who had 5000 men at Crump's Landing.

Otherwise, Grant seemed curiously incapable of acting, but early in the afternoon General Johnston was killed, and about three hours later, his second, General Beauregard, called off the attack for that day. By evening both Wallace's Division and Buell's men had arrived, and the following morning the battle was renewed with the weight of advantage now on the side of the Union. The Confederates fought desperately all day, but by night were forced to retreat to Corinth, after one of the bloodiest and most desperate encounters of the entire war, more than one fifth of the Union forces and one quarter of the Southerners being killed or wounded, a combined casualty list of nearly 25,000.

It has always been impossible satisfactorily to explain Grant's state of mind and actions preceding and during the battle of Shiloh, as it is called, and Halleck, doubting his ability, came down the river and took command.

With overwhelming force, Halleck continued down the river and occupied Corinth, from which Beauregard had been forced to retire. There the winter was spent, an attempt by Grant to capture Vicksburg with 30,000 men proving ineffectual.

Meanwhile, events had been happening much farther southward. It had been planned for some time to despatch a combined naval and military force to capture New Orleans, and proceed up the Mississippi to effect contact with the Union forces operating from the North. Early in the spring a Union fleet, under command of Captain David G. Farragut, which included boats with mortars on board to bombard Forts Jackson and St. Philip, guarding the stream below New Orleans, and troop-ships carrying 25,000 men under the notorious General Benjamin F. Butler, had reached the mouth of the river. The Confederates had a few iron-clad vessels on which they were counting to prevent Farragut's passage. His vessels and gunnery, however, proved more than a match for both iron-clads and forts, and by the first of May New Orleans, the largest city of the South, had been occupied by the combined Union forces.

The charming, leisurely old city, largely French in blood, was hotly Southern in sympathy, and the presence of an army of occupation was, as always everywhere, extremely irritating. The population was by no means all composed of Southern "aristocrats" nor were the troops all composed of Northern gentlemen who might show consideration for the feelings of the conquered. There were many cases of soldiers being insulted on the streets, especially by women, who are always likely to be more bitter than men in their war-time antipathies. General Butler, who had become the military governor, and who was afterward known as "Beast Butler," could think of

GENERAL ORDER ⎱   Headquarters Department of the Gulf, ⎱
No. 28. ⎰   *New Orleans, May 15, 1862.* ⎰

As the officers and soldiers of the United States have been subject to repeated insults from the women (calling themselves ladies) of New Orleans, in return for the most scrupulous non-interference and courtesy on our part, it is ordered that hereafter when any female shall, by word, gesture or movement, insult or show contempt for any officer or soldier of the United States, she shall be regarded and held liable to be treated as a woman of the town plying her avocation.

BY COMMAND OF   MAJOR-GENERAL BUTLER
GEO. C. STRONG, A A. GEN., CHIEF OF STAFF

GENERAL BUTLER'S ORDER NO. 28
From the Manuscript Division, Library of Congress.

no better means of protecting his men from the "insults" of the women than to issue his famous order declaring that thereafter any woman found insulting a Union soldier would be treated as a "woman of the town plying her avocation."

The insulting brutality of such an order would have been bitterly resented in any civilized community. One has only to think what would have happened had it been issued, for example, by General Gage when the British

54

troops were garrisoning Boston in 1774. Butler's order was, indeed, emphatically denounced in the British Parliament, and afforded the opportunity for our minister, Mr. Adams, to score one of the prettiest diplomatic triumphs of all time over the, on this occasion, unwary Lord Palmerston. Butler's order secured its immediate object in New Orleans, but otherwise its effect was extremely bad in that it served to confirm the Southerners in their generally erroneous opinion of Northerners as low, common, and determined on insulting the South.

While bad blood was thus being rapidly fomented in New Orleans by Butler, who was outlawed by President Davis, Farragut had succeeded in pushing some of his vessels far enough up the river past the Confederate defences to get in touch with Grant, but Vicksburg could not yet be taken, and the complete severing of the Confederacy on the line of the Mississippi had to await the following year. Minor fighting in Kentucky and Tennessee during the remainder of 1862 was without definite influence on the larger strategy of the war, and may be disregarded, except to note that both States had come under Union control.

We must now turn to the East, and see what progress was made in 1862 toward a second objective, the capture of the main part of the Confederate forces before Richmond. We shall find it a disappointing year, although with plenty of action.

There were various routes which McClellan might

have taken toward the rebel capital and its defending forces. The Army of the Potomac numbered over 100,-000 superbly drilled men, thanks almost wholly to the general himself, who, however, seemed both uncertain and loath to use the weapon he had forged. Had he decided to proceed southward, keeping himself between Washington and the enemy, he could have counted upon using the whole available Union forces in the Eastern theatre, which would have added at least fifty per cent to his strength. He preferred to transport all his own troops to the eastern end of the Yorktown Peninsula, and work his way thence toward Richmond, marching with the York and James Rivers on his flanks. This involved not only a division of forces, as the administration not unnaturally insisted upon McDowell remaining with his army to protect the Capital against a sudden attack from Lee should he make a dash in that direction, but also necessitated McClellan's marching through a difficult and none too well-known country with the largest force which had yet been in operation in America.

It was essential for his plan that the James River be clear of rebel vessels and open for his own, as he counted on the co-operation of the navy to protect his flank. During the early part of the winter, however, the Confederates, who were in possession of Norfolk and its navy yard, had built an iron-clad of a new type, with a pointed ram on its bow. This had made itself practically

GENERAL SCHENCK'S OHIO REGIMENTS NEAR FAIRFAX COUNTY COURT HOUSE, VIRGINIA

From the pencil sketch by A. R. Waud. In the J. Pierpont Morgan Collection, Library of Congress.

THE BOMBARDMENT OF "ISLAND NUMBER 10" IN THE MISSISSIPPI

Commencing on March 15, 1862, and continuing until April 7, when the island fell to Commodore Foote in command of the Gunboat and Mortar Fleet.

A Currier and Ives lithograph in the Library of Congress.

COMING INTO THE LINES

Slaves with a "spike" team attached to an old schooner, passing the picket post.

From the etching by Edwin Forbes in the J. Pierpont Morgan Collection, Library of Congress.

master of Hampton Roads, after having destroyed two of the big wooden vessels of the Union navy, the *Congress* and the *Cumberland*. The iron hull of this strange new war-ship made it practically impervious to the shot of that day, whereas its ram enabled it to poke huge holes in the wooden hulls of its opponents and to sink them ingloriously. This vessel, formerly the U. S. S. steam sloop *Merrimac,* but re-christened the *Virginia* by the Confederates when they had altered her to an iron-clad and added her ram, was to meet her match on March 8, in one of the historical naval battles of the world.

THE "MONITOR" AND THE "MERRIMAC"

A Swede, John Ericsson, then resident in New York, had produced in the *Monitor* a hitherto unknown type of vessel, heavily iron-clad, looking much like an oval raft with a revolving iron turret which enabled her to fire in any direction. She was unwieldy and unseaworthy, but when the *Merrimac* started out on that day from Norfolk to sink another of the wooden ships of the Northerners, she was met by this weird-looking monster, and after an engagement in which neither vessel was destroyed was forced to retreat to Norfolk. Her power was over, and when, in May, the Confederates evacuated that city, on account of McClellan's operations, they destroyed their ram before leaving.

According to Henry Adams, who was then in London,

acting as private secretary to his father, the American Minister, a profound impression was created among English naval and military circles by the appearance of the iron-clads in action. It has been said by leading American historians, indeed, that the *Monitor* and the *Merrimac* caused the abandonment of the old wooden navies of the world and began a new era in naval history. This, however, is rather over-stating the case. Iron-clads had been used in the Crimean War, a few years earlier. The French had launched a great iron-clad in 1859, and the European admiralties were already deeply concerned about the possible necessity of rebuilding all their fleets before the *Merrimac* had first slipped out from Norfolk. What the American iron-clads in action probably did accomplish was to settle the disputed point and leave no further room for hesitation. It is a mistake, however, to consider that the new type of iron naval vessel was in any way an invention of our own, though that impression is usually given.

The Confederates everywhere in the eastern theatre of war were heavily outnumbered, and the failure of the campaign of 1862 to show results for the Federals was due to the superior skill of the Southern commanders. To oppose McClellan's advance up the Peninsula toward Richmond, General J. E. Johnston had no more than 60,000 men to McClellan's 100,000. A body of about 11,000 Confederates lay north of McClellan's line of advance but was confronted by McDowell's 40,000 at

Fredericksburg. Stonewall Jackson, certainly the ablest officer next to Lee, even if not as some military authorities think abler than Lee himself, was in the southern part of the great Shenandoah Valley, which at its northern end gave easy access to Harper's Ferry, from which place descent might be made on Washington, 60 miles to the southeastward. Jackson, however, was opposed by General N. P. Banks with a slightly stronger force than his own, while Frémont had another 15,000 ready to invade the valley from the west, and there was another Federal force of 7000 stationed at Harper's Ferry. Two smaller Confederate forces, one of 3000 and another of about 6000, could be counted on in the valley, but here as elsewhere the disparity of numbers was greatly in favor of the North.

The Federals, however, both military and civil, threw away their chances. The Confederates had left only slender forces to impede McClellan's march up the Peninsula, but that cautious commander took a whole month of siege work to clear them from his path, and it was not until the middle of May, when the rebels had withdrawn after their delay had been accomplished, that the 100,000 Union troops were set in motion toward Richmond.

McClellan, who in his own opinion never had enough men for any task, had asked to have McDowell and his 40,000 sent around by water to join his own force, but this would have left Washington defenseless before the

swift-moving Lee. Stanton properly insisted that Mc-
Dowell should remain between the capital and the enemy,
and march to join McClellan overland by way of Fred-

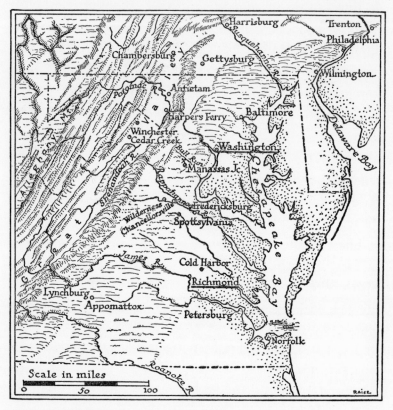

BATTLE–FIELDS IN THE EASTERN THEATRE OF WAR

ericksburg. McClellan's plan of campaign was to advance slowly, taking no chances, and, counting on artillery and siege operations, to win through to the Confederate capital.

On paper, the theory was sound enough, and the Confederates admitted that they would be defeated if they allowed themselves to accept McClellan's methods. They declined to do so, and their success against overwhelming odds and a perfect paper plan would indicate that the latter was not so sound as it looked. Nor can the blame be laid upon Stanton for not allowing the Federal capital to remain wholly undefended by putting all McDowell's 40,000 men on transports and sending them around by sea to McClellan, who already immensely outnumbered his enemy. The brilliant audacity with which the Confederate generals were about to act might well have cost the Federals their seat of government had McClellan had his way against the civilian Secretary of War.

The first move was in the Shenandoah Valley, where Jackson so outplayed his adversaries that, after defeating Milroy's force 25 miles from Staunton, he frightened the life out of Frémont with his 15,000 men and left that general in a funk for days. Jackson then attacked Banks, whom he chased all the way to Winchester and from there up the valley and across the Potomac. At Harper's Ferry he seemed to threaten Washington to such an extent that McDowell was recalled from Fredericksburg, so that McClellan lost any possible aid from that quarter. Jackson, however, had no idea of descending on Washington, and still less of being captured. He had accomplished the most important object, which was so to disarrange the Federal plans as to ruin McClellan's cam-

61

paign against Richmond. Therefore, as quickly as he had advanced, he passed down the valley again, inflicting one or two more stinging defeats, and saved his force and his booty for use against McClellan.

That general was not altogether happy. The Peninsula was difficult marching country and in May the heavy rains had swollen the streams and rivers. On the 31st, two of his corps, under Keyes and Heintzelman, were separated from the main forces by the Chickahominy, and the opportunity being instantly recognized by General Johnston, the Confederates fell upon them. The attack, however, was not as vigorous as it should have been and the chief result of the battle of Seven Pines or Fair Oaks, as it is called, was the appointment of General Lee to succeed Johnston in chief command, the latter having been dangerously wounded.

LEE AND McCLELLAN

The next movements were the result of the contrasting psychology of Lee and McClellan. After Seven Pines, the latter continued his slow "digging-in and siege" method, which Lee knew would be fatal to Richmond if allowed to continue. The difficulty with the method appears to have been that Lee could himself decide whether or not it should continue. As a result of his adverse decision he ordered Jackson to join him from the valley and to attack McClellan's right flank while he himself attacked directly in front, hoping to force a retreat or to cut off McClellan's line of communications.

In spite of Jackson's being late, Lee's plan succeeded in a considerable degree. Fitz-John Porter, who was protecting the Federal right, was forced to retreat from his position at Gaines's Mill, and McClellan had to shift his base to the James River. His move had left Lee uncertain, and McClellan thus gained 24 hours for an orderly withdrawal. The battle at Malvern Hill, July 1, was unquestionably an unwise attack on Lee's part, but the various engagements of the preceding week, known altogether as the "Seven Days' Battles," had pushed McClellan to Harrison's Landing on the James. The Confederate losses, of about 20,000, had been nearly 25 per cent greater than those of McClellan, and the Army of the Potomac was not defeated. In April, however, a Union army of 100,000 had faced a Confederate one around Richmond of only 60,000. As a result of two months' campaigning, it had come to pass that the Federals were outnumbered by their immediate foe at the beginning of Lee's move against McClellan.

That general now again asked for reinforcements and the chance to make another move against Richmond, this time by way of Petersburg. Around the question of McClellan's military ability has raged one of the classic controversies of American history. It is one which it is quite impossible for a layman to decide, more especially as the military experts themselves are by no means agreed.

Whatever may be said of McClellan as a commander, and there is much in his favor, he unquestionably greatly over-rated himself as a man, and in that respect his own words make the case against him. His despatches both to Lincoln and Stanton are almost incredible in their arrogance, and, a matter which has to be considered in a democracy at war, the public at large, whether justly or not, had lost confidence in him. In July he was recalled to Washington, and his army was withdrawn from the Peninsula and moved to Northern Virginia. The Peninsula campaign was over, and Richmond had not been taken.

General Halleck, who, in the West, had been fortunate in the successes won for him by his subordinates, was brought east and made commander of all the Union forces, with the rather bombastic General Pope in command of a force of about 43,000 men made up of the combined forces of Frémont, Banks, and McDowell. The North was still experimenting with generals.

So, likewise, was Lee, and Pope was an opportunity for him. Combining with Jackson, the Confederate commander, knowing that it would take a fortnight or more for the McClellan forces to be transported from the James to the neighborhood of Pope, completely baffled that over-confident leader, and having driven him back to Bull Run he there won a second and more resounding Confederate victory, August 29–30. Outwitted at every turn in a brief campaign, Pope lost 14,000 men and the confidence of every one.

By September 4 the Confederates were crossing the Potomac, twenty-five miles from Washington, and the following day Lincoln orally gave command of all the forces to McClellan, who still had the unbounded admiration of his soldiers. Lee had had no intention of at-

—◦—
From Washington.
ADVANCE OF THE CONFEDERATE ARMY—THE WHITE HOUSE IN SIGHT—STRAGETIC MOVE-MENTS OF THE CONFEDERATES.

WASHINGTON, September 7.—Reports f rom vari-ous points on the other side of the Potomac repre-sent everything quiet last night and this morning.

The Confederates are now said to be within five miles of the President's House, and three miles of Arlington Heights.

A WASHINGTON DESPATCH IN *THE CHARLESTON COURIER,*
SEPTEMBER 11, 1862

From the Confederate Museum, Richmond.

tacking Washington but was advancing into Maryland, where he expected to find Southern sympathy strong enough to win that State over if supported by the presence of his army. A push up into Pennsylvania might divide the North even more dangerously than the South could be divided by Union control of the Mississippi, and even in the western theatre of operations the Confederates were pushing back Union forces across Kentucky and were threatening Cincinnati.

So far, the Republican administration in Washington had little to show the people, and the mid-term elections, always likely to be dangerous for the party in power unless all has been going well, were only a month off. The change in a few months from seeing a Union army within 20 miles of Richmond and expecting to capture it, to having Lee and 60,000 Confederates swinging northward through Maryland, was creating dismay and terror in the North, and also having dangerous effects in Europe, as we shall note later. The crisis was of the first magnitude, and it is interesting to observe how much the element of luck can play in the decision of fate by arms.

There was, as Lee had expected, very strong Southern sympathy in Maryland, but this was mostly confined to the eastern portion of the State, and the Southern general at Frederick found it difficult to get sufficient supplies for his troops. As he could not live on the country it was necessary to open a line of communication down the Shenandoah Valley. By chance, however, Harper's Ferry was in possession of a Union garrison, which under ordinary rules of war should have been withdrawn as Lee had advanced. Indeed, this had been advised by McClellan. Nevertheless no withdrawal had been effected, and thus when Lee pushed ahead to Hagerstown he had to despatch Jackson to capture the ferry. This divided his army.

McClellan had taken several days after his reappointment to reorganize Pope's forces, and, as usual, grossly over-estimated the strength of the enemy, which he set at double the real figure. On September 12, a week after he had taken command, he had reached Frederick in pursuit of Lee, and there by luck a despatch from Lee to D. H. Hill was picked up, revealing Lee's plans and the fact that at the moment the Confederate army was split. McClellan should have taken advantage of his information without delay, but his own cautiousness, increased by telegrams from Washington, made him hesitate.

A few miles to the west were two gaps in the "South Mountains," the rampart of the valley, and eight miles beyond these, in the valley, were the roads connecting the two parts of the enemy army. Instead of seizing these at once, McClellan waited, and when he moved on the 14th the gaps had already been occupied by the Confederates and were carried by the Federals only with severe losses. That same morning, Lee had discovered that his enemy was in possession of the missing despatch to D. H. Hill, and immediately moved southward from Hagerstown, taking up an entrenched position on Antietam Creek. From that place he sent new orders to Jackson to join him. That general captured Harper's Ferry, with its garrison of 12,500, the morning of the 15th, and hastened to join Lee. He could not reach him, however, until the morning of the 16th, whereas McClellan was facing him by the previous noon.

Instead of throwing himself on Lee's army, then in a desperate plight, either on the afternoon of the 15th or the morning of the 16th before Lee could be reinforced by Jackson, McClellan contented himself with making reconnaissances and plans, with a skirmish, until the 17th, when he had to encounter the reunited Confederate armies. Even so, he had 87,000 men to Lee's 55,000, magnified, however, in McClellan's mind to double that number. Lee had taken up a strong position, and the battle that ensued, known from the Creek as Antietam, was one of the bloodiest of the war, about 23,500 men being killed and wounded, of whom slightly over half were Northerners. The conflict was a series of confused attacks, and it has been debated whether the sum of them was a Union or Confederate victory. The following day, McClellan, although numerically far superior, declined to renew the struggle, and on the 19th he unforgivably allowed Lee to retreat unmolested across the Potomac into Virginia.

However, the danger to the North from the Army of Virginia was now over, and jubilation replaced the grim fear of recent weeks. Nevertheless, as McClellan did nothing to follow up Antietam and permitted Lee to retreat southwards along the Shenandoah Valley, the mistrust of him by both President and people increased again. Lincoln begged him to pursue Lee and to prevent the Confederates from getting once more between him and Richmond, but in vain. On the 7th of November he was again deposed from command, and the wholly inadequate General A. E. Burnside was unfortunately named in his place.

At Fredericksburg on December 13, in the last attempt for a decision in 1862, the new commander with 113,000 men faced Lee trying to force his way back to Richmond. The Confederates, stationed on Marye's Heights and well defended, received the useless attack which Burnside launched against them. The Federals had to charge across a plain, completely covered by the rebel artillery and the rifles of those placed behind a stone wall at the base of the height. It was not war but murder, yet six times Burnside ordered the charge across dead bodies through the sheets of flame. Nothing more magnificent or futile has ever been seen in the annals of war. At the end of the day nearly 8000 men lay dead on the field, sacrificed to Burnside's obstinacy, and the total Federal loss for the fight was over 12,500 to less than 6000 Confederate casualties. It was clear that Burnside could not be retained in command, and the search for a general had to go on.

The year 1862 had been marked by momentous events other than military. In spite of England's proclamation of neutrality, the Confederacy had continued hopeful of recognition by both that country and France, and meanwhile was endeavoring to buy vessels of war from English builders. The British Government had forbidden its subjects to build or equip any war-ships which might be used by either belligerent, but unfortunately although Parliament had passed an Act to that effect in good faith the Act had been carelessly drawn. On the principle that a person should be considered innocent until proved guilty, it had provided for punishment of the offenders and confiscation of the vessel only after proof of the offence, which raised very difficult legal questions in any case that might arise. In March, 1862, a small vessel was built and allowed to sail, and though seized at Nassau was released by the court there. This *Florida* case was merely the precursor of the much more serious one of the *Alabama* a few months later. The Confederates, having succeeded in getting the *Florida* to sea, made a contract with the firm of Lairds at Liverpool to build the commerce-destroyer which was afterwards to cost England dear.

Our minister, Charles Francis Adams, procured evidence, which he considered overwhelming, that the vessel was being built for the Confederacy, and presented it to Lord John Russell. The Confederate agents had covered their tracks as well as they could, and, as first submitted, the evidence was not considered sufficiently conclusive to warrant the British Government in preventing the sailing of the vessel, on which work was being rushed, although high legal opinion was in Adams's favor. Finally, however, a full set of the documents in the case was sent to the Queen's advocate, Sir John Harding, who had just gone insane, a fact known to no one at that moment but his wife, who left the papers for five days without any one's seeing them. On July 28 the attorney-general and solicitor-general received them and the next day immediately declared the evidence conclusive and advised Russell to have the vessel seized without an instant's delay. Unfortunately it was

THE WAY LINCOLN WILL BE LIFTED OUT OF WASHINGTON CITY
BY GENERAL LEE

*A cartoon from "The Southern Punch," Richmond, Va., May 7, 1864,
in the Library of Congress.*

too late, for, being warned, the Confederates had got her to sea before she was finished, that very morning.

That the British Government, enmeshed in legal red-tape, had been careless cannot be denied, but even

71

Adams, who had no love for the English in general or Russell in particular, later declared that the Foreign Minister had not been actuated by any motive of ill-will, and that on the whole he was favorable rather than hostile to the North.

This, however, was not true of all English or, notably, of French statesmen. In the summer and autumn of 1862 the stoppage of cotton exports from the South was exerting its fullest effects on both European nations. The number of cotton operatives out of work in England rose to 550,000 by the end of that year, and the unemployed in France were estimated at 300,000. The French Emperor, Louis Napoleon, was pressing hard to have England join him in recognizing the Confederacy, and France certainly, and England possibly, would have done so by autumn had it not been for friends of the North in the British Cabinet. As we have seen, by September the fortunes of the North were at a low ebb. The attack on Richmond had been abandoned and Lee was marching into Maryland, threatening Washington and Philadelphia. The war, which a large section of English opinion believed was only for forcible retention of the South and not for the freedom of the slave, was dragging on with no prospect of Northern victory. At that crisis in our affairs, however, the English prevented Napoleon from taking hostile action against us.

Meanwhile, Lincoln was to clear away one source of misunderstanding. As we have seen, he had not believed it to be either his duty or right as President to interfere with slavery within the States where it was legal. He had also framed for himself, looking forward to a successful end of the war and the need for receiving the seceded States back into the Union, the working theory that those States had never in truth been out of it, and that there should be as little interference with them legally as possible. After the war began, there was the additional problem of retaining the loyalty of such border States as were also slave States. What gradually changed his mind as to the problem of slavery and emancipation can never be known, and we can only follow his actions.

THE EMANCIPATION PROCLAMATION

On July 22, 1862, he surprised his Cabinet by announcing to them that he intended to issue an emancipation proclamation freeing all who should be slaves within the rebellious States on January 1, 1863, and suggesting some form of compensation to their owners. It was pointed out to him, that although most of the Cabinet agreed with the substance of his proposition, the time was singularly inopportune in view of the bad military situation for the North. Agreeing with this, Lincoln laid aside the idea of an immediate proclamation.

On August 20, Horace Greeley published in *The Tribune* an open letter to the President complaining of his hesitating attitude toward slavery. To this Lincoln

THE PRAYER OF TWENTY MILLIONS.

To ABRAHAM LINCOLN, *President of the U. States:*

DEAR SIR: I do not intrude to tell you—for you must know already—that a great proportion of those who triumphed in your election, and of all who desire the unqualified suppression of the Rebellion now desolating our country, are sorely disappointed and deeply pained by the policy you seem to be pursuing with regard to the slaves of Rebels. I write only to set succinctly and unmistakably before you what we require, what we think we have a right to expect, and of what we complain.

II. We think you are strangely and disastrously remiss in the discharge of your official and imperative duty with regard to the emancipating provisions of the new Confiscation Act. These provisions were designed to fight

IV. We think timid counsels in such a crisis calculated to prove perilous, and probably disastrous. It is the duty of a Government so

V. We complain that the Union cause has suffered, and is now suffering immensely, from mistaken deference to Rebel Slavery. Had

VI. We complain that the Confiscation Act which you approved is habitually disregarded by your Generals, and that no word of rebuke for them from you has yet reached the public ear. Fremont's Proclamation and Hunter's
As one of the millions who would gladly have avoided this struggle at any sacrifice but that of Principle and Honor, but who now feel that the triumph of the Union is indispensable not only to the existence of our country but to the well-being of mankind, I entreat you to render a hearty and unequivocal obedience to the law of the land.

Yours,   HORACE GREELEY.
New-York, August 19, 1862.

EXCERPTS FROM HORACE GREELEY'S LETTER IN *THE TRIBUNE,*
AUGUST 20, 1862

PRESIDENT LINCOLN'S LETTER

EXECUTIVE MANSION,
WASHINGTON, August 22, 1862.

Hon. Horace Greeley:

DEAR SIR: I have just read yours of the 19th, addressed to myself through THE N. Y. TRIBUNE. If there be in it any statements or assumptions of fact which I may know to be erroneous, I do not now and here controvert them. If there be in it any inferences which I may believe to be falsely drawn, I do not now and here argue against them. If there be perceptible in it an impatient and dictatorial tone, I waive it in deference to an old friend, whose heart I have always supposed to be right.

As to the policy I "seem to be pursuing," as you say, I have not meant to leave any one in doubt.

I would save the Union. I would save it the shortest way under the Constitution. The sooner the National authority can be restored, the nearer the Union will be "the Union as it was." If there be those who would not save the Union unless they could at the same time *save* Slavery, I do not agree with them. If there be those who would not save the Union unless they could at the same time *destroy* Slavery, I do not agree with them. My paramount object in this struggle *is* to save the Union, and is *not* either to save or destroy Slavery. If I could save the Union without freeing *any* slave, I would do it; and if I could save it by freeing *all* the slaves, I would do it; and if I could do it by freeing some and leaving others alone, I would also do that. What I do about Slavery and the colored race, I do because I believe it helps to save this Union; and what I forbear, I forbear because I do *not* believe it would help to save the Union. I shall do *less* whenever I shall believe what I am doing hurts the cause, and I shall do *more* whenever I shall believe doing more will help the cause. I shall try to correct errors when shown to be errors; and I shall adopt new views so fast as they shall appear to be true views. I have here stated my purpose according to my view of *official* duty, and I intend no modification of my oft-expressed *personal* wish that all men, everywhere, could be free. Yours,

A. LINCOLN.

PRESIDENT LINCOLN'S RESPONSE TO GREELEY'S LETTER IN
THE TRIBUNE, AUGUST 25, 1862

75

replied two days later, saying that "my paramount object in this struggle is to save the Union, and is not either to save or destroy slavery. If I could save the Union without freeing any slave I would do it; and if I could save it by freeing all the slaves, I would do it; and if I could do it by freeing some and leaving others alone, I would also do that. What I do about slavery and the colored race, I do because I believe it helps to save the Union; and what I forbear, I forbear because I do not believe it would help to save the Union."

This was clear enough. Lincoln had long been subjected to pressure from various groups to come out for abolition, but this had had no effect upon his singularly independent mind, and we look in vain for any certain influence which made him decide the fateful question within a week or two after answering Greeley. At the Cabinet meeting of September 22, he read a few pages from Artemus Ward's "High-handed Outrage at Uticy," which had struck him as funny, and then, becoming serious, informed his advisers that he had asked them to meet so that they might hear what he had decided to publish to the nation. It was merely for their information, he added, as he had already made the irrevocable decision himself.

He had made a vow, so he said, to God that he would issue an emancipation proclamation when the Confederates were driven out of Maryland. The battle of Antietam had been fought, and Lee was in retreat. He

THROUGH THE WILDERNESS

A battery of artillery dragged through the mud during a spring rain storm.

FALL IN FOR SOUP—COMPANY MESS

Winter camp showing the huts built by the troops. A wagon is coming down the road from the distant camp on its way to the depot for forage.

From etchings by Edwin Forbes, 1876. In the J. Pierpont Morgan Collection, Library of Congress.

WRITING THE EMANCIPATION PROCLAMATION

A Confederate caricature showing Lincoln, his foot resting on the Constitution, and Satan holding the ink pot. The table has negro-head gargoyles and cloven feet, and an all-seeing eye. On the wall to the left is a bloodhound with a shield supported by a negro head.

From the etching by Volck in the Library of Congress.

would fulfill the vow. Then he read the proclamation which on the following day, September 23, he published to the people, declaring that after January 1, 1863, all slaves held within the States which were in rebellion would be "thenceforward and forever free." He suggested colonization somewhere of the freed negroes, and eventual compensation to owners in both the loyal and rebel States.

Although with one or two exceptions the members of his Cabinet agreed, the effect of the proclamation on the public at large was disappointing. The South, naturally, regarded it as confiscation and an attempt to rouse a servile revolt, but the North, which might have been expected to receive it with enthusiasm, was unimpressed, and the election the following month went against the administration. In England, however, the response was immediate and favorable. Whatever the President's motives may have been, he had now indubitably linked the cause of the North with freedom.

When the first of January came, Lincoln issued the proclamation indicated by his preliminary one in September, declaring all the slaves in the rebellious States to be free from that date, and warning them against indulging in any violence. For long opposed to slavery as an institution, Lincoln had not considered that it could be interfered with under the existing Constitution, and there was nothing in that instrument warranting the emancipation proclamation, unless we accept the theory

77

which he now evolved that "the Constitution invests its commander-in-chief with the law of war in time of war," and that slaves being property, as property, either in the hands of citizens or their foes, they could be seized for war purposes.

Whatever hopes the end of 1862 might be bringing to the Southern slaves it was bringing little comfort to the harassed President. Although his party still had a slender majority in Congress as a result of the elections, his own hold on it was threatened. The President no more than any general had won the confidence of the nation, and in mid-December had come Burnside's crushing defeat at Fredericksburg. A group of Republican senators, headed by the trouble maker, Charles Sumner of Massachusetts, determined to force the President to change both his plans and his Cabinet at their dictation.

Within the Cabinet, Chase, the Secretary of the Treasury, shared the mistrust of Lincoln, and had been both indiscreet and disloyal in expressing criticism of him. Seward had long since recovered from the Presidential aspirations for himself which still troubled Chase, but was the main object of senatorial attack. To relieve Lincoln of embarrassment, he tendered his resignation. The President then called a joint meeting of the other Cabinet members and of the senatorial committee, at which meeting Chase was put in the awkward situation of having to reaffirm what he had told the senators as to the incapacity of the administration or else to defend it. He chose to adopt the latter course and to eat his words, thus playing unfairly with both sides. The following morn-

An Uneasy Head

Lincoln takes great trouble to make the "loyal States" regard him as "the head of the nation." He seems to have no fear that "the nation" may become sensitive enough to hide its head in very shame, or that it may get so itchy in that region as to scratch its crown to pieces, or so crazed as to knock its skull against a stone wall, or so tired of life as to tie a rope around its neck and hang itself, leaving the head to bleach under all weathers, as a warning for all time, to all nations. At present "the head of the nation" is "turned;" yet, it fits the body very well, and every disease to which it is a victim has a suffering sympathy through all the members; so the head is likely to last as long as the nation, and to lie meanwhile, as uneasily as any that wears a crown.

EDITORIAL COMMENT FROM *THE SOUTHERN PUNCH*, RICHMOND, VA., SEPTEMBER 5, 1863
From the Library of Congress.

ing, there being nothing else for him to do, he also resigned.

Both men, however, were essential to Lincoln. Seward had developed into a capable statesman, was loyal to the President, whom he had now come to trust, and was indispensable in the State Department. Chase was a very difficult man to get on with but was doing excellent work in the Treasury, and with a country plunged into gloom and uncertainty it was no time to confess further failure by dismissing the leading two members of the Cabinet. Lincoln had handled the situation with extreme skill. He could afford neither to be dictated to by the Senate nor to alienate its support. The resignation of Chase, which followed from the President's confronting him with both the senators and his own colleagues, and his forced retraction of his accusations, enabled the President to decline to accept either resignation and to retain his Cabinet as before with both Chase and Seward in it. As Lincoln characteristically remarked when he got Chase's resignation: "Now I can ride; I have got a pumpkin in each end of my bag." The Cabinet crisis had passed.

If the President could retain his statesmen, he had yet to continue his experiments with generals. The frightful and unnecessary slaughter at Fredericksburg had rendered Burnside useless as a commander, and in January, 1863, that officer was replaced by General Joseph Hooker, "Fighting Joe," as he was nicknamed, the choice being Lincoln's own in default of a better. The general was full of life and energy and his popularity and dash did much to restore the morale of the troops at a critical moment of deep depression, but he was not capable of planning campaigns on a grand scale, and was much outclassed by his opponents Lee and Jackson.

Lee, in Fredericksburg, had 60,000 men, whereas Hooker had 130,000, and with this numerical superiority he conceived the plan of cutting off Lee's communication with Richmond with one force and turning his left flank with another. In the three days' battle of Chancellorsville, which was brought on by Lee's divining all of Hooker's plans, May 2–5, the Union commander by poor generalship gave up every advantage he had held and was forced back across the Rappahannock with the severe loss of over 17,000 men. It might have been a complete rout had the Confederates not suffered one of the heaviest possible strokes in the wounding of Stonewall Jackson on the first evening of the fight. There was more or less confusion and the general with a small reconnoitring party had got in front of his own lines. On galloping back in the dark, he and his escort were mistaken for Federals, and were fired on by their own men. Jackson, severely wounded, died eight days later from pneumonia. A deeply religious man and one of the finest characters which the Scotch-Irish strain in our nation has produced, he was also one of the ablest generals on either side in the war, and his loss to Lee and the South was irreparable.

Replacing Jackson as well as he could with General R. S. Ewell, Lee determined on another advance into Northern territory, through the Shenandoah Valley. Preceded by Ewell and Hill with two corps to clear the valley, by June 27 Lee had his entire forces in Pennsylvania with headquarters at Chambersburg. On the same

81

day Hooker, who had quarrelled with Halleck, who was continuing as military adviser in Washington, was replaced in command by General G. G. Meade, who took over the Army of the Potomac, then at Frederick. Its presence there had been due to Lincoln, who, although his interference with military plans and commanders had frequently been far from wise, had rightly warned Hooker that he should hang on to Lee's advancing army rather than try to capture Richmond in his absence.

Lee had been over-bold in this second attempt to invade the North. His continued success against one Union general after another had made a Union soldier at Chancellorsville say that "it's no use. No matter who is given us, we can't whip Bobby Lee," and perhaps Lee had himself become too confident. For diplomatic purposes in Europe it was desirable that just at that moment the Confederacy should win a bold stroke. Lee counted on Burnside as his opponent, whom he knew he could outplay, and also on rallying disaffected elements to himself in Pennsylvania. On the other hand, he had lost Jackson, and failed to realize that his own presence on Union soil would rally men to the Northern cause rather than to himself. Meade, though not a great general, was a more dangerous opponent than Burnside, and Lee found his army of about 80,000 outnumbered more quickly than he had counted upon by Meade's forces at Frederick.

GETTYSBURG

Therefore, when Ewell's cavalry had got within three miles of the Pennsylvania capital at Harrisburg, they were recalled, and Lee decided to take his stand on South Mountain and await attack. Meade had decided for his part also to await attack, about thirteen miles from Gettysburg at Pipe Creek, just south of the Maryland line. A chance encounter, however, between very small forces of both armies at Gettysburg precipitated one of the decisive battles of the war on ground not selected by either commander.

As the troops from both armies rapidly arrived near the point where fighting had started, the Federals took up their position on Cemetery Ridge and the Confederates theirs on the parallel Seminary Ridge, the result of the encounter on the first day, July 1, being rather in favor of Lee. The next day the Confederates pushed back both wings of Meade's army, and the position was becoming dangerous. The decisive action was on July 3, when Lee ventured on a direct attack against Meade's centre. After some fighting in the morning and heavy cannonading, the charge against the centre as planned by Lee, contrary to Longstreet's advice, was launched. Fifteen thousand men, with Pickett's division of about 5000 leading, started from the opposing height, approximately a mile away, toward the Union lines on Cemetery Ridge. The charge was magnificent but nothing could

83

stand against the concentrated fire of artillery and rifle. A few Confederates actually reached the Union line and planted the Stars and Bars on top of the ridge, but it was all over. Of the 15,000 men who had charged across the little valley and up the slope, 4000 were captured. The rest were killed or escaped back to the Confederate lines. As a result of the three-days' fight nearly 50,000 men were killed, wounded, or missing, 20 per cent of the Union forces and 30 per cent of the Confederates.

The next day Meade made no effort to follow up his success, and at evening Lee withdrew to the Potomac, which was in flood and impassable. There he remained until the 13th, unmolested by Meade, who, after holding a council of war, resolved not to follow Lincoln's suggestion not to let the enemy escape, although his army, greatly superior in any case to Lee's in numbers, had received 40,000 reinforcements, whereas Lee had none. The President, grateful for Gettysburg, but deeply perturbed by the failure to snatch the fruit of victory and perhaps end the war, declined to accept the resignation which Meade proffered.

On the third day of Gettysburg another victory came to hearten Northern spirit. Grant captured Vicksburg. It had been essential that the city, commanding the Mississippi from the high bluff on which it was located, should be taken if the river was to be opened, and the Confederacy cut, but the task offered peculiar difficulties. Assault from the front was impossible, and the city was protected on the northern side by the streams and marshes of the Yazoo Valley.

Several attempts had been made to capture it when in March, 1863, Grant determined to move his troops down the west bank of the river to below Grand Gulf, cross the river there, and then march northward on firm ground against Vicksburg from the south, Porter slipping down-stream past the fortifications to meet him with gun-boats and transports. The latter, although discovered on the night of April 16 when making the attempt, and subjected to a lively bombardment, got through with the loss of only one transport, and the remarkably able campaign as planned by Grant then proceeded without fault.

Capturing Grand Gulf, Grant next took the important railway junction at Jackson, getting between Vicksburg and the army under J. E. Johnston, who was advancing from Chattanooga to reinforce Pemberton, who was defending Vicksburg. The latter, with 30,000 men, made an effort to cut Grant off from his communications, only to find that he had none! For the first time in the war an army was living off the country on enemy soil. Defeated in two minor engagements, Pemberton was forced back into Vicksburg with no hope of aid from Johnston. Grant, having been joined by Sherman and other forces, had about 75,000 men, and settled down to the siege of the doomed town, although one assault was made on May 22 which cost him over 3000 killed and wounded.

With many non-combatants inside the city, which was bombarded from land and river, the situation was desperate and held out no hope. By the beginning of July, Pemberton had lost about 10,000 men, and there was sufficient food for only a few days more for army and citizens. On the 3d he surrendered the city, and his entire force of approximately 30,000 troops, 50,000 small arms, and other large supplies of military stores, Grant allowing the prisoners to return to their homes on parole. When the place was safely his, Grant returned to Sherman a letter which that officer had written strongly advising him against the plan of his campaign, a typical example of Grant's considerate kindness.

The capture of Vicksburg had cleared the Mississippi, split the Confederacy, and cut off the supplies it had been receiving from Europe through Mexican ports. Their objective won, the Army of the Cumberland and other Western troops could now be utilized to capture Chattanooga, gain possession of Tennessee, and prepare the way for an attack on Atlanta and the splitting of the Confederacy in another direction. The only remaining military events of 1863 were in this field.

Chattanooga, defended by the Confederate General Bragg, was difficult to approach and attack owing to the nature of the bold mountain country in which it is located. Like Vicksburg, it was most accessible from the south, but as General Rosecrans, with 70,000 Union troops, was at Nashville, and Burnside at Knoxville.

Bragg expected the attack to be made from the north. Rosecrans, however, without Grant's ability, tried to repeat that general's strategy at Vicksburg, and swung around so as to approach Chattanooga from the south. Bragg could have cut up the Union forces as they wandered about, more or less separated in the broken and unknown country, but did not do so, and when he led his army out about twelve miles from the city to face Rosecrans at Chickamauga he so placed himself as to leave the way open into the city.

When, on September 20, the second-rate, and on this occasion, panic-struck, Rosecrans was defeated, he fled into Chattanooga with a considerable part of the army. Fortunately, General George H. Thomas, a Virginian and one of the ablest generals on the Union side to emerge from the war, held the Federal left wing with 25,000 men against every assault from the Confederates, gaining the nickname for himself of the "Rock of Chickamauga," and saving the day for the Union army. The following evening he was ordered into the city by Rosecrans, who now found himself besieged by Bragg in the place which he had captured.

GRANT ASSUMES COMMAND

The Union general, completely shattered in nerve, sent desperate calls to Washington for help, but his incapacity being proved, Grant was put in command of all the forces in the West, and he in turn made Thomas commander of the Army of the Cumberland, with orders to hold Chattanooga at all costs until it could be relieved. Grant himself then went to the rescue, with Sherman in command of the Army of the Tennessee. When Grant arrived toward the end of October, he found Bragg entrenched on the heights of Lookout Mountain and Missionary Ridge, and he determined to take the offensive as soon as Sherman should arrive with his forces, a month later.

On November 24 Grant ordered the battle to begin, Sherman, Thomas, and Hooker in command of the forces attacking Bragg's centre and two wings. The result was a complete victory for the Union, made notable by the brilliant dash up Missionary Ridge by Thomas's men, who, against orders, pushed straight up the steep slope, driving the Confederates down the other side. Although far less bloody than the battle of Chickamauga, there being only about 11,000 casualties on the two sides as against 36,000 in the earlier engagement, the battle of Lookout Mountain, or Missionary Ridge, was far more important in its results. Bragg was driven southward, and there was no longer a menace to the Federal control of Chattanooga, which was one of the three most important strategic points in the South, the others being Richmond and Vicksburg. Of these only Richmond now remained in the hands of the enemy, and the way was open to Atlanta and the sea for another year's campaigning. Could the South be bisected east and west, as it had been north and south, and could Lee be defeated definitively, the fate of the Confederacy would be sealed.

The year 1863, though thus ending so favorably for the Union, had not been without its great anxieties in foreign affairs as well as on our own battle-fields. Our chief enemy in Europe throughout our struggle was the French Emperor, Louis Napoleon, but there were several European currents of opinion which also had to be taken into account. There had been, as we noted in the previous chapter, the mistrust of democracy on the part of many in the rich and conservative classes abroad. There was the easily understandable failure to realize that the war was really a blow against slavery. There was also, among some French and Spanish plotters, the hope of realizing anew their dreams of American empire.

The last was most nearly attained by the French. In 1861, as they could properly do even in accordance with the Monroe Doctrine, England, France, and Spain had made a joint military demonstration against Mexico in consequence of one of the perennial disputes over financial affairs, but England and Spain had withdrawn their co-operation the following April after satisfactory terms had been made with the Mexicans. France alone continued to exert the pressure of force in pursuance of a greater adventure.

If the Union was to be broken, the Monroe Doctrine could be safely disregarded, whatever Napoleon might wish to do, and if he could secure the independence of the Confederacy he would have a friendly power on his side for French imperial schemes in America. In January, 1863, just after Lincoln had issued the Emancipation Proclamation, Napoleon proposed to Seward that the North recognize the South as successful, an insulting suggestion which was instantly declined. In June, a few days before Gettysburg was fought, a French army captured the City of Mexico. The following year, Napoleon set the Archduke Maximilian up as Mexican Emperor, backed by French bayonets, and, as it was to prove, by the invariably bad faith of the Napoleonic dynasty.

Throughout the war, when our hands were full, we thus had to count on the persistent enmity of the French Emperor, exerted against us in all possible diplomatic ways. On the other hand, in both France and England, notably in the latter, the tide of democratic sentiment among the ordinary people set more and more strongly in favor of the North as the struggle continued. The Emancipation Proclamation had had a great effect on the liberal-minded of all nations, and early in 1863 great meetings were held all over England demonstrating indubitably that the mass of the English people were solidly in favor of the Union.

There was yet, however, ample cause for anxiety. The Confederate agents, Mason in England and the abler Slidell in France, had not only succeeded in placing a Confederate loan of approximately $15,000,000, but were

having vessels of war built in both countries. By carrying on their transactions in the name of foreign firms

---

HENRY WARD BEECHER IN ENG-LAND.

From our Special Reporter.

This distinguished clergyman, having
traversed the cotton-consuming districts,
delivering at many important points lec-
tures on Slavery and the present condition of Lincolnia, made, on a recent occasion, a novel speech at Exeter Hall.

The fame of the orator drew a brilliant
audience. Among the notabilities present were Viscount Palmerston, Earl
Russell, Honorable Mr. Lindsay, M. P.,
Hon. Mr. Roebuck, M. P., and the Duchess of Sutherland.

'Mr. Beecher entered Exeter Hall, with
the Duchess of Sutherland on his arm,
and both under the especial escort of
her Majesty's Secretary for Foreign Affairs. Earl Russell looked as young as
he did twenty years ago, his seizure of
the Confederate iron-clads doubtless giving him renewed assurance of the distinguished consideration of Mr. Secretary
Seward, of the Lincoln dynasty.

PART OF A REPORT OF HENRY WARD BEECHER'S LONDON VISIT
AS GIVEN IN *THE SOUTHERN PUNCH*, NOV. 7, 1863

and even of foreign governments, they made it difficult
to build up a legal case against the ship-builders, and the
prospect, particularly of having the iron-clad rams build-

ing at Liverpool get to sea and perhaps break up the blockade of Southern ports, was a serious one.

Throughout the summer of 1863, Minister Adams worked steadily and skilfully to prevent the sailing of the vessels on completion, and Russell, having learned the danger of too great observance of legal technicalities, finally ordered them seized. Those building at French ports were also detained. The bonds of the Confederacy dropped to 65, and danger from Europe was over, except for the French Empire in Mexico, which we had to wait to deal with when our hands should become free.

During 1864 the most important events of the war at home were Sherman's march to the sea through Georgia, Grant's long-drawn-out fight for Richmond against Lee, the election in November, and the minor operations of Sheridan in the Shenandoah Valley and of Thomas at Nashville.

Lincoln had at last found his general, and early in March Grant had been made lieutenant-general and chief of all the Northern forces. Coming East, he pitted himself against Lee, and taking charge of the Army of the Potomac, numbering slightly over 100,000, he crossed the Rapidan May 4, and penetrated the wooded country of tangled growth known as "the Wilderness" in a renewed attempt to approach Richmond from the north.

The Lee-Grant campaign which followed was one of the most desperate of the war and notable for marking the transition to the modern form of trench warfare and

THE POSITION AT COLD HARBOR, JUNE 2, 1864

Bottom, A. R. Waud's original sketch and (*top*) the reproduction of it in *Harper's Weekly*, June 25, 1864.

A. R. Waud, an artist for *Harper's Weekly* with the Army of the Potomac from 1861 to 1865, made sketches on the field from which wood blocks were made for publication in *Harper's Weekly*. These original sketches are now in the J. Pierpont Morgan Collection in the Library of Congress.

At the right is Gen. Howard's letter of recommendation of the artist.

War Department,
Bureau of Refugees, Freedmen and Abandoned Lands.

Washington, *March 6th* 1866.

To all agents of this Bureau and others whom it may concern.

I take great pleasure in recommending to your favorable notice Mr. A. R. Waud. Artist for Harper Bros' publications who is travelling thro' the South for the purpose of making sketches for their publications. Mr. Waud I had the pleasure of knowing in the field, whilst I was in command of the Army of the Tennessee. and I found him to be a genial, educated gentleman and worthy of the confidence of all officers of the government whether military or civil — Respectfully —

O. O. Howard
Maj. Gen.

STREET IN FALMOUTH, VIRGINIA

GENERAL GRANT WRITING TELEGRAM THAT THE ARMY HAD CROSSED THE RAPIDAN
From pencil sketches by A. R. Waud in the J. Pierpont Morgan Collection, Library of Congress.

the advent of the spade. Grant had scarcely got across the Rapidan when he faced Lee, who disputed his advance in the two days' battle of the Wilderness, May 5 and 6, which proved only a draw in spite of heavy casualties, involving for Grant the loss of nearly 18,000 men. As Lee blocked the way, Grant tried to outflank him, only to find the Confederates entrenched again in his path. The Union leader also entrenched and then followed the five days' battle of Spottsylvania Court House, in which Grant lost about 16,000 more men, bringing his total losses to about 34,000 in a little over a fortnight. Grant, however, had entrenched his will as well as his army, and simply announced that "I propose to fight it out on this line if it takes all summer." It was to take more.

On whichever side he tried to outflank Lee, the Southerner was there ahead of him, blocking the way. On June 4, Grant made an assault at Cold Harbor, flinging 80,000 men against the Confederate lines, an effort that none believed would succeed and which Grant afterwards acknowledged to have been a mistake. It was over in less than half an hour, the Union loss of 7000 being more than ten times that of Lee. The total losses thus far had been about 55,000 Federal killed and wounded against Confederate losses estimated at between 20,000 and 30,000, and Grant had not as yet got nearer to Richmond than had McClellan.

He now decided to follow McClellan's earlier plan,

that is, to transfer his army to the Peninsula and work up along the James toward Richmond from the southeast. He had at the beginning of the campaign sent General Butler to take Petersburg and cut off Lee's communication, but that general fought Confederate women more fiercely than he did Confederate soldiers, and had allowed himself to be "bottled up" by the forces under Beauregard. On June 15 Grant himself ordered an assault on Petersburg, which failed with the loss of 10,000 more Union men. For more than a month he besieged the town, and on July 27 tried again to force an entry after having sprung a huge mine under a part of the Confederate defences. Once more there was no gain, and a loss of 4000. Until the following April, Grant was to remain without moving. Ugly rumors that his success at Vicksburg had been chance and that he was really an incapable man who had taken again to drink spread through the North, which counted its casualties of over 70,000 husbands and sons, forgetting that comparatively the South had lost as heavily and that the inevitable end was drawing nearer.

Grant had counted on two minor operations to assist him while he was facing Lee near the Rapidan. Both failed, for just as Butler did nothing to capture Petersburg, so Sigel, who was to have cleared the Shenandoah Valley, allowed himself to be completely beaten by General Early. Indeed, by July 11, following the old route down the valley and around by Frederick, Early was within four miles of Washington itself, which he might have captured had he been quick enough. United States paper dollars fell to less than forty cents. However, having delayed, Early was forced to retire by reinforcements sent to the capital by Grant, and having burned Chambersburg, retreated up the valley, which was now to be cleared of all Confederate forces and completely devastated by Sheridan.

On September 19, that general defeated the enemy at Winchester and three days later at Fisher's Hill, burning and destroying as he went until it was said that even "a crow flying over the country would need to carry his own rations." The object was to prevent any further threats to Washington and the North by that route, but answering the cry of rage which went up from the South, Early again advanced only to be defeated at Cedar Creek on October 19. Sheridan was at Winchester, twenty miles off, when he heard of the attack, but rode at top speed to rally his forces which had almost been routed by the Confederates. As a result of the turned tide, the Confederates finally retreated from the valley, which was the scene of no more military operations for the rest of the war.

SHERMAN'S MARCH TO THE SEA

We now have to turn to Sherman and the West. That general's work was the capture of Atlanta and the cutting of the Confederacy. Opposed to him was one of the ablest Southern commanders, J. E. Johnston, with perhaps 70,000 troops. Sherman, in command of the Army of the Cumberland, had approximately 100,000. Early in May, Sherman began his advance, Johnston steadily falling back before him. There was constant skirmishing, although no battle except a minor engagement at Kenesaw Mountain, in which the Federal loss, about 3000, was nearly four times that of the rebels. Thomas, who was with Sherman, disapproved of such useless attacks, and Sherman returned to his former tactics. Johnston continued to fall back, and by July 17 Sherman was across the Chattahoochee River and preparing to besiege Atlanta. The same day, most unwisely, President Davis removed Johnston, with censure, from his command, replacing him by General J. B. Hood.

Hood, being forced by the conditions of his appointment to substitute fighting for Johnston's tactics, fought without avail three battles in ten days, but on September 2 had to evacuate the capital and leave Atlanta to Sherman. Hood now decided to move westward and strike at Sherman's long line of communication, but the latter sent Thomas to oppose him, the Union strength being such that while Sherman could have with him 60,000 men in Atlanta, a force of equal strength could be gathered near Nashville for Thomas. In a masterly little campaign, although marked by his usual caution, Thomas finished all hopes for the Confederacy in Tennessee when he finally inflicted a very heavy defeat on Hood at Nashville on December 16.

Meanwhile, Sherman had determined to cut all communications, even telegraphic, and to march across the richest part of the Confederacy to the sea, subsisting his army on the country. He proceeded to wage war in accordance with his belief that "war is hell," and that the quickest and therefore the most humane way in the long run to end it is to inflict as great damage on the enemy as is possible with the least delay. He left Atlanta on November 16, part of his forces having started the day before. Lincoln and Grant were to know nothing of his whereabouts except from Southern newspapers until December 14, when a despatch announced that he was within ten miles of Savannah. On his march of 360 miles, he deliberately destroyed, in a belt 60 miles wide, all of the property possible which might in any way enure to the military benefit of the enemy, and much more that could not, his own estimate being that he had ruined property to the amount of $100,000,000, of which four fifths was mere waste without military advantage. Savannah was evacuated without a fight, and on December 20 Sherman took possession of the city.

On June 19, the U. S. S. *Kearsarge* had met the *Alabama* off Cherbourg on the coast of France, and had sunk that vessel after it, with the smaller ones escaped from England, had done damage to United States commerce estimated in the later arbitration at $15,500,000. On August 5, Farragut, with eighteen ships, had slipped past the forts guarding the entrance of Mobile Bay and had defeated the Confederate fleet gathered there, gaining possession of that valuable port, although the city itself was not captured until the following spring. With Mobile and New Orleans in Federal possession, the Mississippi in Federal control for its entire length, the Confederacy west of that river no longer strong enough to be any menace, with no fear of further enemy thrusts up from Tennessee or through the Shenandoah Valley, with the railroads and military stores destroyed through the heart of the Confederacy, with Sherman ready to march northward from Savannah and Lee outnumbered by Grant, the end was in sight.

All of this, however, was far from being obvious in the spring and summer, when a war-weary North had to face a Presidential election in the midst of a great conflict, the most serious ordeal of that sort which any modern democracy has been called upon to face. On the 7th of June, Lincoln had been unanimously nominated for a second term by a convention of Republicans and War Democrats, who named Andrew Johnson of Tennessee as Vice-President. The call for the convention had been worded to include all who stood for Union of whatever party, and the first plank in the platform reiterated this in the statement that, "laying aside all differences of political opinion," it was the highest duty of every American citizen to "maintain against all their enemies the integrity of the Union." It approved the President's war policy and aims, and, among other things, de-

GENERAL GEORGE A. CUSTER SALUTING ROSSER, HIS FORMER CLASSMATE

Rosser, graduating from West Point as Virginia seceded, joined the Confederate Army. He later engaged in engineering and was Chief Engineer of the Pacific Railroad in 1881-1882. The meeting shown above took place at Woodstock Races, October 9, 1864.

CONFEDERATES TAKING THE OATH AT RICHMOND, 1865

From the pencil sketches by A. R. Waud in the J. Pierpont Morgan Collection in the Library of Congress.

THE CHRISTIAN COMMISSION IN THE FIELD AT GERMANTOWN, VIRGINIA, 1863

HEADQUARTERS OF THE FIRST BRIGADE, HORSE ARTILLERY, AT BRANDY STATION,
VIRGINIA

From Brady photographs in the Library of Congress.

nounced the French attempt to set up an empire in Mexico.

Prior to the Republican Convention, a group of radicals of all sorts, such as Elizabeth Cady Stanton, Wendell Phillips, Frederick Douglass and others, had approved of a convention which had nominated Frémont on the heterogeneous platform which such groups usually produce, including a plank limiting the office of President to one term.

There was no danger from them. The danger was from the Democrats and even more from those Republicans who were opposed to Lincoln. The Democratic Convention met at Chicago on August 19, and adopted a completely defeatist platform, demanding an immediate cessation of hostilities and loudly denouncing the acts of Lincoln's administration. General McClellan was nominated on the first ballot, and although he repudiated the platform his ambition and vanity prevented him from declining to run on it.

The campaign before the American people thus afforded the peculiar spectacle of a civilian President running on a no-compromise war platform and a general of the army running on a pacifist and defeatist one. At the end of August it seemed impossible that Lincoln could win. In July he had had to call for another half million volunteers and one of the hated drafts, which we shall discuss in the next chapter, was scheduled for September 6. The people were weary of the endless war, and in *The Tribune* Greeley was assailing the President with profound bitterness. Luckily, the week of the draft,

THE HERO OF ANTIETA.

GEN. GEORGE B. McCLELLAN,
DEMOCRATIC CANDIDATE FOR THE PRESIDENCY OF THE UNITED STATES.

BROADSIDE ON WHICH WAS PRINTED McCLELLAN'S LETTER OF
ACCEPTANCE OF THE NOMINATION
From the Rare Book Room, New York Public Library.

Sherman took Atlanta, and gave encouragement to the drooping Union spirits.

Although McClellan saved a good many votes for himself personally by the rather odd method of repudiating the proclaimed views and principles of the party which had made him its leader, the result of the election proved an overwhelming victory for Lincoln, whose popular vote was 2,214,000 to McClellan's 1,802,000, and whose vote even in the army was 117,000 to the general's 34,-000. Owing to the usual vagaries of our electoral system, the President's electoral vote defeated his opponent 10 to 1 (212 to 21), instead of the mere 2.3 to 1.8 of the people's votes; but even so Lincoln had won a popular majority of about a half million, and in spite of all the discouragements of a prolonged war, the democracy of the North had shown itself capable of making the wise decision at the polls.

The doom of the Confederacy could not now be long postponed. There had already been abortive efforts to compromise, mostly got up by self-appointed agents, and on February 3, 1865, there was a meeting of official delegates at Hampton Roads, Lincoln attending in person. There was, however, no real chance of a negotiated peace. Lincoln might offer to end hostilities if the Confederacy would submit to the Union and accept emancipation as an accomplished fact, with the promise to try to have Congress pass some sort of compensation measure, but Jefferson Davis could not agree to anything except on the primary basis of recognition of Southern independence. The conference having failed, there was nothing to do but finish the fight and let arms decide.

There could be no doubt now what that decision would be. The South had at last lost courage to go on. It still had resources both in men and supplies, but the will to fight longer what seemed a hopeless and endless struggle had gone. In the autumn of 1864 Davis had admitted that two thirds of the soldiers were absent from their regiments, mostly without leave. There was no longer any expectation of foreign recognition. The blockade was tightening. Sherman's march had made a deep impression. The women in innumerable homes were tiring, and, as in the Revolution, the men at the front got piteous messages describing conditions on farms and plantations.

On February 1, Sherman left Savannah and began his march northward. There was much plundering on the way, and, on the 17th, drunken Union privates set fire to the railroad station at Columbia, and for two days there was a reign of terror in that city. Sherman's orders had specifically stated that the public buildings, railway property, factories, and machine shops were to be destroyed, but that libraries, asylums, and all private dwellings were to be immune. Months of deliberate destruction and looting, however, had let down the morale of his army, which included, as armies always do, a large number of the lower sort who asked nothing better than the chance to pillage. There is no question that the troops behaved very badly, and in spite of efforts to control them, the capital of South Carolina was left a mass of smoking ruins when Sherman marched out of it on the 20th. Two days before, the Confederates had been forced to abandon Charleston, and there again the Union troops wreaked vengeance.

9ᵗ Apl '65

Genl
        I have recd your note
of this date. Though not enter
taining the opinion you express
of the hopelessness of further resis
-tance on the part of the Army
of N. Va. I reciprocate your
desire to avoid useless effusion
of blood, & therefore before Consider
-ing your proposition ask
the terms you will offer, on
Condition of its Surrender
                Very respt your Obt Svt
                        R E Lee
                        , Genl

Lt Genl U. S. Grant
  Commd Armies of the U States

FACSIMILE OF NOTE FROM LEE TO GRANT, APRIL 9, 1865
One of the series of surrender correspondence, facsimiled by Ely B. Parker.

In the Manuscript Division, Library of Congress.

Moving northward, Sherman was confronted by Johnston, but beat him back, and by March 23 had joined General Schofield at Goldsboro, thus receiving 20,000 reinforcements, 160 miles from Richmond. From Goldsboro he intended to march to the assistance of Grant.

THE FALL OF THE CONFEDERACY

Grant, however, was not to need him. By April 3 he had forced Lee to evacuate Petersburg, and in consequence of threatening his railway communications had caused the Southern commander to abandon any further attempt to defend Richmond, which was now open to the Federals. Davis and the Confederate Government fled, and Grant took possession of the capital. Lee was now in retreat, and had to turn toward Lynchburg when Sheridan captured the railway at Danville. The Southern army was melting rapidly by desertions, and on April 9 Lee asked for a meeting with Grant at Appomattox Court House.

The terms of surrender of the 26,765 men, all that were left of Lee's former magnificent army, were quickly arranged. Grant, rough and uncultured as he was, displayed again and at their finest his instincts of considerate thoughtfulness which made him, in spite of all his shortcomings, one of the great gentlemen in our history.

According to the terms agreed, the Confederate troops were to be released on parole. Officers were to retain their side arms, which saved the gallant Lee and others the humiliation of surrendering their swords, and were also to keep their horses and personal baggage. To the suggestion of Lee that many of the privates owned their own horses also, Grant immediately responded by adding that they as well as officers might keep them, as they might be useful "for the spring plowing." Lee said the action "will do much toward conciliating our people," and the terms were accepted. Enquiry showed that the Confederates were badly in need of food. Grant ordered that rations be supplied to them. As word of the surrender spread through the Union lines, shots were fired in rejoicing. At once Grant ordered them to cease. "The war is over," he said, "the rebels are our countrymen again: and the best sign of rejoicing after the victory will be to abstain from all demonstrations in the field." Lee rode back to his own lines. Scarcely able to speak for feeling, he could only say to his veterans, "We have fought through the war together. I have done the best I could for you. My heart is too full to say more."

In the course of a few weeks, the other armies had also surrendered and the trial by combat had ended.

CHAPTER III

BEHIND THE LINES IN WAR TIME

BEFORE continuing the narrative of political events, which will lead us into what, on the whole, was the most disgraceful period of our national life, we must stop to consider what was going on among the civilian population behind the lines, both North and South, during the four years of war. Such a struggle, under modern conditions, is bound to affect profoundly the life of any people. Not only in a thousand minor ways does it alter all the accustomed routine and habits of daily living, but it also emphasizes existing tendencies to such a degree as to make it appear as though it had almost completely changed one's accustomed world. Indeed, in some respects the greatest wars do so, but we must distinguish between merely temporary influences, the acceleration of existing tendencies, and the new factors introduced. We shall consider first the more local conditions North and South, and then note some of the larger results of the contest on national life and outlook.

EFFECT OF WAR ON NORTH AND SOUTH

In the North as well as the South, the ordinary citizen was affected in two ways, in his direct relation to the government, and in his relations to the general economic and social conditions engendered.

Looking first at the North, we are struck by the fact that, precisely as it was in England, public opinion was confused in the beginning as to what the war was really being waged for when it broke. Writing from Massachusetts to a friend in London some three months after Fort Sumter had surrendered, Nathaniel Hawthorne voiced the confusion of many when he said: "We also have gone to war, and we seem to have little, or at least a very misty idea of what we are fighting for. It depends upon the speaker; and that, again, depends upon the section of the country in which his sympathies are enlisted. The Southern man will say, 'We fight for States' rights, liberty, and independence.' The Middle-Western man will avow he fights for the Union; while our Northern and Eastern man will swear that from the beginning his only idea was liberty to the blacks and the annihilation of slavery."

Although this confusion, as we saw, was to some extent cleared by Lincoln's Emancipation Proclamations of September, 1862, and January, 1863, it was never completely clarified in the North. Throughout the four years a considerable party in that section was wholly opposed to the war. Forming themselves into an organization called at different times and places the Knights of the Golden Circle, Order of American Knights, and Sons of

"There are many complaints, Davy, about that."—*King Henry IV.*, V. 1.

There was a Stern Statesman astute,   who so often went in to *recruit*,
That a Rattlesnake fat   revolved in his hat,
While a Copperhead squirmed in his boot.
15

FROM *YE BOOK OF COPPERHEADS*

Drawings and verses by Charles Godfrey Leland.. Published in Philadelphia, 1863. This book was republished in Indianapolis as a campaign document in 1864.

From the Rare Book Room, Library of Congress.

Liberty, with the notorious Clement L. Vallandigham of Ohio as chief official in 1864, the party was defeatist and disloyal, not seldom using terroristic methods against those who were supporting the government. Apart from these "copperheads," as the members of this group were popularly called from one of the most dangerous of American snakes, the North was far from a unit either in aims or prosecution of the struggle.

As Hawthorne pointed out, Union sentiment was

strongest in the West and Abolitionism in the East, particularly New England. In so far as the latter section was vocal through its authors and orators, it cared little enough for mere Union. The chief Abolitionists, as we saw in an earlier chapter, had long been preaching disunion, and the chief concern of this strong New England group appeared to be lest their skirts might be soiled by continuing the bonds that united them to slave States. More than a dozen years earlier, at the time of the Texas controversy, Lowell had written in the first series of his *Biglow Papers:*

> "Ef I'd *my* way I hed ruther
> We should go to work an' part,
> They take one way, we take t'other,
> Guess it wouldn't break my heart."

After civil war had begun, Hawthorne wrote to a friend: "We shall be better off without the South—better and nobler than hitherto—without them." Even the gentle Quaker poet Whittier had compared Southerners to demons, and in writing and speaking against slavery not only the extreme Abolitionists but others also had, by their fiery, intemperate, and often untrue denunciations of the Southern aims and character, done their best to instil into the Northern mind a hatred of the South and its people almost greater than the hatred of slavery itself.

For this group, the war was not a war for union but primarily a war to free the slave and to punish a people whom they had been taught to think of as almost inhuman aliens, cruel and immoral. They considered that the Southerners were not merely caught in the toils of an economic system which neither they nor Lincoln could see how to change, but were wilfully ruling by blood and lash, that they were men and women so lost to all humanity as to make the destruction of the Union preferable to the North's having any more connection with them. We shall see later the terrible results of the joining of this group of moral fanatics with others in the history of reconstruction. During particularly the earlier stage of the war, if this group cared little about a war for Union, which Lincoln proclaimed the struggle to be, the Western and other Unionist groups cared little about waging a war which should be fought for the ends of the Abolitionists, whose aims and methods they had long bitterly denounced.

Turning to the question of military service, we may note that, owing to much overlapping in various ways, it is impossible to arrive at any accurate estimate of the numbers of troops who served in both armies. In the North, the enlistments were almost 2,900,000, but it is probable that only about 1,575,000 different individuals actually were in service at one time and another. Of these, 359,528 died, 110,000 either on the battle-field or from wounds.

Perhaps no other great nation in history has been less militaristic than our own, with the exception of China, and the raising of troops has always presented difficulties, until the World War, when the lessons from previous ones were utilized from the start. On April 15, 1861, Lincoln in the North called for 75,000 volunteers for

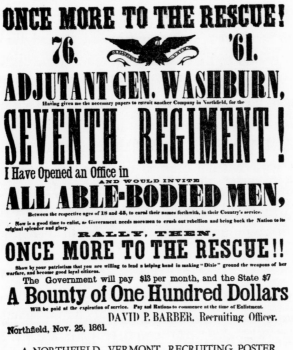

A NORTHFIELD, VERMONT, RECRUITING POSTER

From the Rare Book Room, New York Public Library.

three months' service only, and this small number, for so short a term, out of that section's population of 19,-000,000 (not counting the border States) promptly enlisted. May 3, he called for about 80,000 more, approximately half of whom were to serve in volunteer regiments and half in the regular army for a three-year term.

Until Congress should meet in special session on July 4, the President was in a quandary as to volunteers, the old law of 1795 providing that militia could not be called upon to serve more than three months in any one year. It was for that technical reason and not because he believed in so short a war that Lincoln named the three months' period in his first call, however hopeful Seward may have been of a brief struggle. On the other hand, it is not likely that the North, even in its early burst of enthusiasm, would have voluntarily provided a large army for three years instead of three months.

As it was, when Congress did meet in July, it was believed necessary to offer a bounty of $100 to every soldier who would volunteer, and this system was continued throughout the war. Not only the Federal Government but States, counties, and districts offered bounties also, so that by 1864 volunteers were receiving in some States, such as Massachusetts and Illinois, as much as $1000 and even more for their enlistment. Before the end of the war the system had cost the Federal Government $300,000,000 and the State and local governments $286,000,000 more. It also had the result of encouraging large numbers of unscrupulous men in what came to be known as "bounty jumping." These would enlist in one place, receive their bounty, desert at the first opportunity, go to another enlistment district, and again be paid, often repeating the process many times before being caught.

By the middle of 1862 the need for men was imperative, and in spite of patriotism and bounties they were not coming forward. On July 2 the President asked for 300,000 through the Governors of the States, who instituted State drafts.

"We are coming, Father Abraham, three hundred thousand
   more,
From Mississippi's winding stream, and from New England's
   shore,"

wrote John S. Gibbons, in the editorial column of *The New York Evening Post,* but in fact only 88,000 came.

By the next year the situation was so bad that Congress, on March 3, 1863, enacted a conscription law, which, although based on State population, was for the first time in our history to operate directly on the people by machinery set up by the Federal Government instead of by the individual States. All men between twenty and forty-five were required to register, although certain groups, such as married men over thirty-five, could subsequently claim exemption from service. There were many bad features in the Act, later amended, one of which was the basing of the quota on population instead of on the number of men of military age. At first a good many of the States, particularly in the West, where enlistments had been heavier than in the East, were practically exempt, owing to credits being given for previous enlistments. Although various changes were made in the Act, which remained in force throughout the war, the worst features of all remained, the privilege given to a drafted man to cancel his call on any particular

Avoid the Draft!

HEADQUARTERS PROVOST MARSHAL, SIXTH DISTRICT,
No. 6 Union Buildings, Main street, below De Kalb, NORRISTOWN, June 2, 1863.

PUBLIC attention is solicited to the subjoined circular from the Provost Marshal General. All persons wishing to join any of the Regiments here referred to, will make application to these Headquarters within the next thirty days.

JOHN J. FREEDLEY, *CAPTAIN,*
Provost Marshal, Sixth District.

PROVOST MARSHAL GENERAL'S OFFICE,
WASHINGTON, D. C., May 22, 1863.
All men who desire to join any particular regiment of

CAVALRY

Now in the field, are hereby authorized to present themselves at any time during the next thirty days to the Board of Enrolment, in their respective Districts. The Board shall examine them and determine upon their fitness for the service, and if found to be fit, the Provost Marshal of the District shall give them transportation tickets to the general rendezvous, at the Headquarters of the A. A. Provost Marshal General of the State. As soon as they present themselves at this general Rendezvous they shall be duly mustered by a mustering and disbursing officer, and paid by him the bounty allowed by law.

JAMES B. FRY,
PROVOST MARSHAL GENERAL.

June 2, 1863.

Herald and Free Press Print. Norristown, Pa. All kinds of Job Work done to order.

A RECRUITING POSTER FROM NORRISTOWN, PA.
From the Manuscript Division, Library of Congress.

draft by paying $300, or to avoid service for the entire duration of the war by procuring a substitute for a three-year enlistment.

This meant that only the poor were inextricably caught in the conscription net, and the North was treated to the spectacle of agents roving everywhere to buy men to serve in place of those who did not wish to, and could afford not to. Darkies from the South, the poor or down-and-outs in the North and Canada, even the inhabitants of European poorhouses, were drawn upon, bought and paid for. A district, however, was not submitted to the draft if it filled its quota otherwise, and although over 200,000 substitutes appear to have been purchased, the greater part by far of the men who served throughout the whole war were volunteers, there being over 834,000 volunteers at the time of the four drafts from July, 1863, to December, 1864.

THE RIOTS IN NEW YORK AND ELSEWHERE

The extremely undemocratic aspect of the law and its many inequitable features resulted in much violent opposition, the worst being the draft riots in New York in July, 1863. For four days that city was practically in the hands of a mob. The provost marshal's office was sacked and destroyed, as were the home of the mayor, that of the publisher of *The Tribune,* the Weehawken Ferry House, and other buildings. The Colored Orphan Asylum was burned, and negroes were hunted through the city and a number killed. The draft had to be suspended, both the Governor of the State, Horatio Seymour, and the mayor of the city cravenly assuring the mob that the law was unconstitutional. It was not until Federal troops had been rushed to the scene that order was restored, after a thousand persons had been killed or wounded and about $1,500,000 worth of property destroyed.

ATTENTION!

MERCHANTS, BANKERS AND MERCHANTS' CLERKS AND OTHERS

Meet for Organization and Enrolment

At Two O'clock

AT THE MERCHANTS' EXCHANGE,

111 *Broadway,*

To take immediate action in the present crisis. Military now engaged with the Mob. The Mayor's House being Sacked and Torn Down!!

A HANDBILL OF 1863 DURING THE DRAFT RIOTS IN NEW YORK
From the Rare Book Room, New York Public Library.

Although the New York riots were the most serious, there were minor affairs in other cities throughout the North. In spite of these, however, the drafts were carried out. The results, nevertheless, were far from reassuring. In the draft of July, 1863, of the approximately 292,000 names drawn, the bearers of about 40,000 failed to report. A little over 252,000 men were actually examined, and

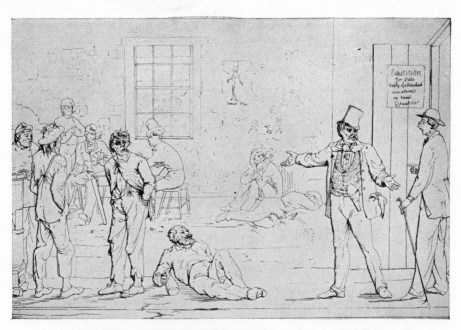

BUYING A SUBSTITUTE IN THE NORTH DURING THE WAR

From the Confederate War Etching by Volck in the Library of Congress.

A SOMEWHAT SIMILAR SITUATION IN THE SOUTH

From an etching by Thomas Worth, in the Library of Congress.

WAR LYRICS.

"Where is our little drummer?"
    His nearest comrades say,
When the dreadful fight is over,
    And the smoke has cleared away.
As the rebel corps was scattering,
    He urged them to pursue;
So, furiously he beat and beat
    The *rat-tat-too*!

He stood no more among them,
    For a bullet as it sped
Had glanced and struck his ankle,
    And stretched him with the dead!
He crawled behind a cannon,
    And pale and paler grew:
But still the little drummer beat
    His *rat-tat-too*!

They bore him to the surgeon,
    A busy man was he:
"A drummer-boy—what ails him?"
    His comrades answered, "See!"
As they took him from the stretcher,
    A heavy breath he drew,
And his little fingers strove to beat
    The *rat-tat-too*!

The ball had spent its fury:
    "A scratch," the surgeon said,
As he wound the snowy bandage
    Which the lint was staining red!
"I must leave you now, old fellow,"
    "O take me back with you,
For I know the men are missing me,
    And the *rat-tat-too*!"

16

THE LITTLE DRUMMER

Pages from "A Selection of War Lyrics" with illustrations on wood by F. O. C. Darley, New York, 1864.

From the Rare Book Room, Library of Congress.

of these over 164,000 secured exemption on one plea or another. Of the 88,170 who were actually drafted, 52,288 bought their exemptions for $300 each, giving the gov-

THE DRAFT.

MERCHANTS', BANKERS', AND GENERAL VOLUNTEER AND SUBSTITUTE ASSOCIATION,

Office, 428 Broadway, New-York.

SIR :—

We beg to inform you that we are now furnishing acceptable *alien* substitutes for men who are enrolled, and men who are not enrolled, for the coming Draft, and also for men who have already been drafted.

The *Provost Marshal General* having officially intimated to accept substitutes for men before the Draft takes place, the present is the best opportunity that will be offered to procure good men at reasonable prices.

Gentlemen will have their substitutes sent to the office of the Provost Marshal, and examined and mustered into the United States' service, and their exemption papers correctly procured, without the inconvenience of their leaving their places of business to attend to it themselves. All inconvenience and trouble will be saved to them, by merely forwarding their full name and place of residence to this office, and their wishes will be promptly attended to.

SIMPSON & McNICHOL,
AGENTS,

THE BEGINNING AND ENDING OF A CIRCULAR LETTER OF JUNE, 1864, REGARDING DRAFT SUBSTITUTES

From the Rare Book Room, New York Public Library.

ernment over $15,500,000. Of the remaining 35,882 men whose names had been turned up, 26,002 bought substitutes and were thus exempt for the duration of the war. Had it not been for the volunteers, the struggle would have ended then and there in defeat, but it is probable that the draft had greatly stimulated the flagging volunteering.

If it was not easy for Lincoln to fill the ranks of the army, the men who were in it were well looked after by those behind the lines. A new era of humanitarianism in military history had been ushered in by Florence Nightingale in the Crimean War only a few years earlier, and when the antiquated medical department of the United States Army found itself helpless before its sudden task of caring for the sick and wounded en masse—there were 90,000 on the Northern side by the end of 1862—a civilian organization on a national basis, the United States Sanitary Commission, rendered admirable service. Clara Barton and Louisa M. Alcott were merely the two most famous of the many nurses it put in the field. Not only caring for the sick and disabled but also supplying the well with many comforts, the Sanitary Commission was the first national organization of the sort which we had developed. Money for it was raised in part by the holding of "Sanitary Fairs," those at New York and Philadelphia alone netting a million dollars each. Another organization, chiefly concerned with distributing Bibles and otherwise ministering to the moral welfare of the men, although also catering for their physical needs, was the Christian Commission, which expended $6,000,000 in all, and like the Sanitary Commission was nation-wide in its organization.

Very large sums were spent by States and smaller political divisions in caring for the families of the poorer soldiers, and the war seems to have given a considerable impetus to the more ordinary charities of peace times. One of the difficult problems was that of the disposition of about 300,000 negroes who had either escaped from

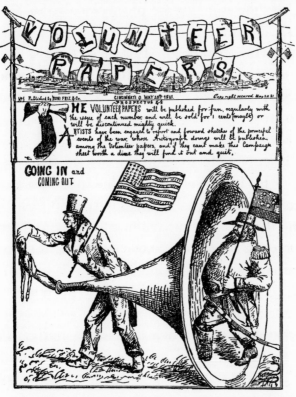

A FOUR–PAGE MAGAZINE, WRITTEN AND ILLUSTRATED BY
VOLUNTEERS IN CINCINNATI, MAY, 1861
From the Rare Book Room, New York Public Library.

the South or were taken over by the government as parts of the South were conquered by the Union armies and the owners of the negroes fled. To a considerable extent these derelict slaves were gathered together into camps, where conditions for the most part were extremely bad, the mortality in them rising, according to a government official, to 25 per cent in 1864. When conditions were revealed, however, a wave of missionary emotion swept over the North, and much was done to ameliorate the situation. It was probably true, nevertheless, that in the long run the harm done to the cause of the negro by Northern animosity against him, which was strong, was not so great as that by the unintelligent and purely emotional fervor raised on his behalf.

It is impossible to estimate exactly the cost of the struggle to either North or South, but for the former the increased expenditure of the government above normal during the war years was unquestionably more than $3,-000,000,000. More than $2,600,000,000 was raised by the sale of bonds, some yielding investors as high as 7.30 at purchase, the total bonded debt of the government reaching practically $3,000,000,000, after adjustment of certain claims, by 1868. Three other chief sources of revenue were tapped—internal taxation, import duties, and the issue of paper money, the latter two having lasting results.

The system of internal taxation, which yielded over $356,000,000, was rather chaotic, and it began to seem as though almost every object and occupation was taxed in one way or another—liquor, tobacco, bank checks, advertisements, all sorts of businesses, and incomes, and almost innumerable other things. Before the war was over, the income tax, declared unconstitutional long afterward, was levied at 5 per cent on incomes from $600 to $5000

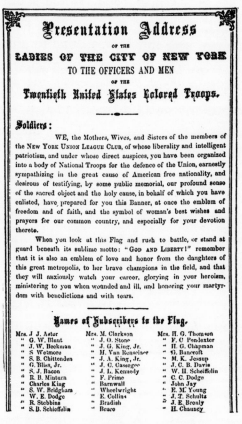

BROADSIDE OF THE ADDRESS ACCOMPANYING THE PRESENTATION OF A FLAG TO COLORED TROOPS, PROBABLY IN 1863
With names of part of the subscribers.
From the Rare Book Room, New York Public Library.

and 10 per cent above the latter amount. It has been said that in levying internal revenue taxes the government went on the theory that "wherever you see a head, hit it," and owing to duplications and the taxation of the same article in its various stages of manufacture or sale, it was estimated that the taxes actually collected ranged from 8 to 15 per cent on every finished product.

From the tariff of 1846 to that of 1860, there had been little agitation on the subject of protection, and rates had tended toward lower figures. For the purpose of winning votes in the election of 1860, in some of the manufacturing States, notably Pennsylvania, the Morrill Bill had been prepared, considerably increasing the duties on iron and wool for protection rather than for revenue. This Act, finally passed in 1861, had been a vote-getting and not a war measure, but it was scarcely passed when the war made its heavy demands for increased revenue. By successive Acts the average duty levied rose to 37.2 per cent in 1862 and over 47 per cent in 1864, but the essential feature of these new tariff measures was the emphasis laid on protection, and, in not a few cases, the flagrant granting to special industries of the opportunity to make excessive profits by government aid. This, in the long run, was to prove of more importance than the raising of slightly over $300,000,000 toward national expenses during the war.

FINANCIAL DIFFICULTIES

Although throughout the contest the government insisted upon customs duties being paid in gold, the metal

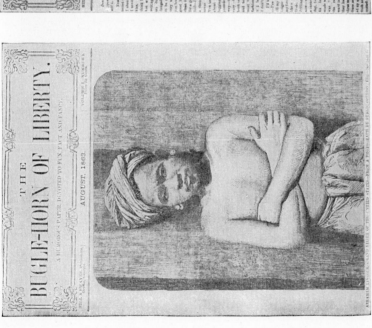

The first issue of *The Bugle Horn of Liberty*, inaugurating a series of "portraits of the kind of men at the head of the Northern Government," carried this design said to be "if not a likeness of the man (Lincoln) who desires so much to govern us, the exterior corresponds with his acts." The second number pictured Horace Greeley, "an entirely original 'pictur.' We do not publish the same picture more than once. We change our base every time."

From the Rare Book Room of the Library of Congress.

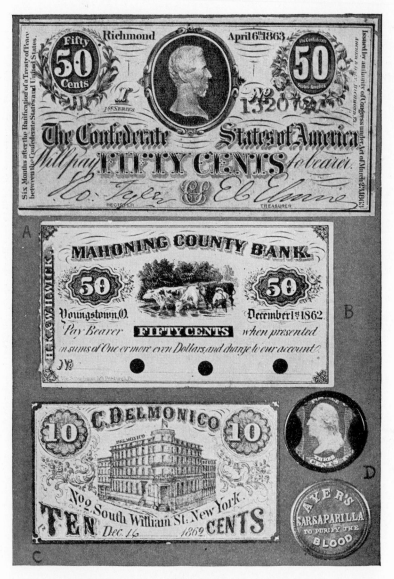

A. CONFEDERATE STATES OF AMERICA 50-CENT BILL, 1863

B. MAHONING COUNTY BANK, YOUNGSTOWN, OHIO, BILL FOR FIFTY CENTS, 1862

C. SCRIP ISSUED BY DELMONICO'S RESTAURANT, NEW YORK, 1862

D. FACE OF ENCASED POSTAGE STAMP MONEY PATENTED 1862, WITH REVERSE, WHICH WAS USED FOR ADVERTISING

From the Chase National Bank Collection of Moneys.

disappeared from circulation almost immediately. In February, 1862, Congress authorized the issue of paper money to the extent of $150,000,000 and made the "greenbacks," as the notes were called, legal tender for all purposes except customs duties and interest on the national debt. There was nothing back of this paper except the credit of the nation, and as, by successive issues, the amount rose to $431,000,000, and the changing fortunes of the war made redemption problematic, the greenbacks fell in value until at one stage a paper dollar was worth only thirty-five cents in gold. At the end of 1861 all banks had suspended specie payment, and it was not until the country went back on a gold basis in January, 1879, that our paper money returned to par.

In 1863 the currency which the people had to use was in confusion. Not only was there the issue of greenbacks, fluctuating in value, but there were the government "shin-plasters," bills for small amounts to take the place of those metal coins other than gold which had also disappeared. Private concerns issued small bills, postage stamps were largely used, and 1300 banks in the North were issuing their bills in denominations up to $1000, it being estimated that there were over 8000 different varieties in circulation, without including innumerable counterfeits.

Partly to clear up this situation, and partly to assist the sale of the huge blocks of government bonds, a National Bank Act was passed in February, 1863, providing for the creation of banks which should belong to a "national" instead of State systems. These were to be supervised by national examiners, and were to issue bank notes to the extent only of 90 per cent of the United States bonds held by them, the government assuming responsibility for the ultimate redemption of all the notes as issued. Few banks were formed under this system during the war, but just at the end of it, in 1865, when the government laid a tax of 10 per cent on all notes issued by State banks, many institutions changed over and became "national." For almost exactly fifty years the new system remained the foundation of our banking currency.

There was another way in which the citizen found his life directly touched by the fact of war. We know at present of no other form of government which, on the whole, suits our modern problems and temper better than democracy. Nevertheless, popular government has its limitations. As history has shown over and over again, in many countries in the last century at times of really great crisis (usually evolved from war conditions) democracy has had to submit itself temporarily to a practical dictatorship and to yield up some of its prerogatives and safeguards.

Whether or not this may eventually prove to be an insuperable weakness in the system, only the future can disclose. It will depend in part on how frequently, in peace as well as in war, great crises may arise and on how rapidly the democratic peoples themselves may advance not simply in knowledge, but in wisdom and freedom from passion and prejudice.

There never was less of a tyrant in heart and mind than Lincoln, and yet many of his acts led him to be so considered by numerous Northerners who were as loyal as himself to the cause of Union. His situation was difficult. The North, as we have seen, was not only not a unit in its war aims, but throughout the struggle there was a very large element in it which was opposed to carrying on the fight at all. The problem of just how far freedom of speech and press can be maintained in war without danger to the nation is an extremely complex one, depending upon a very exact balancing of the value as against the danger of the opinions of the protesting minority.

Although suppression was not carried so far by Lincoln's administration as later by Wilson's, in some respects the earlier control of citizens was more rigorous. At the very beginning, when it was uncertain which side Maryland would join, Lincoln suspended the writ of habeas corpus in that State, without constitutional authority to do so. The following year he gave the force of an executive decree to the arbitrary arrests which had been made by the Secretary of War, suspending the writ throughout the United States for all persons who should "give aid and comfort to the rebels," discourage enlistments or engage in "any disloyal practice."

It was not until after the war was over that a decision

was rendered on the question by the Supreme Court, in the case of L. P. Milligan, who with two other "Sons of Liberty" in Indiana had been sentenced to death by a military commission in 1864, a sentence not carried out because Lincoln did not sign the order. When Milligan's case, after Lincoln's own death, reached the Supreme Court, that tribunal handed down an emphatic opinion, declaring that under no circumstances could a civilian be subjected to military trial where the civil courts were functioning. It is uncertain how many civilians were executed as traitors during the war, but more than 13,000 found themselves in prison on various charges.

Turning now from the consideration of how the Northerner was directly acted upon by the government owing to the war, we must inquire into how he was moved by the general social and economic influences resulting from it.

The first thing to note, in contrast to what we shall find in the South, is that, after a panic at the start, the North fairly buzzed with an amazing prosperity throughout the struggle. The causes of the preliminary panic are not far to seek. The months between the election of Lincoln in 1860 and the actual beginning of war in April, 1861, were months of intense anxiety. No one could tell what was coming, whether it might be safe to borrow or lend, to buy or sell, or to engage in any business undertaking. The South, largely agricultural, with less than a quarter of the number of Northern business houses, owed Northern business men about $300,000,000. There was the fear lest, in case of war, this debt might become an almost total loss, as in fact it did, New York firms alone losing $160,000,000 when the war started.

Even before that, the banks from Philadelphia southward had temporarily suspended, and, especially in the West, the smaller banks failed in every direction, 89 out of 110 in Illinois breaking within a year. One of the causes of the collapse was that the Western banks in particular had secured their currency by deposit of State bonds. The Southern bonds, paying higher rates of interest than the Northern ones, had been preferred by the bankers, those in Illinois, for example, thus finding themselves, at the opening of hostilities, with $9,000,000 of enemy bonds to secure their own bank notes.

The reasons for the abounding Northern prosperity which so soon followed are more varied. The fundamental basis of economic life in America has always been agriculture. It had been the enormous development of cotton culture in the South which had riveted slavery on that section, made it wealthy, and caused it to believe that it would be bound to succeed in war because the world would not be able to get along without its product. Now a peculiar combination of circumstances was about to make the Wheat Empire of the North rival the Cotton Kingdom of the South.

LAND AND AGRICULTURE

For any great expansion of Northern agriculture four factors would have to be present in combination—land on terms which would allow of rapid settlement, power (either mechanical or human) to work it, transportation facilities for distributing crops raised on it, and markets large enough to absorb them.

For several decades prior to the war, there had been constant demand from the West for free land, a demand opposed by the South, which did not wish to see the non-slave States grow too rapidly in population. In 1862, the Republicans, redeeming their campaign pledge of 1860, passed the Homestead Law, signed by Lincoln May 20, by which an actual settler who should remain on his quarter section of 160 acres could acquire title to it without any payment whatever to the government. The dream of the West had at last come true. In the same year, the Morrill Act, sponsored since 1857 by Representative Justin H. Morrill of Vermont, became a law. Under this Act, designed to promote the establishment of agricultural colleges, the Federal Government donated to the States 30,000 acres of public lands for each representative they had in Congress, for the purpose of providing funds from land sales with which to found the colleges. In addition to these two sources of free or low-priced land, there was yet another in the huge land grants which had been made to the railroads to hasten their construction since 1850, and which were to continue throughout and long after the war until they were to reach the imperial total of nearly 160,000,000 acres.

Thus, almost coincident with the beginning of the war, there was an ample supply of land to be had, much of it, for the first time in our history, since the beginning of colonization, wholly free of cost to actual settlers.

Farming, either on a small or large scale, required labor, and the war naturally took thousands of men off the farms to put them in the army. This shortage of labor was more than overcome in three ways. As in the Revolution, the women left at home on countless small farms and little patches turned to and did the men's work, but in addition, although immigration was slight in 1861 and 1862, it rose rapidly and during the five war years 800,000 people arrived in the North from Europe, of whom over 80,000 were carried straight to the farms of the West by one railroad alone. Although many remained in the centres of the East, this access of population made possible the big emigration, which also took place among native-born Americans from East to West. Within two and a half years after the passage of the Homestead Act, nearly 20,000 farms had been settled under it, besides the large number established from the other lands obtainable.

Added to this great increase in agricultural man power, came the yet greater one of mechanical inventions. The McCormick reaper, although patented in somewhat crude form in 1834, really profoundly altered life for the larger-scale farmers only on the eve of the war. A reaper, operated by one man, would cut in a day approximately ten times the acreage the man himself unaided could have cut with a scythe, and the constant difficulty in securing labor, in a country where an ambitious man found it comparatively easy to be his own master, gave a great impetus to the use of machinery under the new conditions which developed after 1860.

It was not the McCormick reaper alone which came into use but such machines as the horse-rake, grain drills, rotary spaders, and other mechanical aids. In the dozen years before the war about 85,000 mowers had been manufactured, but in the four years after 1861 there were sold over 165,000. At the Iowa State Fair in 1859 there were 26 entries of agricultural machinery. In 1865 there were 221. It was estimated in 1864, apparently without exaggeration, that a young man could buy an 80-acre farm in Iowa, fence it, build his house, and pay for the whole out of his first year's crop besides putting over $500 in the bank. Such Western States as Iowa and Wisconsin furnished respectively 75,000 and 90,000 men to the army, yet the population rose rapidly and it was noted that "houses and barns and orchards have sprung up as if by magic."

The transportation problem had been settled by the network of railways which in the decade before the war had been connecting the West with the centres and ports of the East. The country had, indeed, been much over-built, that fact having, as we have seen, been one of the causes of the serious business panic of 1857. But with the Mississippi closed to traffic by the war, the whole business of the West had to be handled by the new railroads, which were most fortunately ready built to carry it. Owing to competition between the trunk lines themselves and also with boats on the Great Lakes, freight charges actually decreased while the prices of farm produce were soaring, and the Western farmer was having boom times.

The last problem was that of markets to absorb the enormous increase in production. There was, of course, an increased demand at high prices within the North itself. As we shall see, it was a period of great industrial activity. Besides the natural increase in our own population, there were the 800,000 immigrants to be fed. But the greatest increase in demand came from Europe. Great Britain, more and more dependent on overseas countries for her food supplies, had crop failures in 1860, 1861, and 1862, and in one of these years the failure was of all Europe and not merely of Great Britain. Before 1862 we had been shipping abroad only 20,000,000 bushels of wheat (half of all our grain exports having gone by way of New Orleans), but by 1862 the North was shipping 60,000,000 bushels. British imports of that staple suddenly increased eight times, while its cotton imports from the South fell to almost nothing.

England needed Southern cotton to keep its workers employed, but even more it needed Northern wheat to keep them alive. As a consequence, our Northern farmer, at least in the West where the nature of the land was adapted to machinery, had ceased to be merely a weather-wise manual laborer and had become a capitalist and a business man. The West had had ample trouble before the war, and was to have again, but in those years of the first harnessing of the machine, of war prices at home and of dire need abroad, the West was wallowing in money and out of debt.

At the opening of the war, about 88 per cent of all the manufacturing of the nation was carried on in the Northern States, and conditions were to make the manufacturer as prosperous as the farmer. Not only is war wasteful of goods but government contracts are notorious for creating high prices and hidden fortunes. The 85,000,000 pounds of peace-time consumption of wool, for example, rose to over 200,000,000 pounds, of which more than one third was used in making uniforms for the army. Mills paid all the way from 10 to 40 per cent dividends and the shoddy cloths sold made millionaires, in countless cases as shoddy themselves as the materials they produced. The war tariffs also gave manufacturers new "protection," and by helping to limit competition increased business and profits at the expense of the consumer.

PROSPERITY IN THE NORTH

As it did in agriculture, machinery also enormously increased the output in many other lines, and even the production of the very machines themselves created great

GROVER & BAKER'S
CELEBRATED
FAMILY SEWING MACHINES.

THESE MACHINES ARE UNDOUBTEDLY THE BEST SEWING MACHINES made for fine and coarse work.
They are Noiseless, easy to learn, simple, and not likely to get out of order.
WARRANTED.
City acceptances, orders on factors, taken in payment. To those who have not the whole amount, arrangements can be made by monthly payments.
H. W. KINSMAN,
AGENT FOR G. & B.'S S. M. CO., 249 KING-STREET.
July 18   c   2

AN ADVERTISEMENT FROM *THE CHARLESTON COURIER,* OF 1860, IN-DICATING THAT DEFERRED PAYMENTS IN SELLING ARE NOT A VERY RECENT IDEA, AND A SINGER SEWING MACHINE OF 1863–1865

manufacturing businesses. Reapers and all other farm machinery had to be made as well as sold. The sewing machine, which had been invented in 1849 and developed in the decade before the war, not only revolutionized the ready-made clothing and other industries, but by 1864 the manufacturers of the "Singer" and "Wheeler & Wilcox" were exporting 50,000 machines a year. The contracts for hundreds of thousands of pairs of shoes at a time for the army could be readily filled because of the invention by Lyman R. Blake of a machine which could sew the soles on uppers. This machine, properly called the Blake in Europe though in America it was given the name of its financial promoter, Gordon McKay, made it possible for the man operating it to turn out a hundred times the number of shoes per day that had been possible under the old hand method. Put on the market in 1862, it was merely one of the most conspicuous examples of what was occurring to Northern industry in the midst of war.

With production speeded a hundredfold by machinery, with an unlimited market to absorb production at war prices, industry boomed and huge profits were made. To a greater or less degree, this was true of almost all lines, even cotton textiles recovering as parts of the South were conquered by the North and the raw material could be secured from them and elsewhere. But the war prosperity of the North was not to be due alone to ordinary war-time conditions, man's ingenuity, and a coincident vast stride forward toward the machine age. The crop failures of Europe were not the only strokes of luck.

Petroleum and its possible commercial value had long been known, but the oil had been found only on the surface of the ground or streams, and had been used mostly in small quantities in patent medicines. In 1859, after many trials, a well was driven which yielded by pumping 25 barrels a day, worth $1000. In the wilds of Venango County, Pennsylvania, where most of the land had been worth only $3 an acre, one of the most colossal of modern industries was to take its start. Before the middle of 1861, scarce six weeks after war had begun, the first flowing well was discovered, producing $10,000 a day. In the three years from 1862 to 1865, over 300,-000,000 gallons were produced, 30,000,000 had been exported, and untold millions of dollars of profits had been made in the most spectacular fashion which perhaps has ever been seen. The Aladdin's lamp of Eastern legend produced no such fortunes as the kerosene lamp of our fathers' day.

No such sudden wealth had ever come to men before except in the rarest of mining discoveries, and even then not in such stupendous amounts. Even mines, however, were to add new and unexpected wealth to the North. The gold yield of California had been decreasing when in 1859 the Gregory Lode was discovered in Colorado, and a few months later the famous Comstock Lode in Nevada. The former started a gold rush comparable only to that of California, and "Pike's Peak or Bust" became the slogan of thousands who toiled across the plains in covered wagons, buggies, or even on foot, pushing their few goods ahead of them on carts. Although discovered just before the war, the output was chiefly important in the war years, during which the Colorado mines yielded perhaps $22,000,000, the Comstock Lode $52,000,000, and others found in Idaho possibly $14,000,000 more.

All of this wealth and of boiling business activity was naturally reflected in prosperity for the railroads. There was not much new railway building during those years, and the mileage already in existence, which had seemed so much more than adequate in 1857, was taxed to its utmost. On many of the most important lines, the tonnage handled doubled during the war, and prices of rail stocks soared. The Far West had, indeed, yet to rely for communication on the "Pony Express" and the overland mail coaches, but in 1862 Lincoln signed the bill authorizing the building of the Union Pacific, though this, the first transcontinental line, was not completed until 1869.

The only large industry in the North which suffered from the war, and there had been causes undermining that for some time previous, was shipping. Not only did capitalists have more lucrative opportunities for employing their wealth in other ways, but with the danger of capture at sea no American shipper would use a vessel under our flag if a neutral could be had. The war gave the last blow to our merchant marine, which declined 1,000,000 tons during it, and after peace came we were willing to leave the carrying trade to the British.

In the midst of all this genuine prosperity in the North, unhappily, fraud and corruption were rife. Washington, with huge government contracts to be given out, was the centre of the disease, which spread every-

California.—The Overland Pony Express, bringing California advices to April 20, reached St. Joseph's on Monday, making the connection between the Pacific and Atlantic shores in less than ten days. The first express going westward had accomplished the journey in nine days, to the astonishment and joy of Californians The news by this arrival is interesting. The Bulkhead Bill had passed the Legislature, and been transmitted to the Governor, who had already signed a large number of bills. The Legislature was to adjourn to-day. The mining news continued to be encouraging. Immense sums had been realized in the Nevada region, and Washoe was still a topic of great excitement. The steamer *John L. Stephens* sailed for Panama on the 20th, bearing nearly $1,300,000 in treasure for New York.

A news item from California in *The Charleston Courier*, July 14, 1860.

A Wells Fargo Pony Express Stamp.

Reward Circular.

From the Jesse Charles Harraman Collection, in the Library of Congress.

THE DAYS OF THE PONY EXPRESS AND STAGE COACH

where. The scandals of the War Department under Cameron became notorious. When Stanton took over the post of secretary, he had an investigation made which revealed loose administration and enormous plunder. A senator had taken a $10,000 bribe from a manufacturer for securing a contract. One lot of claims pressed against the government for $50,000,000 was quickly scaled down to $33,000,000 when the investigation started. A large proportion of the guns supplied to the soldiers were shown to be of inferior quality, and the shoddy cloth for uniforms was a crime. Conditions were better under Stanton, but even he could not prevent graft on a gigantic scale, something which no American Secretary of War has been able to accomplish completely.

The rapidity with which money was being made, especially by people who had not been used to it, brought about that wild extravagance familiar in every great war, though each generation forgets what its predecessor has been through. Never had such quantities of silks, satins, velvets, jewels, and other luxuries been sold. The "most prodigious" diamonds were sold by Tiffany as fast as that shop could import them. Groups of prominent women tried to stem the tide by organization and pledges, but to little use. The flood gates were open. Theatres and opera were crowded as though no war existed. The new millionaires of manufacturing, government contracts, oil, gold, and all the rest, set a vulgar and ignoble pace, and to a great extent the people at large followed.

Under the combined pressure of extravagance, war-time demands, and depreciating paper currency, prices for goods and food soared. As usual, the smaller "white collar" people and the laboring classes suffered most, or gained least. Salaries and wages did not keep pace with the rising cost of living. It was during the war and immediately after, that the labor movement, halted by the panic of 1857, took on its modern national features, the American form of labor unions, the union label, and the nationalizing of unions, employers' organizations, and contracts. Although there were comparatively few strikes of importance, there was some fighting for higher wages and also for lessened hours of work from the ten a day of unskilled labor, the twelve of workers in woollen mills, the sixteen of street-car men.

If wages did not keep pace with prices, so long as the war lasted there were some compensations for the working class, such as the huge sums paid in wages to the men at the front, the hundreds of millions in bonuses, and the money given in charity to soldiers' families. What we think of as a peculiarly contemporary problem today, what we call "technological unemployment," due to the throwing of hands out of work owing to machinery or more efficient production, had already made its appearance. One large group of wage earners, who had performed most useful service to the public, that of seamstresses, suffered greatly and permanently. The wide-spread use of the sewing machine, and the change in trade conditions and taste which brought about the development of the ready-made clothing business, left many thousands of honest women without work.

On the other hand, we have to contrast extravagance, low wages, high prices, and special causes of unemployment with other figures. In 1864 the largest savings bank in New York City increased its depositors by 13,000, of whom 600 were these same seamstresses. There were 200,000 new depositors in the State, and this was true of other sections. The business of life-insurance companies more than doubled, and accident insurance was introduced, the new companies immediately doing a large business.

EDUCATION AND THE ARTS

Although education suffered from the war, it should be noted that in addition to the government grants under the Morrill Act, private benefactors, such as Ezra Cornell and Matthew Vassar, to name only two, gave over $5,-000,000 in the war years to various institutions, and such notable ones as the Massachusetts Institute of Technology, Cornell, and Vassar all had their inception during the struggle. Although attendance in the men's colleges fell off, that in the public schools increased tremendously, and the shift from men to women teachers throughout the country dates chiefly from this period. The tendency had been present for some time but the large number of men teachers who went into the army (5000 or one

EIGHT HOURS LABOR

IN SHOE-MAKING, OR ONE HUNDRED POUNDS OF CORN.

The most disagreeable labor is entitled to the highest compensation.

MAY 18, 1827.

CINCINNATI, OHIO.

Due to _William Morton._

Number—, F——street. Bearer,

LABOR for LABOR

Time is Wealth.

100 100

The above is one specimen of what money ought to be. It should be issued by those men, women, and children who perform some useful service, but by *nobody else*. It should command LABOR FOR LABOR in equal quantities, and the most disagreeable should be highest paid.

Perhaps no class or person is to blame, but the most fatal element of confusion, oppression, and violence ever introduced among mankind is the passing off of metals or any other natural product of the earth, or the earth itself as *pay for labor!* It defrauds, starves, and degrades, and then insults labor, and makes it a thing to be shunned and avoided, and forced upon whoever can be made to bear it. This is the origin of all forms of slavery, in all civilized countries, and of all poverty and crime, the *insecurity of condition*, the worship of money, the antagonisms of classes, and the crisis of these times. Whereas, if Labor were equitably rewarded (with an equal amount of labor), the hardest worker would be the richest man, and all would choose a portion of labor as a means of health and pleasure. For further explanations, see the works mentioned on the opposite page.

This is addressed in a friendly spirit to all parties and nations. *YOU HAVE NO TIME TO LOSE!*

JOSIAH WARREN'S PROPOSAL FOR THE SOLUTION OF MONEY AND LABOR DIFFICULTIES IN 1827 WAS THAT LABOR BE PAID IN KIND

From *"The Labor Movement—The Problem of Today."*

141

half the whole force in Ohio in the first two years) made a permanent change. In Illinois schools, for example, in 1860 there were 8223 men and 6485 women; in 1865, 6170 men and 10,483 women.

The drama of war, at least in modern times, begets surprisingly little of permanent literature. Noting the efforts made in the first few months after Sumter to translate the emotion of the moment into verse, Hawthorne wrote to a friend that "Ten thousand poetasters have tried, and tried in vain, to give us a rousing 'Scots wha hae wi' Wallace bled.' If we fight no better than we sing, may the Lord have mercy upon us." Under the old conditions of warfare, unless a country were actually over-run by the enemy, war, if it were not an inspiration, at least did not greatly affect the literary life of a nation, and during the years of England's great struggle against Napoleon, such authors as Coleridge, Wordsworth, Lamb, Jane Austen, Scott, and others could continue unaffected to add to the glories of literature.

The Civil War marked, half-way, the transition to modern military conditions, in which the entire people, and not merely the army itself, is warped and strained by the presence of war. The greatest drama of blood and suffering in our history, it left us a comparatively scant legacy from the men of letters. Thoreau died in 1862, his *Maine Woods* and *Cape Cod* being published posthumously in 1864 and 1865. Hawthorne died two years after Thoreau, long ill, leaving nothing but one bit of journalism on the war. Longfellow, largely untouched, published his *Tales of a Wayside Inn,* and devoted himself to his inferior translation of Dante. Motley, serving as Minister to Austria, was turning out volumes of his

A CONFEDERATE AND A UNION CIVIL WAR SONG

From the Confederate Museum, Richmond, and the Rare Book Room of the New York Public Library.

History of the United Netherlands. Holmes published his novel *Elsie Venner* in 1861, and then was silent except for a few war verses for which his delicate social muse was unfitted. Melville wrote some war poems, far below the level of his best work. Mark Twain, twenty-six years old when the war came, having tried a bit of soldiering and not liking it, wandered off to the Hawaiian Islands. William Dean Howells, having at twenty-three years of age written a campaign life of Lincoln in 1860, had received the post of American Consul in Venice and remained there, mostly silent, until peace came in 1865.

Whittier was touched by war but his war pieces are far from the best of even that minor poet. Lowell tried to revive his dialect preaching in a new series of *Biglow Papers* but failed, and the only work of his that will survive perhaps as poetry rather than history from these years is the *Commemoration Ode,* written after peace came and under the inspiration of the death of Lincoln. Of the leading men of letters, the only one who rose to a new height was Whitman in his succession of war poems gathered together in 1865 under the title *Drum Taps.*

These last were not popular in their day, however, and the war literature of the people was mostly the work of minor figures, many of them now little read if even known—Henry H. Brownell, E. C. Stedman, Lucy Larcom, G. H. Boker, and a host of others. Of minor verse, the many songs for the soldiers have lasted longest. Julia Ward Howe tried to raise the literary quality of these in her *Battle Hymn of the Republic,* but this never took the popular fancy as did *John Brown's Body; Tramp, Tramp, Tramp, the Boys are Marching; Marching Through Georgia; The Battle Cry of Freedom;* or more sentimental songs such as *When This Cruel War Is Over,* and Walter Kittredge's *Tenting on the Old Camp Ground*.

THE GETTYSBURG ADDRESS

But of all the written or spoken words brought forth by the war those that will last longest in the heart of the American people were not from man of letters or noted orator but from the simple, self-taught President himself, Abraham Lincoln. Dedicating the national monument on the field at Gettysburg on November 19, 1863, in the midst of struggle, he made the brief speech now carved in marble on his Memorial in Washington.

"Fourscore and seven years ago our fathers brought forth on this continent a new nation, conceived in liberty and dedicated to the proposition that all men are created equal.

"Now we are engaged in a great civil war, testing whether that nation, or any nation so conceived and so dedicated, can long endure. We are met on a great battle-field of that war. We have come to dedicate a portion of that field as a final resting-place for those who here gave their lives that the nation might live. It is altogether fitting and proper that we should do this.

"But, in a larger sense, we cannot dedicate—we cannot consecrate—we cannot hallow—this ground. The brave men, living and dead, who struggled here, have consecrated it far above our poor power to add or detract. The world will little note nor long remember what we say

145

here, but it can never forget what they did here. It is for us, the living, rather, to be dedicated here to the unfinished work which they who fought here have thus

Four score and seven years ago our fathers brought forth, upon this continent, a new nation, conceived in Liberty, and dedicated to the proposition that all men are created equal.

Now we are engaged in a great civil war, testing whether that nation, or any nation, so conceived, and so dedicated, can long endure. We are met here on a great battlefield of that war. We have come to dedicate a portion of it as a final resting place for those who here gave their lives that that nation might live. It is altogether fitting and proper that we should do this.

FIRST PAGE OF THE SECOND DRAFT OF LINCOLN'S
GETTYSBURG ADDRESS
From the Division of Manuscripts, Library of Congress.

far so nobly advanced. It is rather for us to be here dedicated to the great task remaining before us,—that from these honored dead we take increased devotion to that cause for which they gave the last full measure of devotion; that we here highly resolve that these dead shall not have died in vain, that this great nation under God shall have a new birth of freedom, and that government of the people, by the people, and for the people, shall not perish from the earth."

CONDITIONS IN THE SOUTH

When we turn to consider the conditions behind the

Confederate Army Correspond- Yankee Army Correspondent on ent on the Battle-field. the Battle-field.

AS A CARTOONIST FOR *SOUTHERN PUNCH* VIEWED WAR CORRESPONDENTS IN OCTOBER, 1863
From the Rare Book Room, Library of Congress.

lines in the South we find a situation which, although sadder than in the North, was in many ways simpler.

In the matter of preserving the constitutional liberties of the individual under stress of abnormal conditions, the Southerner fared somewhat better than the Northerner. Davis, like Lincoln, had to encounter a consider-

147

able amount of defeatism, pacifism, and disloyalty, on the part both of individuals and of organizations. For most of the war the writ of habeas corpus was suspended, but by the Confederate Congress instead of by the questionable executive decree of the President. Moreover, no Southern newspapers were forced to stop publication, as were some in the North, and the freedom of the press was maintained. The Southerners, partly from their nature and partly from the sort of life that most of them led, had a more lively sense of personal liberty than had the Northerners, and this combined with the doctrine of States' Rights helped to keep Davis more strictly to the letter of the Constitution than was the case with Lincoln in the North.

Allowing for the impossibility of estimating accurately the number of men who actually served in either army, one fact emerges indisputably from the most conservative estimates for either side. The white population of the North, not including the border States, was about 19,-000,000; that of the seceded States about 5,500,000, or about 5,000,000 deducting those in the loyal mountain sections who were useless to the Confederacy. These figures give the North nearly four times the white man power of the seceded South. Moreover, we may note that the South did not use negro troops, a law permitting the enlistment of negroes being passed only a month before Appomattox, whereas the North used about 100,000.

If we accept the figure of about 1,750,000 for the number in the Union army, and 800,000 in the Confederate, we find the number serving in the South in proportion to population more than two to one as compared with that in the North. The total number of Northerners killed in

HAVING BEEN SOLICITED BY MANY GENTLE-MEN to raise an ARTILLERY COMPANY for the Confederate service, during the War, any Volunteer wishing to join will find an opportunity by applying at 89 Church-street. Equipments and rations furnished. August 26   ·CHARLES E. KANAPAUX.

VOLUNTEER RECRUITING IN THE SOUTH

An advertisement from "The Charleston Courier" of September 10, 1861, in the Confederate Museum, Richmond.

battle was 110,000 and of Southerners 94,000, and the total dead from all causes in the Northern army 359,528 and in the Southern 368,000. Thus the South lost four times as many dead in proportion to population as did the North, and these various ratios are borne out in general by the number of veterans surviving on each side in 1890. Such figures need no comment to emphasize the far more intense suffering of our Southern States, and throw a flood of light upon comparative conditions both during and after the war.

It is quite true that the South as well as the North had

(Left) "BAH! MONEY'LL MAKE THINGS ALL RIGHT YET!"
War profiteers flourished in 1863 on both sides as this drawing from *The Southern Punch* shows.

(Right) THE SOLDIERS' FRIEND
This maiden, whom *Southern Punch* featured in November, 1863, had "knit more than five dozen pairs of socks since the war commenced and she is still knitting!"

its slackers, its bounty scandals, and its deserters. Lincoln's call for troops in April, 1861, was immediately echoed by Davis in the Southern call for 32,000 volunteers for a year. Later calls, from the States as well as the

Confederacy, resulted in the formation of the first armies, but by April, 1862, Davis, like Lincoln, had to resort to conscription, and all white men between eighteen and thirty-five, unless falling into certain exempt classes, were made liable to service. Passed by the Confederate Congress, the Conscription Act at once raised the question of States' Rights, on which the Southern States had seceded, and South Carolina in particular denied the constitutionality of any such legislation.

The many classes of exemption provided—such as school teachers, druggists, printers, editors, legislators, artisans of one sort and another, and slave overseers—resulted in a somewhat disgraceful scramble on the part of many to fill such posts, and also created much ill feeling. The constant desertions from the ranks all through the war were also a source of weakness to the Confederacy, if not the chief contributing cause to its final downfall. But although there was some disorder, there was no such rioting in the South as in the North, and the statistics quoted above tell their own story of the greater and more willing sacrifices made by Southern than Northern whites for their cause.

On the whole, throughout the four years, the white South was far more intent than the North solely on waging the war, and not on economic exploitation and money-making. Contrasted with the rise of wheat in the North we have to watch the cotton crop decline from over 4,500,000 bales in 1860 to 500,000 in 1864 and 1865, much of which, being merely stored, was ruined and a total loss. No gold and silver and oil were discovered in

Hard Winter Ahead.

This pent-up Utica of ours is over-crowded. Refugees from every section of the Confederacy have come hither in search of safety and something to do. Every railway train bears a living freight of visitors to Richmond on transient business.

Every article of wearing apparel, every mouthful of food, every Calcutta Black Hole of a room, every cart-load of fuel, commands fabulously high prices.

Where this diabolism will stop, no one can tell. Men who extort $75 per pair of coarse shoes, $200 for a pair of boots, from $75 to $100 for a pair of coarse pants, $25 to $30 for a meagre load of coal—and so on, till one gets out of breath in the recital of these robberies—we say, men who will do this now will not scruple to extort still more on the advent of cold weather.

PRICES AND CONDITIONS IN RICHMOND IN OCTOBER, 1863
From "Southern Punch," in the Rare Book Room of the Library of Congress.

the South to make fortunes overnight. The limited manufacturing equipment at the beginning of the war was scarcely sufficient to take care of the military needs. The railroads, instead of becoming prosperous hauling the tonnage of new industries, could not even be properly repaired for want of iron for rails and rolling stock. The lack of food in some sections, and particularly the difficulty of supplying the armies, was due to lack of transportation facilities rather than to lack of foodstuffs themselves.

With the upset conditions, the constant inflation due to declining paper money, and the opportunities which war always offers, there grew up on a smaller scale the same new-rich class in the South as came into existence in the North. After Richmond became the capital, there was a more than doubling of its population, a real-estate boom, and Southerners lamented the wild extravagance and luxury to be seen there, just as the more sober elements in the North lamented the excesses in that section. The winners of Southern government contracts, the owners of manufacturing plants, and others, made large and quick profits. These, however, were all estimated in Confederate money, which, at the end, became mere worthless paper. Not a dollar of the Southerners' currency, or of their State or Confederate bonds, was worth anything when peace came.

DIFFICULTIES IN THE SOUTH

The difficulties of financing the war in the South were incomparably greater than were those in the North. The people responded liberally to the first loan in 1861, but that exhausted practically all the specie available. The blockade of Southern ports cut off almost all possible income from customs duties. An internal revenue Act, similar to that in the North, was passed, but there

GENERAL ORDER.

HEAD QUARTERS,
DEPARTMENT OF WESTERN VIRGINIA,
Charleston, Va., Sept. 24, 1862.

General Order, No.

The money issued by the Confederate Government is secure, and is receivable in payment of public dues, and convertible into 8 per cent. bonds. Citizens owe it to the country to receive it in trade; and it will therefore be regarded as good in payment for supplies purchased for the army.

Persons engaged in trade are invited to resume their business and open their stores.

By order of   **MAJ. GEN. LORING.**
H. FITZHUGH,
Chief of Staff.

A BROADSIDE DESIGNED TO INSTIL CONFIDENCE IN
CONFEDERATE MONEYS

From the Rare Book Room of the New York Public Library.

was not the same wealth to be taxed, and much resentment was aroused. The one foreign loan, of $15,000,000, did not go far. The result was the issuing of over a billion dollars of paper which formed the only currency, steadily sinking in value to ultimate zero.

Moreover, with the exception of Lee's two raids, practically all fighting and destruction of property took place on Southern soil. The rich and beautiful Shenandoah

Valley was left desolate. The track of Sherman's march was a broad swath of ruin. The country between Richmond and Washington was said to be a desert. Columbia, Charleston, and other cities were wrecks of their former wealth and beauty. Railroads were lines of rusty and twisted iron. The rolling stock was dilapidated. When, after peace was declared, a Union commission was sent South to investigate, they found destitution everywhere, and in some cases men and women walked thirty miles to obtain food at the Federal agencies.

Banks, life-insurance companies, all Southern investments representing capital based on Confederate money and bonds, crashed and became as worthless as the paper they were based on. Even those Southerners who thought they had money when the war ended found it could buy nothing. Over 3,500,000 slaves, worth at an average of $500 each, about $1,750,000,000, had been freed. Practically all that was left to the Southerner were his lands and his houses with their contents, if the houses were still standing. During all the war the slaves had been docile and loyal. Many had fled to the Union armies after the Emancipation Proclamation, but these were few compared to the total, and, though slavery was wrong, it is a commentary both on the negro nature and on the wild ravings of the Northern Abolitionists that a Southern governor, Walker of Florida, could say after the war was over that "Our women and infant children were left almost exclusively to the protection of our slaves and they proved true to their trust. Not one case of insult, outrage, indignity, has come to my knowledge."

The slaves unquestionably welcomed their freedom, not only for the obvious reasons which would have operated with a white man under similar conditions but because to a great extent, in their ignorance, they thought it meant that a millennium was coming for them in which they would not be free *to* work but free *from* work. Major Henry Hitchcock, who was on Sherman's staff on the famous march through Georgia, gave many glimpses of conditions in his letters home. Nowhere, he wrote, did the slaves show any resentment against their masters, but everywhere a desire for freedom.

How quickly ruin could overtake a wealthy Southerner may be noted from one of Hitchcock's letters on the march. "We passed 'Shady Dale,'" he wrote, "this A.M.—not a town or village but the farm of one man, containing 7600 acres—250 negroes. An old man, Mr. Whitfield, worth (before the war) a million. We are told he left yesterday or this morning, having collected his horses and mules and ordering the negroes to bring them along. But the darkies wouldn't follow him, and instead they remained with the stock and joined the Yanks in high glee."

The South had been weak in its educational institutions for long before the war (many Southern boys of the richer class going north to college, largely to Princeton and Harvard), and during the struggle education in the South, even such as there was, went rapidly backward. Before the war was over, conscription had been made to include white men from the age of seventeen to fifty. Recalling that four times the number of men and

THE

GAME OF MATRIMONY:

OR,

WHO WILL BE MARRIED FIRST.

HOPE HAD NOT BEEN ABANDONED BY THE KNITTING YOUNG LADIES, AS PROVED BY THIS GAME WHICH WAS POPULAR IN PHILADELPHIA IN 1862.

From the Rare Book Room of the Library of Congress.

boys in proportion to population in the South were in service as compared with the North, and that even in the North college attendance fell off heavily, we can realize how little opportunity for college education there was in the South from 1861 to 1865. The University of Virginia, the best in the section, which had 600 students in 1861 had only 40 in 1863, and the buildings of one of the most flourishing of Southern institutions—the Virginia Military Institute—were burned by Union troops in 1864.

In any case, the intellectual life of the South had been retrograding for a generation before the war, as we have already noted. To a great extent "the South" had come to mean the South of South Carolina and the Gulf States which were the first to secede, the South of the black belt and the great cotton plantations, a very different South from that of Washington, Monroe, Pinckney, Madison, Marshall, and Jefferson.

In spite of the charm of social life, the black belt was an intellectual desert. As contrasted with the great Southerners just named we may quote the words of one of the new leaders, W. L. Yancey of Alabama, to indicate the boastfulness and barrenness that to a great extent had overtaken the South since King Cotton had made his slaves and magnates. Speaking of the lack of Southern literature, Yancey could say, with applause, that "our poetry is our lives; our fiction will come when truth has ceased to satisfy us; as for history, we have made about all that has glorified the United States."

It is not strange that of the war literature of the South, mostly occasional verse, nothing remains which ranks high as literature. Among the best contributions, per-haps, were Hayne's *Battle of Charleston Harbor*, Timrod's *Ode on the Confederate Dead* (1867), and F. O. Ticknor's *Little Giffen of Tennessee*. The song, both words and music, which the South made peculiarly its

THE DIFFICULTY IN SECURING HOOPS LED TO TRAILING SKIRTS WHICH SOMETIMES LEFT CONSTERNATION IN THEIR PATH

From a rare copy of "The Bugle Horn of Liberty," published at Griffin, Georgia, in September, 1863. In the Rare Book Department, Library of Congress.

own, *Dixie,* was written in 1859 by a Northerner, Daniel D. Emmett of Ohio, for his troupe of negro minstrels in New York; and the words of the fine *Maryland, My Maryland* by James R. Randall of Baltimore were, it is true, by a Southerner, but by one in a Union State and in that northern South which had unfortunately abandoned leadership to the Rhetts and Yanceys of cotton and bombast.

159

INFLUENCES FROM THE CONFLICT

Passing from the more local conditions and effects of the war in the two sections, we may now consider some of the broader influences stemming from the conflict. Chiefly these were the abolition of slavery, the tremendous impulse given to the forces of nationalism, and the subtle influence on our political thought.

Of the moral effect of Abolition it is not necessary to speak at length. With almost negligible exceptions, practically all Americans, even the sternest of Puritans in Massachusetts, like all the world, had had no qualms about the righteousness of slavery in the seventeenth and at least the early eighteenth century. But in the world of the nineteenth it had become an anachronism, and its moral effect upon both slave and owner was bad. The civilized world had moved toward a wholly new grouping of ideas and sympathies, and slavery in the South, so long as it remained, ate into our whole national life like a cancer. The operation for removal, unnecessarily brutal and performed without the anæsthetic of financial compensation which the British Empire had administered in similar case, had been performed. The patient had nearly died, both from the disease and the operation, but in 1865 the way was open for recovery, and renewed health in harmony with the moral and economic environment of a new age.

For forty years it had been increasingly evident that

the Union could not endure half slave and half free, Lincoln's "house divided against itself." No real Union could have been lastingly achieved had the South merely been conquered, and its "peculiar institution" remained to make the same trouble in the future that it had in the past. In that sense, Abolition was a Union measure even more than a war measure.

The constitutional question of Union had also been settled, as brutally, if one will, as the slave question. Both were settled not by arguments and reason but by force. Nevertheless, they were settled. Although no one doubted in our earlier history that slavery was morally just and no one could rightly affirm, not even Lincoln, that it was not constitutionally legal and protected, yet it had been extirpated by war. So, although I think it cannot be questioned that the original States in 1787 would never have formed the constitutioned Union if they had explicitly understood that under no conditions whatever could they ever extricate themselves from it, that question also had been settled by war. In the seventy odd years since 1787 the moral emotions of the world had changed as to slavery; and the political emotions of the larger part of the American people had changed as to the indissolubility of the Union. The majority and the minority, on both questions, had found argument a futile weapon at last. The questions had to be decided, and it was from the mouths of rifle and cannon that the decision was rendered. After 1865 there could be no chattel slavery in the United States; after 1865 no State of the United States could dream of peaceable secession.

The mere settlement of the question of the indissoluble nature of the Union, however crudely determined, in itself came, in course of time, to increase national sentiment. It was not only in the eyes of Europe that the United States, having survived a disastrous civil war, assumed a new power and greatness. For our own citizens, also, there came a new sense of the nation, no longer constantly trembling on the brink of dissolution, but one and indivisible forever.

Apart from the military decision, there had been many influences at work during the war to turn our minds from localism or sectionalism to nationalism. The greatest breeder of sectionalism, slavery, had gone. On the other hand, under stress of war necessities, the Federal Government had made great strides in enforcing the obedience and gaining the supreme loyalty of all citizens, regardless of State or section. For four anxious years the fate of the nation and of every citizen had depended on the acts of that government, and it emerged, with Lincoln at its head, with vastly enhanced prestige and power. Just as the firing on the Stars and Stripes at Fort Sumter in 1861 had revealed in a flash the unsuspected sentiment for Union among the people, so the years of war had developed the emotion of nationalism.

War-time conditions in business had also contributed strongly to the nationalizing of our minds. The rapid increase in the use of machinery, the greater interdependence of the different sections, the increasing scale of business, the improved transportation, the wider markets, all tended toward nationalization. Labor found that with manufacturing developing almost as actively in Ohio as in Massachusetts, local unions would no longer serve, and the first national organization of labor resulted, as did the first national organization of employers, in certain lines. Demands on Congress for tariff favors and the need of business men in different sections for joint consideration of their problems, now no longer local, but national, called for conventions and organizations, of which the National Association of Wool Manufacturers, and the American Iron and Steel Association were examples.

The telegraph had brought the different sections of the nation into instantaneous communication with each other since S. F. B. Morse had invented it in 1844, but it was only during the war that the Western Union installed the first transcontinental line. It was also during the war that the consolidation of all the telegraph companies (more than fifty local ones in 1851) took place so rapidly that by 1866 the Western Union had absorbed practically all the other companies into one national system owning 75,000 miles of wires. Similar tendencies were at work in the many consolidations of local railways into larger systems, and, indeed, in countless ways throughout the business world.

The vast increase in private fortunes also contributed indirectly to nationalism. By the end of the war it was stated that there were several hundred millionaires in New York City alone, and several worth some scores of millions. A. T. Stewart, in 1863, was paying an income tax on over $1,800,000 a year income, and Cornelius Vanderbilt and W. B. Astor on approximately as much. Such aggregates of capital sought employment on a scale which could no longer be confined to business in a single locality. All the units in the economic system increased in size—fortunes, incomes, the capitalizations of corporations, the sphere of operations.

The business leaders were almost forced to think in national terms. The more aggressive owners of local concerns, as in the telegraph business, almost by force of circumstances, found themselves striving for a national monopoly. The owners of local railways began to dream of "transcontinentals." Partly owing to the closing of the Mississippi at the beginning of the war, one third of the meat packing business of the entire West had been quickly concentrated in Chicago, where the great Union Stock Yards were established, and the number of hogs slaughtered rose from 275,000 in 1861 to 900,000 at the end of the conflict. Concentration and consolidation came about naturally—indeed, inevitably—from the conditions, and both meant that the business men must think in terms of the nation instead of a locality.

Nationalism was to bring standardization, and the first

great step had been taken when the South was forced to make its labor system, and its own peculiar type of social and economic life, conform to that of the rest of the nation. The business men had not wished to disturb existing business relations. The politicians of the sections had contended for power. The Abolitionists had seen slavery as a moral blot on the country of which they were also citizens. The South had insisted upon individualism, its right to continue to think along the old lines even if the North, and the rest of the world, had begun to think differently. Its theory of secession and States' Rights was an assertion of individualism against nationalism and enforced uniformity. In this also, the South was fighting against the time spirit, which for the past two generations has seemed insistent upon bringing the entire world into conformity, until all over the globe we shall wear the same clothes, do the same things, read the same books, see the same films, think the same thoughts and become eventually, perhaps, as uniform and dull as bees in a hive or ants in a hill.

The last of the three effects of the war which we mentioned was the subtle one upon our political thought. Our theory of government had always insisted that all just governments derive their power from the consent of the governed. There had, indeed, been awkward difficulties with the theory, such as Indians, women, and slaves, but the world had not troubled itself very much as yet, politically, with any except men, and men who were white, and the difficulties had been brushed aside. What, however, became of our theory when we insisted upon governing, with a consent given unwillingly, if at all, and only as a result of conquest by force, five or six million whites who had fought for four years against us to be left in peace? They were not of alien race. They were not minors or idiots, and they formed more than a quarter of the population of our nation.

The fact was that our theory had broken down, and on a vast scale. In a democracy there is no better rough and ready mode of governing than by the will of the majority, but, to be workable and to make a contented nation, that theory presupposes that every possible protection shall be given to a minority. The huge rift made in our fundamental theory by the Civil War is not unconnected with the imperialism of the Spanish War and the increasing tendency to ride rough-shod over the wishes or sensibilities of minorities if a majority can win to power.

CHAPTER IV

THE AFTERMATH OF WAR

THROUGHOUT the war, the problems of reconstruction of the Union had been occupying the mind of Lincoln. These problems were of great complexity and were at once economic and political. Of the first magnitude was that of the negro. In the seceded States there were approximately 3,500,000 former slaves to less than 5,500,000 whites, and in some of those States the negroes were practically as numerous as the whites, or even more so. For example, in Alabama in 1860, the numbers had been respectively 437,770 negroes to 526,-271 whites, in Georgia 465,698 to 591,550, in Louisiana 350,373 to 357,456, and in South Carolina the 412,320 negroes heavily outnumbered the 291,300 whites.

In many cases free American negroes had done well, and there had been a few conspicuous ones, such as Frederick Douglass, the Abolition orator, Ira Aldridge, the tragedian, and Elizabeth Greenfield, the singer, who had gained even European reputations, Aldridge having received decorations from the King of Prussia and the Emperors of Austria and Russia. Nevertheless, whatever capacities the negro might show for development, the fact remained that the vast mass of suddenly freed slaves were illiterate, unused to thinking for themselves, and ignorant of the world outside the plantations on which they worked, except in so far as they might have been sold from one locality to another. Thrown unexpectedly on their own resources, how would they take their freedom, and how quickly would they adjust themselves to the responsibilities of free life and of the modern wage system?

In innumerable cases the ex-slaves simply remained working for their former masters on a sort of wage basis, but in many others they had strange dreams of what freedom meant, and toward the end of 1865 the idea was spread that every negro was to receive "forty acres and a mule" on New Year's Day. The Freedmen's Bureau, created by Congress on March 3 of that year to aid the negroes, did good work with Major-General O. O. Howard at its head, in spite of incompetent and grafting agents. The shift from the economic system of slavery to that of wages might have been made with less friction and difficulty than had been anticipated by the South had it not been that political questions were to hamper the transition.

As we have seen, Lincoln's theory had been always that the seceded States had never been out of the Union at all, and he hoped to effect reconstruction with a minimum of restrictions upon the Southerners who had returned to their allegiance. By 1863 three of the Confederate States had come under Federal control again—Tennessee, Louisiana, and Arkansas—and the problem of administration had then arisen.

Although on the first of January of that year, Lincoln had issued his Emancipation Proclamation, he was not personally in favor of granting the emancipated slaves the suffrage, except in certain cases, and any such sudden alteration in status would have been, when avoidable, wholly contrary to his cautious approach to all problems of such magnitude. Having appointed military governors for the three States, he offered in the Proclamation of Amnesty on December 3, 1863, pardon to all their citizens, with broad exclusions, who would take the oath of loyalty to the United States. He also offered them the opportunity of re-establishing their State governments and of re-admission to the Union as soon as one tenth of the voters had taken the prescribed oath. Congress would have to decide upon the question of seating such senators and representatives as might be sent from the newly established States, but Lincoln himself wished to have the transition from secession to re-establishment made as simple as he had suggested in the Proclamation.

The States named, or the ten per cent loyal electorate in them, accepted the offer, and in 1864 organized new governments. Congress, however, long restive over the war-time encroachment of the Executive, and hostile to the South, declined to seat members from the reorganized States, and in the so-called Wade-Davis Bill insisted that Congress, and not the President, had the responsibility for reconstruction. It then outlined another plan, including, among other changes, an increase to fifty per cent of those who must take the oath of allegiance. This

With malice toward none; with charity for all; with firmness in the right, as God gives us to see the right, let us strive on to finish the work we are in; to bind up the nation's wounds; to care for him who shall have borne the battle, and for his widow, and his orphan to do all which may achieve and cherish a just, and a lasting peace, among ourselves, and with all nations.

THE LAST PAGE OF LINCOLN'S SECOND INAUGURAL ADDRESS
From the Division of Manuscripts, Library of Congress.

bill Lincoln vetoed by the method of not signing it within ten days, whereupon its chief sponsors, Senator Benjamin Wade and Representative Henry Winter Davis, issued an outrageous public manifesto July 4, 1864, accusing the President of base motives in not having approved of it.

Forces, of which we shall presently take note, were aligning themselves in the North against any conciliatory attitude toward the beaten South. Whether even Lincoln could have made headway against them and saved the South the bitterness, and the North the disgrace, of the next few years is at least open to question. Lincoln was, however, to have no opportunity. In March, 1865, in his second Inaugural, he had urged his countrymen not only to continue the struggle to the end but to think also of the future reunion. "With malice toward none; with charity for all; with firmness in the right, as God gives us to see the right, let us strive on to finish the work we are in; to bind up the nation's wounds; to care for him who shall have borne the battle, and for his widow, and his orphan—to do all which may achieve and cherish a just and a lasting peace, among ourselves, and with all nations." In conversation he had answered the suggestion that President Davis of the Confederacy should be hanged, with the quotation "judge not, that ye be not judged." At a Cabinet meeting he warned that there was too much desire in the North for "bloody work."

THE ASSASSINATION OF LINCOLN AND ITS EFFECTS

Lee had surrendered to Grant at Appomattox on April 9, and the war was known to be over, though peace was not actually proclaimed until August 20, 1866. Lincoln had gone to confer with Grant and had remained with him until the day before the surrender, then returning to Washington. The long vigil was over, and he had lived to see the Union restored. On the evening of the

14th, he was seated, with his wife and some friends, in a box at Ford's Theatre, and all eyes were on the stage when suddenly a shot rang out. One of a small group of conspirators, John Wilkes Booth, a half-insane actor, brother of the great Edwin Booth, had gained access to Lincoln's box, and shot the President in the back of the head. Leaping from the box to the stage, the assassin shouted to the audience the motto of Virginia, "sic semper tyrannis," and in spite of a broken leg, escaped to a waiting horse by the stage door. The unconscious President, carried to a house across the street, lingered until early morning when he peacefully died.

Born of a shiftless and in general a run-out stock, Abraham Lincoln had slowly and patiently trod his spiritual as well as political way from a squalid frontiersman's log cabin to the war-besieged White House in Washington. Mostly self-taught, feeding on the Bible, Shakespeare, and Blackstone, he had been slow to mature. As different from George Washington as any backwoodsman could be from a tide-water magnate, nevertheless the great founder of the nation is the only character in our history with whom Lincoln himself can be compared. Mistakes he made in plenty—mistakes in politics, in taste, in trying to run military affairs in the early days of the war—but in the four years and more of the nation's agony which he spent as its head, he steadily grew. Of all the statesmen around him, in Cabinet or Congress, there was not one who could have led the nation as did this raw and uncouth man whom they had looked down upon and thought to control and guide.

War Department. Washington. April 20. 1865.

$100,000 REWARD!

THE MURDERER

Of our late beloved President, ABRAHAM LINCOLN,

IS STILL AT LARGE.

$50,000 REWARD!

will be paid by this Department for his apprehension, in addition to any reward offered by Municipal Authorities or State Executives.

$25,000 REWARD!

will be paid for the apprehension of JOHN H. SURRATT, one of Booth's accomplices.

$25,000 REWARD!

will be paid for the apprehension of DANIEL C. HARROLD, another of Booth's accomplices.

LIBERAL REWARDS will be paid for any information that shall conduce to the arrest of either of the above-named criminals, or their accomplices.

All persons harboring or secreting the said persons, or either of them, or aiding or assisting their concealment or escape, will be treated as accomplices in the murder of the President and the attempted assassination of the Secretary of State, and shall be subject to trial before a Military Commission and the punishment of DEATH.

Let the stain of innocent blood be removed from the land by the arrest and punishment of the murderers.

All good citizens are exhorted to aid public justice on this occasion. Every man should consider his own conscience charged with this solemn duty, and rest neither night nor day until it be accomplished.

EDWIN M. STANTON, *Secretary of War.*

DESCRIPTIONS.—BOOTH is 5 feet 7 or 8 inches high, slender build, high forehead, black hair, black eyes, and wears a heavy black moustache.
JOHN H. SURRATT is about 5 feet 9 inches. Hair rather thin and dark; eyes rather light; no beard. Would weigh 145 or 150 pounds. Complexion rather pale and clear, with color in his cheeks. Wore light clothes of fine quality. Shoulders square; cheek bones rather prominent; chin narrow; ears projecting at the top; forehead rather low and square, but broad. Parts his hair on the right side; neck rather long. His lips are firmly set. A slim man.
DANIEL C. HARROLD is 22 years of age, 5 feet 6 or 7 inches high, rather broad shouldered, otherwise light built; dark hair, little (if any) moustache; dark eyes, weighs about 140 pounds.

GEO. F NESBITT & CO., Printers and Stationers, cor. Pearl and Pine Streets. N. Y.

CIRCULAR ISSUED BY WAR DEPARTMENT OFFERING REWARD FOR CAPTURE OF MURDERER OF PRESIDENT LINCOLN

From the original in the Rare Book Room of the New York Public Library.

Inferior to Washington in some respects, he surpassed him in others, and no other President in the long line has equalled him in that love of the nation which included the humble with the great, the common man and the rebel with the distinguished and the loyal. In the sad and patient eyes of Lincoln, we were indeed one nation, indissoluble, united, beloved.

The assassination of the President was the murder of the moral leader of the nation, the removal of the one individual who might perhaps have been able to overcome the forces of party, greed, and revenge which were gathering from all quarters, like foul birds that feed on carrion, to wreak their lusts on the prostrate South and the entire country.

Vice-President Johnson, who by Booth's insane act now became President, was in many respects a strong and able man, but some of his qualities and his lack of others made him futile as the interpreter to the nation of its own best self, and instead of ruling the whirlwind he became its victim, both in his own day and for long after. It is only in very recent years, since war-time passions and misrepresentations have been lulled, let us hope forever, that Andrew Johnson, after a generation of malignant aspersion even by historians, has come to be appraised at his true worth.

Born one of the Southern "poor whites" in a log hut in Raleigh, North Carolina, he inherited with his extreme poverty a deep resentment against the rich and patrician classes of his section. Left fatherless at three years of age, apprenticed to a tailor, he learned without schooling to read but could not write until later taught by his young wife. Having moved to Tennessee, he rose

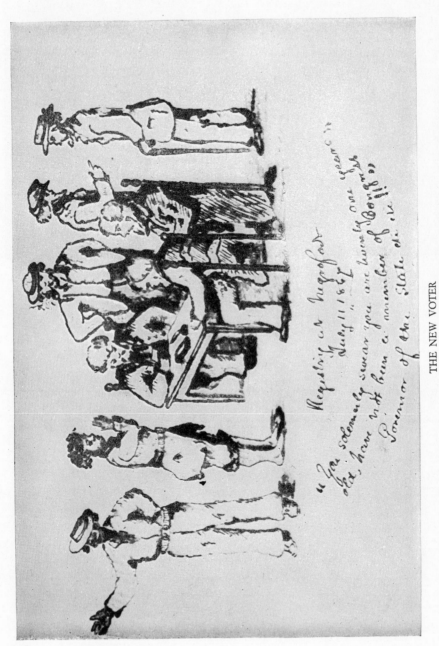

THE NEW VOTER

From the original sketch made by Dr. Bracket at Negrofoot Precinct, Hanover County, Virginia, July 11, 1867.

Now in the Confederate Museum, Richmond.

FUNERAL OF PRESIDENT LINCOLN, APRIL 25, 1865

The magnificent funeral car was drawn by sixteen gray horses richly caparisoned with ostrich plumes and cloth of black trimmed with silver bullion.

A Currier and Ives lithograph in the Library of Congress.

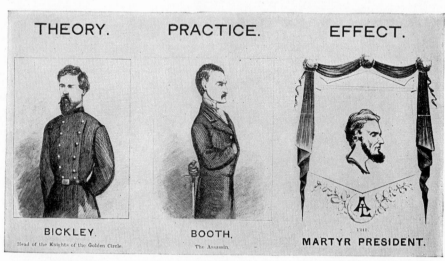

THEORY. PRACTICE. EFFECT.

BICKLEY.
Head of the Knights of the Golden Circle.

BOOTH.
The Assassin.

THE
MARTYR PRESIDENT.

THE TEACHINGS OF THE KNIGHTS OF THE GOLDEN CIRCLE WERE HELD RESPONSIBLE BY A CONTEMPORARY CARTOONIST FOR LINCOLN'S DEATH

From the Library of Congress.

from one political position to another until, when the war came, he had become not only United States senator, but the only member of the Senate from a seceded State who remained loyal to the Union. Lincoln made him military, as he had already been twice civil, governor of his State, and in 1864, by Lincoln's own wish, Johnson had been put on the ticket as Vice-President. Although he had been a Democrat, he had become a Republican from desire to save the Union. It was thought his presence on the ticket would emphasize the Republican claim to be the party of Union men of all political faiths; would reward Johnson for his loyalty; and perhaps would do something for Union sentiment throughout the nation by giving high office to a loyal Southerner.

Johnson's nomination, however, had been resented by the radical Republicans, largely because he had been a Southern Democrat. When, as a result of Lincoln's assassination, he was suddenly raised to the Presidency, it was certain that he would be bitterly attacked. Unfortunately, although honest, courageous, and intellectually capable, Johnson could not manage men or guide and create public opinion, while his lack of tact, his proneness to descend to the level of stump speeches in his political utterances, and one or two unhappy occasions when he appeared to be the worse for liquor in public, gave his opponents weapons which they were not slow to wield against him. Probably no other President has ever been so persistently and unfairly attacked by the press and his own party as was Johnson, who, nevertheless, was not himself altogether blameless.

For a very brief time it appeared as though the new President might, as result of his long dislike of the Southern aristocratic class, be precisely the man whom the radicals wanted for their attack on the South. But, whether sobered by responsibility of office or for other reasons, Johnson quickly made up his mind to fight the radicals and to attempt to carry out Lincoln's wise and large-hearted plan for reconstruction. Retaining all the members of his predecessor's Cabinet, he was unanimously supported by them in his belief that there was no need for a special session of Congress—not due to meet until December 4—and that he should begin the work of reconstruction by executive action alone.

This he did on May 29 by issuing a Proclamation granting amnesty to all rebels on condition of their taking an oath of fealty to the United States, and although certain classes were not included, notably ex-officers of the Confederate army and navy and all having taxable property in excess of $20,000, even these were assured of liberal treatment if they would petition for pardon. By midsummer, Johnson had also appointed provisional governors for seven of the Confederate States, and in practically all of these, in accordance with his suggestion, conventions had been held which had repealed the secession ordinances, adopted new constitutions, and elected members of Congress for the coming session.

As was to be expected after four years of war and the overturn of the social and economic system, there was more or less unrest and disturbance in the South, which was much exaggerated by the hostile Northern press and politicians. In the autumn, Johnson sent Carl Schurz on a tour through the section to investigate conditions, and Schurz made a report which more than suggested that the South was not loyal and that it intended to keep the negroes in some sort of serfdom, thus providing the radicals with precisely the sort of ammunition they wished for their campaign. General Grant, however, making a similar report at the same time, took exactly the opposite view on these points.

Schurz later on in his career was to do some good work for civil service and other reforms, but at this stage it is rather difficult not to lose patience with this young German of thirty-six who had been in America only thirteen years and whose chief claim to importance was his influence with the German vote and his services to the Republicans in the campaign of 1860. The campaign services in the Middle West must have been considerable for, in 1861, when he was only thirty-two and could not have been a naturalized citizen for more than three or four years, Lincoln had appointed him Minister to Spain.

JOHNSON AND RECONSTRUCTION

During the summer of 1865, public opinion was not unfavorable to Johnson's policy of reconstruction and conciliation, and we must examine some of the forces and causes that were to wreck both it and him. One section of Northern opinion had been outraged during the war by what it considered the usurpation of legislative power by the Executive, and by its genuine fears for constitutional liberty aroused by Lincoln's suppression of freedom of speech and of the press, as well as the suspension of *habeas corpus*. Naturally Congress was particularly jealous of its own prerogatives, and now that the war was over, and a Johnson instead of a Lincoln was in the White House, the members of this group would strive strenuously to regain control of policies and action.

There were also the extremists who had preached hatred of the South and who exalted the welfare of the negro above that of his former master. The leaders of this group were Representative Thaddeus Stevens of Pennsylvania, and Senator Charles Sumner of Massachusetts. Stevens, who at seventy-three had become almost the dictator of the House of Representatives, and was rumored to be the keeper of a mulatto mistress, was an able, narrow, intense, harsh, and vindictive old man, unlovely in almost every aspect of his character. The North, he claimed, had the right to take "the lives, liberty, and property" of all Southerners, whose States should be considered as conquered provinces, from which their inhabitants should be driven out to be replaced by Northerners. Sumner was of different type, but in his way as narrow and fanatical as old Stevens himself. Nothing would satisfy the Massachusetts senator but immediate and complete equality of the former slave with the whites. The difficulties of practical statesmanship meant nothing to this doctrinaire who had come to hate the Southern white as much as he claimed to love the Southern black.

There were also other considerations, though less openly discussed. If the Southern States were allowed to send members to Congress there was the question of the ascendancy of the Republican Party. The old compromise had provided that representation in the House should be based on the number of whites plus three fifths of the slaves, but slavery having been abolished by the Thirteenth Amendment to the Constitution (adopted in 1865), the entire black population of the Southern States would have to be included in the basis for representation, which would largely increase the number of Southern members in the lower House. As the Southern whites were almost unanimous against the Republican Party, this new situation evidently called for shrewd political manipulation and consideration.

As one constituent wrote to the negrophile Sumner, the Southern whites would certainly unite with the Northern Democrats, but if the negroes were given the vote, they might be used to offset the whites, maintain Republican supremacy, and thus ensure a continuance of the high tariff. How terrible to think that the free-trade South, beaten in war, its slaves confiscated by the North, might ruin Northern manufacturers, who had just been tasting the joys of high protection, by out-voting them in Congress! As one Northern governor expressed it, the readmission of the Southern States to the Union would be unwise until "their ideas of business, industry, money-making, spindles, and looms were in accord with those of Massachusetts," or until, as the Massachusetts reformer, Wendell Phillips, suggested, the North had been able to make over the "South in its own likeness." If Johnson had his way in reconstructing the South on Lincoln's plan, what might not become of the Republican Party, of Republican congressmen, of the Republican tariff, and of Northern Republican manufacturers?

Unfortunately, whereas on the one hand, Johnson was not fitted to guide the public opinion of the North on questions of economic and constitutional policy, on the other, the Southerners played into the hands of the radical groups in the North who did know how to inflame, if not to guide, popular prejudices. After all the passion of civil war, it was unquestionably a delicate matter to seat "rebels" and "traitors" in Congress again to help govern the country just as though nothing had happened. Had the war been merely a putting down of insurrection in one or two States, whose members of Congress would be in negligible minority when returned, the problem would not have been serious, but, as it was, a good many people in the North were genuinely uneasy when contemplating the danger of a large bloc of Southern congressmen once more in power.

In a situation calling for great self-control, confidence, and magnanimity on the part of the North, and of tactfulness on that of the South, both sides acted with a minimum of these qualities. Naturally the ablest men in the South had occupied high military or civil positions during the war, and so had been prominent actors in the drama of rebellion. The few who, like General Thomas, had taken the Union side, could hardly be expected to command the immediate suffrages of their Southern fellow-citizens. So, unfortunately, it came about to a great extent that the South elected to Congress the very men whom the suspicious North regarded as the leaders in the fomenting of rebellion, and the feeling of fear and resentment reached a high pitch when even Alexander H. Stephens, the Vice-President of the Confederacy, was chosen unwisely by the Georgia legislature to represent that State in the United States Senate.

Moreover, the laws passed by Southern legislatures with regard to the emancipated slaves, which legislation was known collectively in the North as the "black codes," aroused feeling in that section to an extent which was wholly unwarranted. Owing to the overwhelming proportion of whites to negroes in the North there was no Northern negro problem. Even so, however, in only six Northern States was a negro permitted to vote. After peace came, there was economic chaos for a while in the

South. The negro, with false ideas of what freedom meant, was not inclined to work but much inclined to wander. For his own good, until he had learned to adjust himself to the new condition of being his own master, with the responsibility of looking after himself and his family, he had to be controlled to some extent.

The codes recognized his freedom, and gave him almost all the rights of any ordinary citizen, although he was not allowed to vote or sit on juries; was required to have some means of support; and subjected to penalties for breaking labor contracts. In a few States, the codes went too far with respect to the labor clauses, but on the whole they were framed justly in accord with the real conditions which confronted the Southerners. But the North preferred theory to reality, and shutting its eyes both to its own refusal to give the Northern negro the vote and to the dangers in the South, raised a hue and cry about the oppression of the negro by the Southern whites, who, it was claimed, were trying to nullify emancipation.

Such was the situation when Congress met in December, 1865. There were some fair-minded conservatives in it, but the leaders of the two houses, Representative Stevens and Senator Sumner, were bitterly opposed to Johnson's plans, Stevens dominated by his hatred of the Southern white, and Sumner by his doctrinaire love for the negro, which, regardless of conditions, led him to be satisfied with nothing less than the immediate enfranchising of the slave of yesterday. Nor were the President's foes all in the Capitol. Like John Adams, sixty-five years previous, he had retained the whole of

A CONTEMPORARY VIEW OF THE NEGRO'S PLIGHT AT THE HANDS OF THE POLITICIANS

The "change of face" (and views) after election may be seen by turning the picture sidewise.

From the Rare Book Room in the Library of Congress.

his predecessor's Cabinet, to be repaid with treachery, Stanton, the War Secretary, remaining with him as adviser only to reveal all the Cabinet secrets to his foes.

In February, 1866, Congress passed a bill prolonging the life of the Freedmen's Bureau, the organization already mentioned which had been created in the preceding March with rather broad powers for relief and supervision of the freed slaves. The powers now conferred were much wider, and the Bureau was given the right to invoke military authority when civil rights were denied to the negro. This bill Johnson at once vetoed as unwise and unconstitutional, and unfortunately made some speeches in which he bitterly attacked Stevens and Sumner in particular and Congress in general. It was now open war between the Executive and the legislature, a war which could not have been averted but which might not have been so disastrous for Johnson and the nation had the President shown himself more adroit in the management of men.

In April, Congress passed a Civil Rights Bill over the President's veto, and also, with a more than two-thirds vote, an amendment to the Constitution to be presented to the States for ratification. This amendment, in five sections, provided that no State could pass any laws depriving the negro of any of his rights as a citizen; that if he were not given the suffrage in any State its population basis for representation in Congress would be proportionally reduced; that all the Confederate and State debts in the South incurred for the war were void; that no claim could ever be made for compensation for the emancipation of the slaves; and that no person could hold Federal office who had ever held such office and then engaged in rebellion.

The amendment, which it was understood would have

to be adopted by any Southern State before it could be fully reinstated in the Union, was approved by Tennessee in the summer, and its senators and representatives were seated in Congress. The other Southern States all refused to accept it, although it was ratified by a sufficient number of the total in the Union to become part of the Constitution in 1868. The radicals were far from satisfied with it, and it is at least open to question whether, even had the South accepted it, such acceptance would have altered the course on which the radicals had determined.

In the autumn of 1866 came the mid-term elections. There was a good deal of conservative sentiment in the North, and in the West there was little enthusiasm to be worked up for Sumner's enfranchisement fanaticism. Johnson, who had tried to save the Homestead Act from rape at the hands of large speculative interests, and who had the democrat's dislike of banks and the machinery of "big business," could have developed a considerable following had he brought into prominence a number of the economic questions, such as high taxation, which were troubling the people. There was really no great unity in the Republican Party, but by not daring to split it, Johnson handed it over complete to the radicals.

THE CAMPAIGN OF 1866

The campaign was one of the most indecent in our annals. The President himself took the stump, and touring the West talked in the wrong way about the wrong things, while the vilification and misrepresentation indulged in against him by the leaders of his own party were almost without parallel. Untrue charges that he was frequently drunk on his tour were spread everywhere, as they have often been against our public men, and were all too eagerly accepted. By some queer trick in our psychology we seem always willing, without proof, to believe the worst of any one who has risen to high position.

The hidden desires of the radical leaders did not make good campaign material. It was therefore determined to appeal to the crudest emotions. The doctrine was preached that if the Southern States were re-admitted to the Union too quickly, there would be danger of a repudiation of the Federal debt. So far did Sumner go with this absurd campaign lie that the Secretary of the Treasury had to appeal to him to stop making his untrue statements because they were greatly damaging the credit of the nation. Neither the credit of the nation, nor of its President, however, meant anything to Sumner and the others if anything could be gained politically by assailing either of them.

The President was denounced as a "traitor," who had been in the conspiracy to assassinate Lincoln, and who was now planning to use the army against Congress. During the summer, there had been riots in Memphis and New Orleans, natural enough under the disturbed conditions, but radical orators magnified these into dangerous plots, and Sumner charged the President with being the abettor of the mobs. "Charles IX of France," Sumner thundered, "was not more completely the author of the massacre of St. Bartholomew than Andrew Johnson is the author of those recent massacres which now cry for judgment . . . and a guilty President may suffer the same retribution which followed a guilty King." The distinguished senator must have known he was lying.

Our new citizen and very hot Republican patriot, Carl Schurz, pronounced that Johnson ought to be hanged, and that he was "worse than Judas Iscariot or Benedict Arnold." Considering the charges which these men brought against the President for his coarseness of speech, it is interesting to note their own. Schurz, claiming that Johnson was the victim of flattery, added "you might even tell him he was a gentleman and he would believe you." Stevens had had inserted in *The Congressional Record* a statement from *The World,* which both he and Sumner repeated, that the President was an "insolent clownish drunkard," a "drunken brute, in comparison with which Caligula's horse was respectable." If this was the sort of talk in which the leaders allowed themselves to indulge, when criticising the President himself for lack of taste and breeding, it is easy to imagine the sort of thing that was hurled at him by stump speakers and the cheap press.

All emotions were played upon. Southerners were called "rebel devils" and "redhanded traitors." On the field of Gettysburg, immortalized by the dead of both sides in the war and by Lincoln's address, Edward Everett, of Massachusetts, now proclaimed that the North would never admit again to a share in the government "the hard-hearted men whose cruel lust of power has brought this desolating war upon the land." The "bloody shirt," that was to keep the Republican Party long in power, began to be waved with frantic frenzy. Congressman Logan said the only way to treat the Southerners was to "take the torch in one hand and the sword in the other . . . and sweep over their territory."

To win the election the President, who was not the man for the place and hour but was honest, was painted as a traitor; the Southerners as still dangerous rebels who must not be admitted to a share of government (until, *sotto voce,* the negroes could be given the vote for the Republican Party); and the one issue of the campaign was made to appear as the saving of the nation from the dangers of reconstruction according to the ideas of Lincoln and Johnson.

It was all good campaigning according to ordinary low political standards to which Sumner, Everett, Schurz, and other reformers and "scholars in politics" stooped, and it won. The radical Republicans secured more than two thirds of both houses of Congress, and the doom of the South was sealed. In spite of the vicious slanders which the party leaders had spread about him, the President acted with dignity after the election, and prepared a markedly conciliatory message for the opening of Congress in December. Unhappily, the leaders made it clear a week before Congress was to meet that they would consent to no truce and that they were determined to crush both the President and the South.

The wild rantings of Stevens left no doubt on that score, and lesser men made the same threats. In a speech at Cooper Institute, for example, Wendell Phillips called for impeachment of "the Rebel in the White House" and added, "let us pray to God that the President may continue to make mistakes." Sumner was more radical and defiant than ever, and it was evident that Congress would be guided by passion only. The places of such great statesmen and compromisers as Clay and Webster had been taken by vindictive and narrow-minded politicians such as Sumner and the dying Stevens. The President put aside his conciliatory and wise message, and sent another, breathing defiance of Congress. The last phase of the fight between the White House and the Capitol had now begun.

Before continuing the story of that to the end, we may turn to two international affairs of importance which were concluded under Johnson in 1867. The President left foreign affairs largely in the hands of Seward, as

Secretary of State, and Seward, who was an expansionist, had tried in 1865 to buy the island of St. Thomas from Denmark. It is interesting to note, in view of what we have said about the change in our political theory with regard to the "consent of the governed," that it was Denmark which insisted upon, while Seward resisted, the taking of a vote of the inhabitants on the transfer. Although this proved favorable and a treaty was drawn up to cede the island and a smaller one, for $7,500,000, the Senate declined to ratify, and the plan fell through.

In 1867, however, Seward was more successful in another direction. Russia suddenly offered to sell us all her possessions in North America for $10,000,000. Seward jumped at the chance, but bargained shrewdly, and finally a treaty was drawn up by which we were to receive Alaska for $7,200,000. Sumner was strongly in favor of making the purchase, and the Senate was also favorably inclined, although the real value of the acquisition was then almost unknown. It is possible that the senators were more inclined to add to our territory in the North than in the South, but the chief determinant in the Alaska purchase was the belief that we were under some obligation to Russia for having offered us her fleet during the Civil War should England or France intervene. The story had some foundation, though not of such a nature as to warrant any such feeling of friendly obligation on our part as oddly developed. When the Senate ratified the treaty, however, it was more with the thought that it was paying an obligation toward Russia than that we were getting an amazing bargain.

The same year saw the clearing up of the French situation in Mexico. As we have seen, Louis Napoleon had taken advantage of our being occupied with war to seize that country, in spite of our protests. When the war was over, Johnson had sent General Sheridan with an army to the border, and renewed our protests to France with vigor. The French people had not been in favor of the adventure, Napoleon had wrongly counted on the success of the Confederacy, and now found himself in an untenable position. Without any qualms of conscience, he broke faith completely with Maximilian, whom he had set up as Emperor at Mexico City, withdrew the French troops, and coldly left Maximilian to his fate. Maximilian was executed by the Mexicans, the empress went insane, and an inglorious and dastardly chapter in Napoleonic imperial policy was closed.

Were it not that his fight with Congress over reconstruction has overshadowed all else in Johnson's unhappy term, his success in clearing the New World in one year from all claims of the two great Old World empires of Russia and France would have received more attention than it has. He secured peaceably the withdrawal of the menace on our south and added nearly 600,000 square miles in the north to the national domain, a country nearly three times as large as France and whose rich possibilities are even today not sufficiently realized.

CONGRESS AND RECONSTRUCTION

We must now return to the drama that was unrolling in Washington. Congress at once took in hand the recon-

THE RECONSTRUCTION DOSE.

JOHNSON OBJECTS TO THE PHYSIC GIVEN TO THE SOUTH
The differences of the President and Congress over the Reconstruction Act.
A cartoon from "Frank Leslie's Illustrated Newspaper," July 13, 1867.

struction of the South, ignoring completely the plans of Lincoln and Johnson. In March, 1867, it passed, over Johnson's veto, "the most brutal proposition ever introduced by a responsible committee," the Reconstruction Act. By this and several supplementary Acts, all the former Confederate States were swept away, and the South was divided into five military districts, each under command of a general who was insultingly made subordinate to Grant and not to Johnson, in spite of the fact that under the Constitution the President is Commander-in-Chief. Although the Fourteenth Amendment had left the question of negro suffrage optional with the States of the Union, and not a single State allowed it south or west of New York, and not even Connecticut in New England, the Act forced it on the ten Southern States, without any constitutional authority.

Under the military governments, conventions were to be called in the ten States, after all the male negroes over twenty-one had been registered as voters, and these "black and tan" conventions then were to frame new constitutions in which negro suffrage must be provided for. After this had been done, the new constitutions approved, and the Fourteenth Amendment ratified by only three fourths of all the States, but by *every Southern* State, then and then only could the seceded States be reinstated by representation in Congress.

The Supreme Court had decided three months earlier, in the Milligan case, already cited, that military courts were unconstitutional except under such war conditions as might make the operation of civil courts impossible, but the President pointed out in vain that practically the

whole of the new legislation was unconstitutional. So
mad had become the course of the radicals that there was
even talk in Congress of impeaching the Supreme Court

FACSIMILE OF PART OF SECTION 2 FROM THE TENURE OF OFFICE ACT
AND THE SIGNATURES TO THAT MEASURE

From the original Act in the State Department, Washington.

for its decision! The legislature had run amok and was
threatening both the Executive and the Judiciary.

On the same day on which Congress passed the first
Reconstruction Act it passed another, also over the veto
of the President and which was aimed directly at him.
From the days of Washington down, the Executive had

held the power of dismissal of a Federal employee from office without consulting the legislature. On March 2, 1867, Congress passed the Tenure of Office Act which not only took away from the President all power of removal, even of the members of his own Cabinet, without the consent of the Senate, but made any infraction of the new Act a "high misdemeanor." Not merely was a broad and important power thus stolen from the Executive by the Senate, but in making infringements of it "high misdemeanors" Congress made the Act a weapon with which it might impeach the President and remove him himself from office if he did not submit to having even his personal advisers forced on him by the Senate. The Cabinet was included in the Act partly to prevent Johnson from getting rid of Stanton, who was working with the radicals and whose secret information was of importance to them.

Although Johnson put the Reconstruction Acts into force, he defied Congress on the Tenure of Office Act, for the purpose of bringing it before the courts for judicial review. As early as January, 1867, Representatives Ashley of Ohio and Ben Butler of Massachusetts were already at work trying to force a bill through for the President's impeachment, and it was clear what would happen if he demanded the resignation of Stanton. In August, nevertheless, Johnson asked him to resign, the situation having become intolerable. Stanton refused in an insulting note.

Johnson then suspended him temporarily and appointed General Grant in his place, who, however, as soon as Congress reassembled in December, at once resigned when the Senate refused to accept Stanton's removal. Johnson then dismissed Stanton and appointed General Lorenzo Thomas. Stanton declined to get out, indulged in an undignified battle of words with Thomas and placed him under arrest. Released on bail, the general had a drink with Stanton, who, however, held his private office by force and would not surrender to the new appointee.

Congress then proceeded immediately to the impeachment of the President, the trial before the Senate beginning on March 4, 1868. This impeachment of President Johnson was not only the most disgraceful episode in the entire history of Congress but one of the most dangerous. The Tenure of Office Act had been merely a trap laid into which the Executive would have to walk, or abdicate to the legislature all power for himself and his successors. The Civil War had threatened the existence of the nation; now the action of Congress threatened the existence of its form of government, for if a political party or faction could depose a properly elected President without constitutional cause, there was little left of the Constitution and the balance of powers.

Although Stevens, almost at the end of his embittered days, was the most virulent against the President, Ben Butler, John A. Bingham, George S. Boutwell, Benjamin

Wade, Thomas Williams, and John A. Logan have to share some of the heaviest of the deserved obloquy of the proceedings. Of the eleven charges made by the House, there was not one which could stand. The President was defended by five counsel, ex-Justice B. R. Curtis of the Supreme Court, William M. Evarts, Attorney-General Stanbery, Judge Groesbeck of Illinois, and T. R. R. Nelson of Tennessee, the first four being men of the highest attainments and standing.

There was no legal basis whatever for impeachment, but the prosecution pleaded as politicians and not as lawyers. Fortunately, the Senate, acting as jury, was presided over for the proceedings by Chief Justice Chase, who kept them strictly within legal bounds. Even so, the President, and the nation, escaped by only a single vote, seven Republicans ruining their futures with the party by voting in his favor, Fessenden, Fowler, Grimes, Ross, Van Winkle, Henderson, and Fowler. It is little to the credit of three others, though it seems to be usually considered so, that they were ready to vote for acquittal if their votes were needed. Johnson was either guilty or he was not, and these three who preferred their careers to their honor were Sprague, Morgan, and Willey.

Johnson's term, however, was within a few months of its end when the final vote acquitted him on May 26, 1868, and the Republicans were looking forward to the fall election. The South had submitted again to force, and under conditions which we shall note later, new constitutions had been adopted in all the Southern States except Mississippi, Texas, and Virginia, embodying negro suffrage, though Minnesota, Ohio, Kansas, and Michigan in the North had rejected it. In order to gain the benefit of the new negro vote, Congress quickly readmitted the seven reconstructed States into the Union during the summer in time for the election.

GRANT NOMINATED AND ELECTED

The Republicans nominated General Grant for President and Schuyler Colfax, the Speaker of the House, for Vice-President, while the Democrats put up a ticket of Governor Seymour and General Francis P. Blair, Jr. Owing to the great popularity of Grant, there was considered to be no doubt of the result of the campaign, which, however, had several points of interest. Grant had voted but once in his life, and then for a Democrat. The two party platforms were also peculiar in that the Republican one rancorously condemned the Republican President, Johnson, whereas the Democratic one applauded him. Both offered the bribe of pensions to the soldier vote, and both twisted the tail of the British lion. The Republicans claimed that suffrage in the South must be a matter for Congressional legislation, but not in the North, whereas the Democrats properly insisted that the suffrage question always had been and should be one for the individual States everywhere in the Union to determine for themselves. They also insisted upon the unconstitutionality of almost the whole of the Acts of the Republican Congress.

Unfortunately, economic questions had also come to the front, and the Democrats took the side of those who wished to tax the tax-free government bonds, which was

IN 1869, DWIGHT L. MOODY, THE FAMOUS EVANGELIST OF THE NINE-
TIES, WAS PRESIDENT OF THE CHICAGO YOUNG MEN'S
CHRISTIAN ASSOCIATION

equivalent to a lowering of interest and partial repudiation, and the party also supported those who wished to pay the bondholders in greenbacks. On these points the Republicans adopted sound principles, and the future position of the parties for some decades was foreshadowed. The Republican Party, with its tariff and favors for business, and its sounder ideas on currency, naturally attracted the conservative business interests, while it swept along a large part of the mob, and tried to keep its hold on the negro vote of the South by waving the bloody shirt and denouncing the loyalty of Southern whites. On the other hand, the Democratic Party, with much to offer in wholesome and progressive doctrines, and in its genuine democracy, was to suffer under the handicap of economic heresies.

For Grant himself, the apparent victory was in reality a profound tragedy. Rarely is the great soldier combined in one person with the great statesman. They were assuredly not in Grant, and the reputation which was so high at Appomattox was to become bedraggled and smirched in eight years of the White House. In the scandals which welled up in his administration, like the back-flow from a sewer, he himself profited nothing and was personally honest, but he had such a singular incapacity for choosing the right men for office, and then was so obstinate in his loyalty to the wrong ones, that the situation created was almost worse than if he had been a less honest but an abler man.

The first blow to confidence in the new President came with the announcement of his Cabinet appointments, which caused a gasp of astonishment throughout the nation. They were most of them, except Judge E. R. Hoar of Massachusetts and ex-Governor Cox of Ohio, practically unknown and small men, three of whom immediately resigned. The appointment of Hamilton Fish as Secretary of State, in place of one of the three, was good, and the only satisfactory portion of Grant's administration was to be in the field of foreign policy.

Less than a week before Grant took the oath of office in March, 1869, Congress put the finish on its Acts for Reconstruction by the passage of the Fifteenth Amendment to the Constitution (adopted by sufficient States in the following year), declaring that the right of citizens to vote should not be denied by the United States or any State "on account of race, color, or previous condition of servitude," thus giving the negroes the franchise throughout the Union.

The amendment pleased those who, without regard to practical conditions, had fanatically demanded immediate equality in all respects between the two races; those who hated the Southern whites and wished to crush them as much as possible; and those who wished to control the Southern vote in the interests of the Republican Party by manipulation of the negro voters. Had it not been for the negroes in the States under Congressional control, 650,000 of whom took part in the election of 1868, Grant, in spite of his personal popularity, could not have won, a majority of the white vote of the nation having repudiated the Republican policies.

Conditions in the South were intolerably bad. Not only in many of the States, as we have pointed out, did the negro population approximate or even exceed the white, but for various reasons large numbers of the latter, including many prominent men, were still disfranchised. Naturally all the better class were solidly Democratic, and in view of the treatment being meted out to the

South by the Republicans, could be nothing else, at least for the time being. The negro vote, mostly illiterate, was the determining political factor, and although the white Democrats tried to win it, the Republicans had little difficulty in controlling it. They could properly claim that it had been the Republican Party which had given the former slaves their freedom, and all over the South through agents of the Freedmen's Bureau and the newly formed "Union Leagues" they swept the negroes into the party fold.

The Republican Party in the South was thus made up almost exclusively of the illiterate ex-slaves and local white leaders of the lowest and most scandalous political type. These were known as "carpet-baggers" and "scala-wags," the former being politicians who had swarmed down from the North with their carpet-bags, to get what pickings they could, and the latter being low-grade Southern whites who helped to organize their negro machines locally for the same reason.

The pickings were, indeed, on a colossal scale. We shall note later such scandals in the North as the Tweed Ring in New York, but there has been nothing in our history to compare with the vast plunder secured under the "carpet-bag régime," in the South of reconstruction days. In South Carolina, of the 144 radical Republican members out of a total of 155 legislative members, 98 were negroes, of whom only 22 could read and write, as were also the State Treasurer and Secretary. This travesty

of an American government, with a Northern carpet-
bag governor at the head, which voted themselves cham-
pagne, gold watches, horses and carriages, and other in-

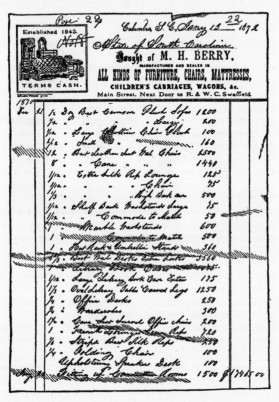

FACSIMILE OF A BILL FOR FURNISHING THE STATE HOUSE AT
COLUMBIA, SOUTH CAROLINA, IN 1872

credible things out of the public money, raised the State
debt in a brief time from $7,000,000 to $29,000,000.

In New Orleans, $17,000,000 of city bonds were issued
at thirty-five cents on the dollar, and the State debt was

increased so recklessly that it has been estimated all the way from $24,000,000 to $50,000,000, and the tax rate rose 400 per cent in four years. The political trash, white and black, grew rich selling franchises, public property,

A CARTOON BY RYLAND RANDOLPH SHOWING THE FATE IN STORE FOR LOCAL CARPET–BAGGERS AND SCALAWAGS

The figures represented two men connected with the university and educational work in Tuscaloosa who were driven out by the Klan.

and political favors for any price they could to get money quickly for themselves. One carpet-bag governor cleaned up a half million dollars in his term. Such régimes could only result in many cases in later repudiation of debts so corruptly incurred, and unfortunately many of these bond issues were sold in England.

It was natural that the Southern whites, to prevent this complete ruin, should wish to regain control of their own States. This was impossible if carpet-baggers and

KU KLUX.

Hollow Hell, Devil's Den, Horrible Shadows. Ghostly Sepulchre. Head Quarters of the Immortal Ate of the K. K. K. Gloomy month. Bloody Moon. Black Night, Last Hour.

General Orders No. 3.

Shadowed Brotherhood! Murdered heroes! Fling the bloody dirt that covers you to the four winds! Erect thy Goddess on the banks of the Avernus. Mark well your foes! Strike with the red hot spear! Prepare Charon for his task! Enemies reform! The skies shall be blackened! A single Star shall look down upon horrible deeds! The night owl shall hoot a requiem o'er Ghostly Corpses!

Beware! Beware! Beware!
The Great Cyclops is angry! Hobgoblins report! Shears, and lash! Tar and Feathers! Hell and Fury!

Revenge! Revenge! Revenge!
Bad men! white, black, yellow, repent! The hour is at hand! Be ye ready! Life is short. J. H. S. Y. W.!!!

Ghosts! Ghosts!! Ghosts!!!
Drink thy tea made of distilled hell, stirred with the lightning of heaven, and sweetened with the gall of thine enemies!
All will be well!!!
By order of the Great
BLUFUSTIN.
G. S. K. K. K

A true copy,
Peterloo.
P. S. K. K. K[1]

"Dam Your Soul. The Horrible *Sepulchre* and Bloody Moon has at last arrived. Some live to-day to-morrow "*Die.*" We the undersigned understand through our Grand "*Cyclops*" that you have recommended a big Black Nigger for Male agent on our sic rout; well sir, Jest you understand in time if he gets on the rode you can make up your mind to pull roape. If you have any thing to say in regard to this Matter, meet the Grand Cyclope and Conclave at Den No. 4 at 12 o'clock midnight, Oct. 1st, 1871.

"When you are in Calera we warn you to hold your toungue and not speak so much with your mouth or otherwise you will be taken on surprise and led out by the Klan and learnt to streick hemp. Beware. Beware. Beware. Beware. Bewars.
(Signed)

"PHILLIP ISENBAUM.
"*Grand Cyclops.*
"JOHN BANKSTOWN.
"ESAU DAVES.
"MARCUS THOMAS.
"BLOODY BONES."

"You know who. And all others of the Klan."

(Above) WARNING SENT BY THE KLAN
From Ku Klux Report, Alabama Testimony.

(Left) A KU KLUX ORDER PRINTED IN THE
INDEPENDENT MONITOR OF TUSCALOOSA,
ALABAMA

205

scalawags could marshal the blacks to the polls. Organizations, therefore, were formed to intimidate the negroes. Among these "White Leagues," "Knights of the White Camelia," and other secret societies, the most noted and effective was the Ku Klux Klan, started in Tennessee in 1866, and later an important weapon throughout the whole South. Riders, robed in white, would appear suddenly in the night and frighten negroes out of their wits in one way and another. At first little violence was used, but when the methods began to prove effective, as was shown by the big drop in Republican votes in 1870, Congress passed the Enforcement Act, imposing severe penalties for infractions of the new Constitutional Amendments, and the South then met force with force. Whatever Abolitionists and theorists like Charles Sumner might say, living in white Northern communities, whites will not consent to be ruled by blacks, and the South was fighting for white supremacy. The only way to combat Congressional legislation had to be violence when other methods failed, and there is no doubt violence was used, and racial bitterness much increased.

In 1871 Congress passed an even more rigid Enforcement Act, and in it gave the President power to suspend *habeas corpus* and to use the army to suppress the activities of the members of the Klan. The Congressional policy had been criminally stupid. No matter what its political faith, the white South could not be expected to submit supinely to be ruled and plundered by its former slaves. The negro fanaticism of a Sumner could result only in arousing passions and delaying a solution of an extremely delicate and difficult problem.

Gradually, however, the whites regained control, and by 1877 throughout most of the South the carpet-bag-negro régimes had ended, and the section had become solidly Democratic, the combined dishonesty and ignorance of the local Republicans making any two-party system impossible. The blacks were frankly intimidated, and negro suffrage was nullified in one way and another. Federal troops were withdrawn and the South was left to manage its own affairs by its own civil governments. Gradually a new order was evolved, though economic recovery was necessarily slow. The former slave learned to work for wages, and almost a revolution in the agricultural conditions of the section can be inferred from the reduction by almost a half, in little more than a dozen years, of the average size of Southern farms. The Old South of the "plantation" days with its romantic dreams had passed into history.

CHAPTER V

WE BEGIN TO LOOK FORWARD AGAIN

THE North also was changing. The South, although not wholly agricultural, had been chiefly so, and when the armies of that section were disbanded the soil called back their men simply and naturally. In the industrial North the problem of re-absorbing nearly a million ex-soldiers peaceably into civil life was properly considered a serious one, and was envisaged with a good deal of misgiving. There, again, it was the land which made the transition from war to peace surprisingly easy. It was not the "old plantation" or the old farm that called the Northern soldier, however, but the new and untamed West.

As seems inevitably to be the case, there was a primary post-war depression in business about two years after the end of hostilities. This short period of bad times in 1866-7 made it more difficult for men to find places in Eastern industry, and thus emphasized the westward drift. There were not only the ex-soldiers who had to find ways of living but the steadily mounting numbers of immigrants, which rose from just under 250,000 in 1865 to 460,000 in 1873.

BUILDING OF RAILROADS

Within three years after the end of the war the Federal Government was distributing 6,000,000 acres a year of public lands, and although much of this went in grants to the railroads, millions of acres had been turned into farms by new settlers. Between 1865 and 1872 the railway mileage of the nation jumped from about 35,000 to double that amount, much of which new building was in the West, where the railroad increasingly displaced the stagecoach. In 1869 the first transcontinental line, the Union Pacific, was completed, after four years' work. Building had been carried forward westward from Omaha and eastward from Sacramento, and the two lines met when an engine from the East and one from the West finally faced each other at Promontory Point.

The work had been colossal. The Central Pacific, for example, had had to climb over 7000 feet through the Sierra Nevada mountains in the first 125 miles. The whole line, traversing the plains and mountains, was, indeed, one of the greatest engineering feats of the time. It is not easy now to realize the difficulties under which it was accomplished. For the western portion, all the machinery, iron, cars, locomotives,—practically everything except timber and water,—had had to be transported all the way from the East to California by way of the Panama Isthmus or around Cape Horn.

When the two lines met, the Central Pacific after

building 688 miles from the West, and the Union Pacific 1086 miles from its starting point in the East, the entire country rejoiced. The actual physical uniting of the two sections was made the occasion of an elaborate ceremony. On the final tie to be placed, which was of polished California laurel wood, a silver plate bore the inscription reading "the last tie laid in the completion of the Pacific Railroad, May 10, 1869," and the rails were spiked to this. For this purpose, Arizona sent a spike made of iron, silver, and gold, Nevada one of solid silver, and California one of gold. This last was driven into position by the presidents of the two roads, each striking it alternately with a sledge hammer made of silver, while the telegraph carried the strokes to all the principal cities of the country. As each stroke thus re-echoed, the bell of the City Hall in San Francisco repeated the sound, and the chimes of Trinity Church in New York played "Old Hundred." As the last blow was struck, cannons roared their salute across the whole continent. If the single line spanning the country was the most spectacular feat of the railway builders of this period, it was perhaps less important than the network of lines being built in every direction in the West, extending settlement and widening markets. The five years before the panic of 1873, for example, saw the mileage in Wisconsin doubled, and in one year more miles were built in Illinois than measured the whole length of the Union and Central Pacifics.

This intensive railway building was partly the result

ACROSS THE CONTINENT—THE FRANK LESLIE TRANSCONTINENTAL EXCURSION

The excursion train is rounding Cape Horn at the head of the Great American Cañon. In the distance
is shown the South Fork of the American River, where gold was discovered in 1848.

By courtesy of the University of California, Extension Division.

A CAFÉ, GLASGOW, MONTANA, IN 1889

By courtesy of the Great Northern Railway Company.

CUSTER'S DEAD CAVALRY AT THE BATTLE OF LITTLE BIG HORN
From Indian Pictographs in the Tenth Annual Report of the Bureau of Ethnology.

and partly the cause of the rapid development of the West. Even during the war, there had been a huge migration, the population of the Western States increasing by more than a million during the conflict. With peace, the rate of increase was immensely accelerated. Of course the basis of Western industry and prosperity was agriculture, stimulated by war prices and a combination of other circumstances. The improvement in agricultural machinery, of which we have noted the beginnings, was rapid, and the few years after the war saw the advent of the self-binding harvester, the Oliver plow, the modern windmill, and the increasing use of steam in threshing. But if the new railways, in too many cases scandalously over-capitalized and flimsily built, were earning in gross twenty-seven per cent of their cost in a year, their business was derived from many industries besides farming. Eastward came not only wheat and corn, but ore for the rising steel and iron industries, metals from the mines, and cattle from the plains. Westward went the tens of thousands of settlers, and manufactured products of all sorts for their needs.

GROWTH OF THE CATTLE KINGDOM

The American has had to learn to adjust himself quickly to fast-changing conditions, and the two decades after the war saw the rise and fall of one of the most picturesque of our varied occupations. It had been found by chance that cattle which wintered on the plains were fatter and gave better meat than those in Texas, and from this discovery grew the cattle kingdom of the great plains, stretching from Texas to Montana. The pushing westward of the railroads and settlers had several effects which facilitated the rise of the cattle kings.

Most important was the problem of the Indian, and war after war now marked the last stage of driving the original occupier of the soil into reserves on lands least desirable for the white men. In 1862 we were fighting the Sioux. In 1864 it was the Cheyennes, the Apaches, Comanches, and others. In 1866 there was the uprising again of the Sioux under Red Cloud, and two years later General Custer broke the power of the Cheyennes under their chief Black Kettle.

Although the Federal troops were winning, there was constant unrest, which was closely linked with the killing of the buffalo, the main source of food and profit to the plains Indians. William F. Cody, better known as "Buffalo Bill," killed personally nearly 4300 of the animals in one year and a half, and although they had been so numerous that a train passed through one herd for 120 miles, the killing was at so furious a rate—5,000,000 in 1873 alone—that the Indian saw his main support disappearing almost as by a miracle. Although one of the chief conflicts occurred in 1876 with the Sioux under the great leader Sitting Bull, the advance of the railroads and the presence of troops gradually opened the plains to the cattlemen and cowboys from the end of the Civil War.

Cattle by the tens of thousands were driven up along the Chisholm and other trails, first to the end of the Kansas Pacific and later up to the newer Santa Fé and the Union Pacific. The day of the steer lay between the earlier one of the Indian and the later one of the settled West, when the farmer won with his enclosed fields and towns against the cattleman who had thrived only so long as a reasonably safe national domain was given him to use without cost or hindrance. But of all romantic pages of our history that of the cowboy has become the most typically American in our own eyes and that of the world at large. The "West" of legend and story and picture is not that of the pioneer farmer and his wife, fighting dust, hard water, droughts, grasshoppers, and loneliness, in too often slovenly, drab, and poverty-stricken homes, but that of the stagecoach, the wild Indians on horseback, and the cowboy rounding up his herds on the "long drive."

Cattle towns sprang up where the cattle were sold. Then came the refrigerator car after 1870, which carried the meat from great packing plants concentrating in Omaha, St. Louis, and Chicago to households in the East which had largely depended hitherto on the local butchers. There had also been a steady drift of other great industries farther and farther west. The manufacturers of agricultural machinery followed the sunset trek of the farmers. While the Armours, Swifts and others were establishing packing houses, Pullman located his car-building plant at Chicago, the great breweries of Pabst and Busch rose in Milwaukee and St. Louis, and the milling plants of Pillsbury and Washburn in Minneapolis. These were but outstanding examples of a new West, a West fatal alike to Indian, buffalo, and cowboy. In spite, however, of growing industrialization, of big enterprises, and of banks, the West was to remain primarily agricultural,—a land of farms and small towns, and its attitude toward political and economic questions was to continue to be that of the small independent producer, often in debt, and opposed to measures which seemed to benefit the creditor and business classes at his expense.

FINANCIAL ORGY IN THE EAST

While the South was slowly and painfully trying to rebuild its economic structure, and the West was booming, the East was having a veritable financial orgy. The vast opportunities afforded by the quick accumulation of capital in the war, the inflation following it, the expansion of the West, the new machinery, inventions, and commodities, were quickly appreciated and embraced by a type of business man as bold, unscrupulous, combative, and selfish as the worst robber barons of the Middle Ages. All business men were not as unsocial, irresponsible, and predatory as Jay Gould, Cornelius Vanderbilt, and others of that brand, but these were outstanding figures in the immediate post-war years.

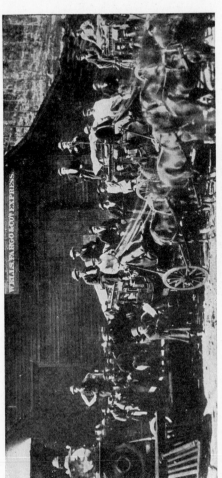

Left: The original express-man, William F. Harnden. He travelled by boat from New York to New Haven, and then to Boston. Henry Wells and William Fargo were in his employ at one time. *Top:* Concord stage coaches ready to start, Reno, Nevada, in the early sixties. *Bottom:* An express-wagon of about 1875.

THE RAILWAY EXPRESS

From the Jesse Charles Harraman Collection, Library of Congress.

HARVESTING IN THE EIGHTIES
The ranch of Henry Best, Sullen County, California.
By courtesy of the University of California, Extension Division.

TWELVE McCORMICK–DEERING 16–FOOT HARVESTER THRESHERS WORKING IN
ONE FIELD, 1933, CUTTING A SWATH 192 FEET WIDE, OR APPROXIMATELY
640 ACRES PER DAY
By courtesy of the International Harvester Company.

The foundation of some of the so-called great American fortunes had been laid in an earlier period, such as those of the Astors and Vanderbilts, but these were enormously increased in this period, and many of the most widely known, such as the Rockefeller, Gould, and Carnegie ones, date only from it.

The Bessemer process for manufacturing steel was invented by Henry Bessemer in England in 1856, but it was after the Civil War that the new age of steel began in America. In 1867 we were making only 2600 tons, but in the next few years such concerns as the Bethlehem Steel Works, Carnegie, McCandless and Co., and others were rapidly expanded and, in spite of the panic and hard times, by 1879 we were producing nearly 1,000,-000 tons annually.

During the war, young John D. Rockefeller had devoted himself solely to money-making, and by 1872 he was already trying to control the entire oil business of the nation. The policy pursued by his firm had been one of deliberate killing off of competitors by any means possible, however ruthless. One of these was the forcing of the railways to grant special low rates to the Rockefeller group, which even forced the roads to pay to them a considerable part of the freight charges received by the lines from Rockefeller's rivals in business. By this combination with the railroads on the one hand and his ability to prevent the passage in Congress of measures directed toward making the railways perform impartially their duties as public carriers, Rockefeller's Standard Oil Company had reached by 1878 the point of practically complete control of the American oil business in all its phases.

The railroads themselves were the footballs of specu-

WHO STOLE THE PEOPLE'S MONEY?
From the cartoon on Tweed and the Tammany Ring by Thomas Nast in "Harper's Weekly," August 10, 1871.

lators, grafters, and bribers, and, in a large number of cases, were built, operated, and their stocks manipulated with the sole thought of personal profit. In the spectacular war between Jay Gould and Cornelius Vanderbilt both of them bought senators at Albany and judges in New York as readily as, though more expensively than, they could have bought hogs. Gould, who by his issues of illegal stock in the Erie wrecked that road, made in that and other ways a fortune of $25,000,000 in not much more than a decade.

Corruption, indeed, was so rife throughout the country as to disgust honest men. As is the case far too often with us, however, they could not be moved to action so long as they themselves were making money, and until the moral stenches in one place and another became so bad as to be suffocating. New York was merely a classic example although, unfortunately, not the only one. There William M. Tweed had made himself head of Tammany Hall and political boss of the city. Almost two thirds of the voters were foreign-born. Using the well-known methods for controlling this foreign vote together with false registrations and illegal naturalizations, and in alliance with the legislature at Albany, it seemed for a while as though Tweed were invincible.

Of course the ignorant and venal foreign voters were merely the debauched tools of the bosses who found their power and profit to rest on an alliance with the big business leaders. When a Mr. Gould or a Mr. Vanderbilt or others of that sort bought an alderman or a senator, a franchise or a legislative Act, they wanted to know what, and for how long, they were paying their money. They wanted to deal with an individual who could "do business" and "deliver the goods," and from their standpoint the boss, then, as he has since, performed a useful function. Political corruption in America can never be wiped out until the American business man, large or small, ceases to seek for himself the fruits of corruption. So long as business, autocratic and unsocial, buys what the boss is there to sell, and so long as democracy tries to clear its life by an occasional uprising at the polls against the boss only, the symbol of its party will properly remain an ass.

Every possible source of graft on city contracts, selling offices, dispensing favors and franchises, was tapped by Tweed and his henchmen, and not content with those, false bills were presented to the Board of Special Audit and paid. By the time the boss was overthrown in 1871, the stealings from the city probably had aggregated close to $50,000,000 if not more. But New York was not alone. Pennsylvania politics, under the disgraced ex-Secretary of War, Simon Cameron, and Matt Quay, were filthy, nor were other States without scandals of their own.

In 1869 the slimy trail, in fact, reached perilously near the White House and President Grant himself. From early in the war, the United States had been off the gold basis, but gold was required by business men for several purposes, such as the payment of customs duties, and shipment abroad to settle the balance of trade. There was therefore a market for gold, where business men bought and sold it for their needs. As the Treasury drew in to itself gold through its customs duties, it was in the habit of selling it to keep the metal from going to such a premium as would make it difficult if not impossible for business men to meet such of their engagements as had to be settled in gold.

Gould conceived the idea of cornering the metal, buying all of the limited amount in the market, and forcing merchants to pay his price for it or go bankrupt. To succeed in this he had to make sure that for the period of his speculation the United States Treasury could be kept from selling any of the government supply. Playing on Grant's vulgar liking for extremely ordinary men provided they had wealth and power, Gould so managed that Grant became the guest of himself and his disreputable associate, the notorious Jim Fisk. The two on several occasions entertained the President, who was no financier, and persuaded him that it would be for the benefit of the country if gold were temporarily at a high price in New York. They had also worked on Grant's brother-in-law, A. R. Corbin, whom they actually bribed with a share in the deal, and $25,000 cash.

Grant, having allowed himself to become converted to the idea that a higher price for gold would benefit the farmer, ordered Boutwell, the Secretary of the Treasury, not to sell any government metal. It was only after the conspiring gamblers had forced the price of gold up to 163½ on Friday, September 24, 1869, and the country was in a panic, that Grant, who had come to realize his mistake, allowed Boutwell to sell $4,000,000 from the Treasury. Gould, who had got wind of the President's change of mind, had quickly sold out on his partners, without letting them into the secret. Fisk repudiated his contracts amounting to $70,000,000, and the corner collapsed. As Fisk remarked, it was now a case of "each man drag out his own corpse."

Meanwhile on what came to be known as this "Black Friday," hundreds of reputable merchants had been ruined while the country as a whole had faced disaster. The President, Mrs. Grant, and his secretary, Horace Porter, were exonerated, but Grant's stupidity and his having allowed himself to be seen as intimate with such notorious crooks and swindlers as Gould and Fisk left a smirch that cannot easily be wiped out, though personally he never had any intention of profiting himself.

Meanwhile, affairs were going far from well in Washington. For some reason Grant had become determined to annex Santo Domingo in the West Indies, and had sent his secretary, O. E. Babcock, there in 1869. That gentleman came back with a treaty of annexation in his pocket. The President unexpectedly presented this to his Cabinet, who were utterly opposed to the project, especially when engineered in such a dubious way. A second treaty, secured rather more according to diplomatic usage, the following year, failed of passage in the Senate by a tie vote, Sumner speaking strongly against it. Grant had already asked his Attorney-General, Hoar, to resign so that he might appoint a much inferior Southerner in his place to buy votes for the treaty. Not long after, he forced his Secretary of the Interior, Cox, also to resign because Grant refused to support him in trying to save the Indian Bureau from plunder by such men as Cameron and others who were friends of the President.

So wide-spread was becoming the discontent with certain aspects of the administration by 1870, that there developed an ominous break in the party ranks. Starting first in Missouri, under the leadership of Schurz, who was now entering upon the greater career which lay ahead of him, and of B. Gratz Brown, a former Democrat, a new party, known as the Liberal Republican, was launched with success in the State elections.

Among other demands made by the leaders of the new organization was a more enlightened policy toward the South, and as a consequence, in the following May, 1871, Congress at last passed a general Amnesty Act by which all but about 500 Southerners were restored to full rights of citizenship, thus taking the last step in giving back home rule to the South. It has been estimated that the Act enfranchised over 150,000 ex-Confederate soldiers, almost the entire number of whom could be counted on to vote for the Democratic ticket.

In view of the coming Presidential campaign in 1872, and the growing dissatisfaction throughout the country with the inefficiency and scandals of the Grant régime, soon to be increased by the investigation into the Crédit Mobilier, it was fortunate that the election year witnessed a signal success for the administration in foreign affairs.

OUR SETTLEMENT WITH GREAT BRITAIN

Negotiations had been begun by Seward under President Johnson to reach a settlement with the British Government for the damage done to our commerce by the *Alabama* and other vessels which had been built in England for the Confederates during the war and allowed to escape. Lord Russell, however, had denied that any just or legal claim existed on our part, while American public opinion was being goaded and driven astray by the wild bunkum of Charles Sumner, who absurdly but dangerously insisted that England owed us not only for the damage done directly to our shipping by the English-built Confederate cruisers, which was estimated at $15,-000,000, but also for the "indirect damages," amounting to $110,000,000, caused by loss of shipping profits due to the fear of the cruisers, and a further $2,000,000,000, or half the cost of the war, because the cruisers had prolonged it!

It is hard to conceive that Sumner could honestly believe that there was any basis in law or equity for such a preposterous claim, though such English-haters as James Russell Lowell was at that time backed him up, and even Grant at first accepted the theory of "indirect" damages. Instead of appealing to popular prejudices like the sonorous senator from Massachusetts, Hamilton Fish, the Secretary of State, quietly carried on negotiations with England, and found the British officials in a more receptive mood in the following year, when the Franco-Prussian War had broken out. In 1871, the Treaty of

A FACTORY OPERATIVE'S
APPEAL,
To the President of the United States.
Respectfully dedicated to all our Fellow Operatives engaged in the manufacture of Cotton and Woolen Goods throughout the Union.

BY WILLIAM FORSTER,
OF FALL RIVER, MASS.

To thee, O Grant, who art our Nation's pride, laying mercenary thoughts aside, we wish to honor thee, and therefore pray, God give thee tuition to recommend the conditions to our Constitution, guaranteeing to every citizen throughout our land, Freedom's fundamental institution.* Ope one night each week for six months in the year where they may meet and generate,† And preserve all pure, free government throughout our Union; making of it one vast communion; a brotherhood of man.‡ We pray for thee and them.

AN APPEAL TO GRANT IN 1869 FOR NATIONAL LEGISLATION TO
SHORTEN THE LABORING HOURS OF COTTON AND
WOOLEN GOODS OPERATORS

From the Rare Book Room, Library of Congress.

Washington was signed in that city, on May 8, becoming a milestone in Anglo-American relations, and indeed, in the history of diplomacy and the settlement of international disputes.

By this treaty both England and the United States agreed to abide by the decision of an impartial board of arbitration, the five members of which were to be appointed by President Grant, Queen Victoria, the King of Italy, the President of Switzerland, and the Emperor of Brazil. The following summer, the five arbitrators met at Geneva, and the whole matter was amicably settled. Charles Francis Adams, who as our Minister to England throughout the war had continually warned Russell of the building of the vessels, was our perfect and natural choice as American arbitrator. England was less happy in her selection of Chief Justice Alexander Cockburn, a somewhat narrow-minded Britisher of the insular and irascible type. The other three, Count Sclopis of Italy, Jacques Stampfli of Switzerland, and Vicomte d'Itajuba of Brazil, were fair and impartial.

The honor of guiding the proceedings, which more than once threatened to break down completely, was due chiefly to Adams, for the American advocate, who presented the American claims, J. C. Bancroft Davis, was as impossible in his way as Cockburn was in his, and, with an eye on the Irish vote at home for the election due in a few weeks, included at first all the nonsensical "indirect damages" urged by Sumner.

The "*Alabama* claims," as the damages to our shipping by the several British-built vessels were called, was not the only subject in dispute, although the chief. The final verdicts were unanimous with the exception of

Cockburn, who disagreed with distinctly bad grace. The United States was awarded $15,500,000 damages, in gold, for the "*Alabama* claims." England, in turn, was given approximately $7,430,000, of which $5,500,000 arose from fisheries disputes and the remainder for damages sustained by her during our war, while a minor boundary dispute was also adjudicated, the two questions being settled by special commissions and the arbitration of the German Emperor. Leading English statesmen, and not Cockburn, were responsible for the settlement of these various sore spots in our relations with the old mother country, and the air once cleared, those relations greatly improved, though it was to take several decades before the two English-speaking nations could be said to be really friendly, and war between them to become almost unthinkable.

Although the Geneva Award and the settlement of all our disputes with the most powerful nation in the world were claims to distinction for Grant's administration, they were the only ones other than the passage of the Amnesty Act, whereas the scandals were becoming more odious as the election approached. Nevertheless, it was clear that Grant would be the leader of the party again, and he was nominated unanimously by the convention held in Philadelphia on June 5, although Henry Wilson of Massachusetts was substituted for Schuyler Colfax as Vice-President.

GRANT'S SECOND TERM

Not only was Grant re-nominated, but the platform, discreetly silent as to scandals, praised the President's "earnest purpose," "sound judgment," and "incorruptible integrity." In our true American party fashion it also claimed for the Republican policies the full credit for winning the war, the "unparalleled magnanimity" shown toward the South [!], the establishment of "universal" suffrage, and—quite blind to what was immediately to come in a Republican administration,—the avoidance of financial crises and the maintenance of prosperity. A protective tariff and a large increase in war pensions were also recommended.

The opposition was confused, although not unimportant. A new party, the Labor Reformers, made its appearance, and adopted a platform which seemed wildly radical in that period, and conservative and sane today, on which Charles O'Conor, an able New York lawyer and reformer, agreed to stand for the Presidency. It was also in this campaign that the Prohibition Party made its first appearance.

More important, however, was the question of what the liberal Republicans would do. Not only had that new party gathered into its ranks many liberal and reform Republicans of the sort which had been prominent in the original founding of the Republican Party, but the President had antagonized important party men who had little in common with the original liberals, men such as Horace Greeley and Charles Sumner. It was also generally understood that the Democrats would probably endorse the candidates named by the bolting Republicans, and that in view of the weakness and scandal of Grant's administration such a combination might have a good chance to win.

If it ever did have such a chance, it threw it away by nominating Horace Greeley for the Presidency and straddling on the tariff question. In retrospect we can see that every other plank except that on the tariff was sound, including the strong condemnation of the scandals of the administration, and the demands for civil service reform and the return to a gold basis for the currency, but no party could win with Greeley for a candidate.

As editor of *The New York Tribune* he had wielded possibly the widest influence of any editor America has seen. He possessed marked ability and had rendered great service, but right as he had been on some questions, he had been as stubbornly wrong on others. Moreover, he had taken up with so many "crank" movements, and was himself so erratic, that the thought of him in the White House could only be looked upon by the people generally as a joke. The first candidate who had been seriously suggested had been Charles Francis Adams, but he had given no encouragement to the plan, and it was understood that the Democrats would not accept him. At their convention in Baltimore in July they did accept

Greeley, with wry faces and deep dissatisfaction, and adopted both the candidates and platform of the Liberal Republicans.

Neither of these, however, seemed possible of acceptance by a considerable section of the Democrats. These refused to follow their party, and at a convention held at Louisville, Kentucky, in September, nominated O'Conor for President and John Quincy Adams, a brother of Charles Francis, as Vice-President.

The result of the election was never in doubt. Grant was re-elected by a larger popular majority than he had received the first time, and the Republicans controlled both houses of Congress by large majorities. Greeley, who had spent years venomously denouncing the party whose nomination he accepted, and who as a rabid protectionist was nominated by free-traders and low-tariff men, was snowed under, and died a few days after the election. With a better candidate it may be questioned whether the result would not have been approximately the same, and it probably would have been. Post-war periods are always periods of low public morals, and just as we refused to be stirred by the scandals of the Harding régime after the World War, because we were prosperous, so the public of 1872 was evidently unmoved by those under Grant. Prosperity, however, in 1872, was soon to give place to one of the worst panics and longest periods of depression in our history, and scandals were to become more odious than ever.

Grant was to be inaugurated for his second term on March 4, 1873. Toward the end of February the Congressional Committee which had been appointed to investigate charges made by *The New York Sun* in regard to scandals in connection with the building of the Union Pacific Railway made its report. It appeared from this that the promoters of the great engineering feat in which we had taken so much just pride, had formed a construction company, called the "Crédit Mobilier," through which they had secured great and corrupt profits to themselves. Fearing adverse legislation in Congress, these men, through Oakes Ames, a congressman from Massachusetts, had distributed blocks of stock among other congressmen where they would "do the most good"; in other words, had bribed members of Congress to wink at and share in corruption.

Ames was found guilty and censured by Congress. The Vice-President of the United States, Colfax, was clearly also involved, and in an unsuccessful effort to prove his innocence revealed that he had been guilty of an even greater breach of political morality. He retired from office a ruined man. The reputation of James A. Garfield, later President of the United States, was also smirched, and although his latest, and scholarly, biographer claims that he was wholly innocent, he was involved in this and another matter in ways that appear to reflect either on his integrity or his good sense, and the best that can be said is that he was somewhat obtuse as to high standards in public office. Others also were entangled, and the nation was widely aroused.

On the last day of Congress, March 3, 1873, the day before Grant was to be inaugurated for his second term, Congress passed an Act raising the salaries of many government officials, from the President down, not only increasing their own remuneration fifty per cent, from $5000 to $7500 a year, but as respected themselves making the Act retroactive so that each member of Congress drew $5000 of back pay. This was so extremely raw as to cause an unexpected outburst of public resentment, and the "salary grab," as it was called, had, in this particular, to be repealed in the next session.

Other scandals were yet to come. In 1875 the frauds on the revenue perpetrated by the "Whiskey Ring" were uncovered, and involved Grant's private secretary, General Babcock, whom Grant shielded, as he did also his Secretary of War, W. W. Belknap, whom he allowed to resign "with great regret" the day before he was to be impeached before the Senate for graft. Frauds in other departments were also uncovered, and the total unearthed in the President's second term amounted to about $75,000,000. If the trail went very close to the White House, it did not, however, quite reach it.

The charge against Grant is that, with apparently a fatal inability to choose either his officials or his friends among the right sort of men, he allowed his mistaken sense of loyalty in private friendship to overshadow completely his sense of what he owed to the public. In many respects he had the same qualities as Harding, though he had an ability and a real greatness that were both far beyond the reach of the later President who allowed his administration to become honeycombed with public scandal precisely as did Grant. One act in Grant's unhappy second term was to prove that he had high political courage and was to do much to redeem his reputation.

In its platform of 1872 the Republican Party had taken the credit for the prosperity which, at least in the North and West, had been enjoyed after the war. It is with no wish to hold a brief for either of our great parties that the fact must be stressed that no party has a monopoly on prosperity. Economic laws continue to operate, and in surprisingly regular cycles, regardless of the political questions of any campaign, and to a great extent it is a matter of luck which party happens to be in power when crises occur. It is an odd fact, however, that the Republican Party has always claimed, and much of its prestige has come from the ready belief given to the claim by the public, that it alone can provide us with prosperous times. The fact is that since the two parties assumed their modern forms, that is from the beginning of the Civil War, the most severe and most numerous periods of depression have been under Republican and not Democratic rule.

The Democrats were in power during the brief depression of 1884-5, the panic of 1893, and the brief depression at the beginning of the Great War in 1914-15;

whereas the Republicans were in power in the small depression of 1865-6, the panic and long collapse of 1873-78, the so-called "rich man's panic" of 1903-4, the panic of 1907, the deep depression of 1920-22 and the great collapse since 1929. It is high time that these facts were recognized, not for the sake of party but for that of clear thinking. Politics have far less to do with prosperity than they are supposed to have, and less than we wish they might have. It is not only unfair but dangerous to blame the Democrats for their three periods of bad times and ignore the far worse times we have had in Republican administrations.

THE PANIC OF 1873

Grant had been elected in part on a platform of prosperity, but he had been in office only a few weeks in his second term when the storm broke. It was to prove one of the most disastrous and prolonged economic catastrophes in our history, and if political ability or foresight can be held responsible for the action of economic laws, the Republicans, who had been in continuous power since the winter of 1861, could not possibly escape responsibility. It would be, however, as unjust to blame Grant and the Republicans for the panic of 1873 as to lay that of 1893 on the shoulders of Cleveland and the Democrats.

It is possible, although the point is much disputed, that had the party been willing to force resumption of specie payments in 1871, when it could have been effected without too great danger of hardship, the severity of the crisis might have been somewhat mitigated, but it assuredly could not have been avoided.

As we have seen, there had been enormous expansion of business and credit after the war, and, as in 1929, men became drunk with the seeming prosperity and the limitless possibilities for the future. Money borrowed from banks in America and from foreign lenders had been poured into new enterprises with utter recklessness. In the four years, 1869-72, for example, the railway mileage of the nation was increased by 25,000 miles, or fifty per cent of the previously existing total. Everybody was gambling on the future. When such conditions exist, it is certain that a crash will come, though it is never possible to forecast its date or the precise happening which will topple over the house of cards.

There were many warnings in 1872, such as the failure of four large savings banks in New York, but such warnings are seldom noted, and business leaders, like Jay Cooke, the great financier of the Civil War, Thomas A. Scott, the vice-president of the Pennsylvania Railroad, and Cornelius Vanderbilt of the New York Central, sailed gaily into the hurricane with all sails spread. In the spring of 1873 there was a disastrous panic on the stock exchange in Vienna. Europe suddenly became cautious. Credit from that source was stopped for us. Our bankers, manufacturers, and other leading business men unexpectedly faced realities instead of dreams. The summer was ominous. Then on September 18, the banking house of Jay Cooke & Co., the greatest then in America, which was too heavily involved in the building of the uncompleted Northern Pacific Railway, closed its doors. The next day nineteen Stock Exchange firms failed. The Union Trust Company of New York followed, and other great firms crashed. The Stock Exchange closed for eight days, but the panic was on, and many banks continued to break.

By November, pig iron could scarcely be sold at any price, and half the furnaces and mills in the country closed down. Building stopped on every railroad, and all hands were discharged from car shops. In many lines it was impossible to sell goods for the cost of manufacture. As the depression continued, there were strikes and violence everywhere, culminating in the first nation-wide railroad strike of 1877. Between 1873 and 1878, over 50,000 commercial houses failed, and the maximum annual figure was not reached until the latter year, after which recovery set in fairly rapidly. But in the now almost classic description of those five years of misery by James Ford Rhodes, they were one "long dismal tale of declining markets, exhaustion of capital, a lowering in value of all kinds of property, including real estate, constant bankruptcies, close economy in business, grinding frugality in living, idle mills, furnaces and factories, former profit-earning iron mills reduced to the value of a scrap heap, laborers out of employment, reductions of wages, strikes and lockouts, the great railroad riots of

OCTOBER

THIS MONTH IS DEDICATED TO THE CALLING IN OF WHITE HATS. EVERYBODY LICENSED TO SMASH WHITE HATS WHEREVER SEEN.

DATES.	DAYS.	SUN RISES. H.M.	SUN SETS. H.M.	MOON RISES. H. M.	"PROBABILITIES."
1	Thursday	5 57	5 42	9 38	Worry the cider out of your apples. Wormy ones make the richest article.
2	Friday	5 58	5 40	10 40	
3	Saturday	5 59	5 39	11 49	Look out for your fall pippins; also, look out for the boys
4	Sunday	6 0	5 37	morn	who hook 'em. This will apply just as well to store-
5	Monday	6 1	5 35	56	keepers as to farmers.
6	Tuesday	6 2	5 33	2 1	Get your potatoes out of the ground and into your cellar.
7	Wednesday	6 3	5 32	3 4	Send to market those that show symptoms of specking,
8	Thursday	6 4	5 30	4 6	and you will make a speck by doing it.
9	Friday	6 6	5 28	5 6	Dig your pumpkins and watermelons.
10	Saturday	6 7	5 27	6 6	J. Bull paid "that little bill."

BRICKTOP'S ALMANAC FOR OCTOBER, 1874, FEATURED THE SEASONAL CHANGE IN HEADGEAR

From the Rare Book Room, Library of Congress.

1877, suffering of the unemployed, depression and despair."

Ugly, sinister and sordid as was much of the political and economic life of this post-war period, it would nevertheless be a mistake to dwell upon these aspects of America in those years to the total exclusion of other and more hopeful ones. Our life was not all political graft and business money grubbing. If big business scarcely as yet recognized social obligations, and had a low code of business ethics, it was indirectly accomplishing much for the comfort and mental quickening of the people. The labor-saving machinery on the farms made the farmer less of a weary manual laborer, and gave him more time and energy for a better rounded life. The network of railways, the quicker postal facilities, the telegraph, the telephone, invented in 1876, the better news service of the papers following the founding of the Associated Press, and such magazines and journals as *The Atlantic Monthly, Scribner's* and *The Nation,* all helped to broaden the daily intellectual interests.

THE FINE ARTS

In the fine arts, a period must be considered as notable in our history which, after the barren decades before, saw the first rise of such artists as Winslow Homer, Whistler, John La Farge, Sargent, Mary Cassatt, Edwin A. Abbey, Joseph Pennell, George Inness, William Morris Hunt, F. D. Millet, Homer Martin, Howard Pyle, Alfred Parsons, Timothy Cole, and Augustus St. Gaudens, many of whom were to continue work to the end of the century and later. There was a strongly marked broadening of American culture, not merely in the small

THE KNIGHTS OF KING ARTHUR'S ROUND TABLE RECEIVING THE BISHOP'S
BENEDICTION

A panel of the Holy Grail Frieze in the Boston Public Library, painted by Edwin Abbey in 1892.

THE GULF STREAM

Painted by Winslow Homer in 1899, now in the Metropolitan Museum of Art.

MADAME GAUTREAU

Portrait by John S. Sargent, painted in 1884, now
in the Metropolitan Museum of Art,
New York.

The Heathen Chinee.

Yet the cards they were stocked
In a way that I grieve,
And my feelings were shocked
At the state of Nye's sleeve:
Which was stuffed full of aces and bowers,
And the same with intent to deceive.

But the hands that were played
By that heathen Chinee,
And the points that he made,
Were quite frightful to see,—
Till at last he put down a right bower,
Which the same Nye had dealt unto me.

13

TILL AT LAST HE PUT DOWN A RIGHT BOWER.

"THE HEATHEN CHINEE," BY BRET HARTE

Illustrated by S. Eytinge, Jr. Published by James R. Osgood in 1871.

In the Rare Book Room of the Library of Congress.

cultivated groups here and there, but of the public at large.

Many more people went to Europe, and if they were not altogether happy in their environment when they returned, they brought with them, in shoals, ideas of what a more finished civilization could offer in addition to the qualities of their own. Criticism, especially of books and politics as provided in *The Nation* under the editorial leadership of Edwin L. Godkin, assumed an importance and achieved a standard that it had never before possessed with us, and in 1875 a professorship of Fine Arts was established at Harvard with the appointment of Charles Eliot Norton. The 1870's also saw the founding of such notable institutions as the Museum of Fine Arts in Boston and the Metropolitan Museum in New York, as well as other lesser ones and the beginning of many important private collections.

Not less hopeful was the change in literature. The position of men of letters was greatly improved by better methods of book distribution, by the rise of such publishing houses as Henry Holt and Company, Charles Scribner's Sons, and E. P. Dutton and Company, and by such opportunities for remuneration as made writing not only a possible career for men without private means but one which might provide them with ample incomes. There grew up a much wider reading public with a catholicity of tastes and interest no longer satisfied, as the smaller public had been, with the Boston and Concord group of Holmes, Longfellow, Emerson, Lowell, Hawthorne, and Whittier.

Two notable points about that group had been its extraordinarily minute geographical locus, and the extent

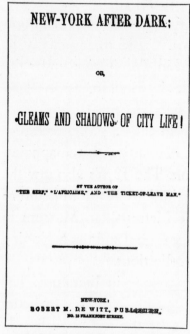

ONE OF DeWITT'S ROMANCES
OF 1866

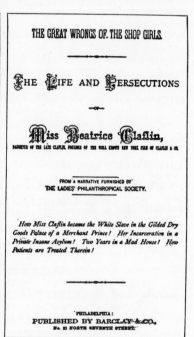

A POPULAR TYPE OF FICTION
OF 1873

From the Library of Congress.

to which its writings served for the most part merely to transmit European culture. The change in the 1870's was marked in both respects. The new authors hailed from all parts of the United States, and dealt almost wholly with the American scene, even though they showed a tendency to drift into New York or Boston. Sarah Orne Jewett painted the slowly decaying life of the old New England, but from the Middle West came

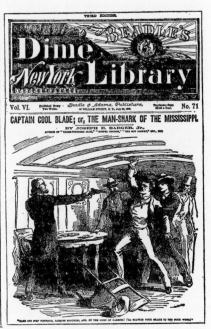

(*Left*) TITLE–PAGE OF ONE OF THE FORERUNNERS, IN 1862,
OF BEADLE'S DIME NOVEL
From the Rare Book Room of the Library of Congress.

(*Right*) BEADLE'S DIME NOVEL
Captain Cool Blade; or, The Man-Shark of The Mississippi was published July 2, 1872.
From the O'Brien Collection in the New York Public Library.

Mark Twain with his *Roughing It* and *Life on the Mississippi;* John Hay with his ballads, and Will Carleton and Edward Eggleston with their tales of Western life. Across the Rockies were Joaquin Miller and Bret Harte with their poems of the Western mountains and stories of rough mining camps, while in the South were George W. Cable, Miss Murfree (Charles Egbert Craddock), and others telling of *Old Creole Days,* of life in the Appalachian Mountains or on the old plantations.

Then, as usual, the mass of the people were contented with less admirable fare, and this period saw the rise of the dime novel devoted to the wild life of the West, and the reading of colossal amounts of sentimental fiction, though the vogue of Dickens throughout the country was astounding. Between the end of the war and about 1875 was the period of the amazing success of the Lyceum and the lecturers of all sorts, from Emerson to the temperance orator John B. Gough, who addressed millions of hearers on every conceivable subject.

If the Lyceum was in a sense the university of the people, the real universities were advancing very rapidly, along with the graft and scandals of business and political life. Post-graduate work, leading to the higher degrees, was inaugurated in America, at Yale, in 1871, and not only was the possible sphere of studies greatly enlarged at many of the colleges throughout the country, but the period witnessed the beginning of the influence of a remarkable group of educators in Charles W. Eliot, Daniel Coit Gilman, Andrew D. White, James B. Angell, and James McCosh.

The age, like all, was full of conflicting currents, and if we have to chronicle the doings in New York, for example, of the Goulds and Vanderbilts and Boss Tweeds, and other such ruck, we must not forget that at the same time in the same city Barnard was reorganizing Columbia, Theodore De Vinne was laying the founda-

THE ABANDON OF YOUTH AS SHOWN IN *CAPERS*, DESCRIBED AS "SOME-THING BETTER THAN SOMETHING TO EAT," PUBLISHED IN NEW YORK IN 1873

From the Rare Book Room, Library of Congress.

tion for the fine art of American printing, the Metro-politan Museum was being established, and many other things were happening in the currents of the most vigor-ous artistic and intellectual life that city had yet known, and this was true of other parts of the country. The 100th anniversary of the Declaration of Independence was celebrated with the Exposition in Philadelphia, one of the earliest of the World's Fairs, and if our own exhibits were rather in the inventive field of farm machinery, the telephone, the new typewriter, and such things than in the arts, and if the taste of it all was rather atrocious, the affair nevertheless marked a certain coming of age in our national life, and a looking forward to new endeavor in many directions instead of backward to the Civil War.

The war was at last passing in influence, and new issues were forming, although neither political party was as yet willing to commit itself positively on any of them. The more important of these, as the campaign of 1876 drew near, were those of national finance and currency, the tariff, and the reform of the civil service. All of them were tinged with strong emotion and had to be discussed against a background of deep discontent.

Both the industrial laboring class and the farmers had been hard hit by the deflation following close on the heels of peace, and by the great business depression which set in with 1873. In each case, national organizations were formed, which were to be of considerable influence, the industrialists forming the Knights of Labor, and the agriculturists the secret organization known as the Grange, which latter by 1874 had a million and a half members and was daily increasing. Industrial labor has open to it the weapons of the strike and mob, and we can consider their grievances better in the next chapter when discussing the riots of 1877 in the first year of the administration of President Hayes, but, although farmers cannot go on strike, their grievances were no less acute than those of the railroad and mine and factory employees.

DIFFICULTIES OF THE FARMERS

In spite of prosperity during the war, and the help of the labor-saving machinery of which we have spoken, the life of the Western farmer in the 1870's was for the most part one of comparative poverty, hardship, deep anxiety, and bitterness. The great mass of our Westerners belonged as little in the romantic picture of cowboys, train robbers or lucky prospectors and cattle kings as did the great mass of antebellum whites in the old South with the aristocratic owners of vast plantations and troops of slaves.

Our Western farmers were small people who had trekked west with little or no capital, to scratch a living out of the boundless prairie. The hard work, loneliness, forlorn living conditions, and the usual hardships of the pioneer, fighting droughts and blizzards, had been bad enough in the boom time when prices were high, but when, after the temporary rise during the Franco-Prussian War in 1870, wheat appeared to have fallen permanently to a price that did not permit a profit, there seemed no hope at all. In 1874 in Kansas and Nebraska the plague of locusts completed the destruction.

The farmer felt rightly that he was fighting for his life not only against poverty and nature but against the capitalists of the great centres. The stocks of the railways had been criminally watered on a vast scale, and on capitalizations that to a great extent represented speculative profits to favored insiders, the owners insisted upon earning dividends by charging rates which often deprived the farmer of all chance to pay the interest on his mortgage and to keep his farm. Corn selling at seventy cents in the East might bring the farmer in the Middle West only eighteen cents or less.

The railroads bribed legislatures to allow them to do as they pleased and seemed impregnable, but if the farmer could not go on strike he decided he could attack the enemy if he could secure control of the legislatures, and this he proceeded to do. In 1871 the farmers won control in Illinois and passed a law aimed against both high rates and discrimination. Other States followed, and a howl went up from the railroad men and the East that radicalism was in the saddle and capital was unsafe.

The rapidity with which the Grange increased its membership further alarmed them. That organization, by arranging for co-operative buying, reduced costs by half for the farmer and cut out the middlemen who had been making high profits. It was natural that the farmer should regard the capitalist as his enemy, whether in the guise of mortgagees, stock-yard owners, railway magnates, or bankers. Feeling himself to be the primary producer of the basis of the nation's wealth, working hard and fighting against heavy odds to keep himself and his family from being dispossessed, the farmer

THE OFFICERS IN POSITION AT A MEETING OF THE GRANGE
From "The Grange," published under direction of William Saunders in 1874.

watched most of the profits from his toil go to men whom he pictured as rich and luxurious, fattening on his labor. For the next twenty-five years, American politics were to be largely influenced by the economic ideas of the West.

One of the chief questions working to the fore in the early 70's was, as we have said, that of finance and currency. There was little or no objection made to the wise measures by which the Secretaries of the Treasury,

Hugh McCulloch and John Sherman, had consolidated the various forms of the national debt and completed the reorganization of the war-time financing by 1878. The main objection to the treatment of the debt had been to its being paid in gold instead of paper, especially as in the case of a number of the issues nothing had been specified as to the nature of the currency in which interest and principal were to be paid. In 1868 the Democrats had advocated payment in greenbacks when not otherwise specified, whereas the Republicans had insisted upon gold, though both parties were split on the question.

The problem of the currency, however, was then, and for long was to remain, a more serious one. In 1871 the Supreme Court, reversing its own decision in the preceding year, had decided that the greenbacks could lawfully be used to fulfill contracts entered into before the Act making them legal-tender had been passed. When they had been issued as a war measure, there had been no intention of keeping them in circulation as a permanent part of our currency system, and by 1868 Congress had reduced the amount outstanding from $433,000,000 to $356,000,000, but at that time we were emerging from the first post-war depression, and the natural demand for currency was rapidly increasing instead of diminishing.

Moreover, as gold was at a premium, the deflation of the currency and the bringing back of our paper money to a parity with gold lowered the prices of commodities, and made it harder for the farmer, for example, to pay his debts, most of which he had incurred in paper money. He was not unnaturally quite blind to the advantages of a high national credit and a sound currency when all he could see was that if he had borrowed $2000 in paper when wheat was $1.50 a bushel he was being asked to repay the debt in gold with wheat at 75 cents. Periods of inflation and deflation affect different classes differently. When inflation is in progress, creditors are bound to suffer by being repaid in money of less value than that which they loaned. When deflation, on the other hand, sets in, it is the debtors who suffer by being forced to repay borrowed money in currency of a higher purchasing power. This cannot be helped, and in innumerable individual cases, in both movements, much hardship is bound to ensue.

Inflation is like an insidious drug. Its first effects, notable in a general rise in prices, appear so pleasant that there is demand for more, but if the process is continued indefinitely it can end only in worthless paper money, as in Germany, where a suit-case full scarcely paid car-fare. Long before that stage is reached, however, all business is disorganized because the founts of credit dry up, any one with money being afraid to lend it lest he be repaid in paper worth far less. It is naturally the wealthier and more experienced portion of the community which best realizes the dangers inherent in a bad currency, whereas the poorer class sees only rising prices and the chance to pay off debts cheaply.

It is said that the cry for "cheap money" always comes from the debtor class. This is not quite true, for a rich man not only has money invested but is apt himself to be a debtor on a somewhat larger scale, but he sees more clearly the essential need for a general basis of stability which can come only from a sound and little-fluctuating currency. The demands for cheap money come from the smaller debtor class, which sees only the chance to pay the debt without realizing the wider significance of a depreciating medium of exchange.

In 1868 the Republican Congress had heeded the discontent of this class, and stopped reducing the amount of greenbacks. Six years later, in April, 1874, they allowed themselves to be so influenced as to revoke their sound-money policy and to pass a bill increasing the amount of paper money again to $400,000,000. It was in vetoing this bill that Grant showed his courage, for the party leaders claimed that if he did not consent to inflation the party would be ruined in the South and West.

In the mid-term election of 1874, the Republicans had lost control of Congress, largely on account of the panic and the scandals of the administration, but, having lost in any case, their backbones were stiffened on the subject of money, and in January, 1875, they passed a bill, which Grant signed, providing for full resumption of gold payments on January 1, 1879, including the retirement by that date of the greenbacks which should by then have been reduced to the amount of $300,000,000. Although, as we shall see, specie payment was resumed on the date named, the greenbacks were not retired, and are today outstanding to the amount of $346,681,000.

Prominent Republicans, like Thaddeus Stevens, had been for cheap money, and prominent Democrats, like that party's nominee for the Presidency in 1868, Horatio Seymour, had been for sound money. The same confusion ruled with regard to the tariff.

The tariff Act of 1864, with its extreme rates, had been considered simply as a war measure to raise revenue, but, as always happens, industries which had made large profits under its protection were loath to give them up when the need for revenue or temporary measures ceased. There were other taxes which were more unpopular with the public at large because more directly felt, and these were done away with first after peace was declared, leaving the revenue to be raised to a greater extent from the tariff duties.

There was a fairly strong high-tariff group among the Democrats, and a section of the Republicans were for tariff reform. For reasons quite other than any controversy over tariffs, the chief stronghold of the Republicans had come to be the Eastern States, which happened to be industrial. The negro vote in the South had largely ceased to count, and the whites in that section had been forced into the Democratic ranks by Reconstruction. The

West was naturally Democratic. Both the cotton growers of the South and the Western wheat farmers had come to believe that the high prices which tariffs made for domestic manufactured goods more than offset the supposed market at home for their produce which protection was claimed to create. On the other hand, the States which were Republican came to demand protection. Moreover, the Republican Party, during the war and after, had been the one which had passed tariff measures, which they were called upon to defend. Being Republican, the Democrats naturally attacked them. It was in this way that the Republicans drifted into being the party of protection and the Democrats of tariffs for revenue only. A little later they both took definite stands and attracted followers of the two schools and the several sections, but in the early 70's there was no sharp line between them.

In view of the scandals, only some of which we have mentioned, among office-holders, it was natural that the more decent element of the community should become interested in a partial reversal of the policy of "To the victors belong the spoils" and demand a reform in the matter of appointment to public office. In the next twenty years this question was to loom large, and a considerable amount of good was accomplished, but along with many upright and able practical men who demanded reform there were many cranks and theorists who did not realize the difficulties in the way. On the other hand, the very "practical" politicians, the bosses of the machines who were accustomed to winning by the use of patronage, were all opposed to any change in the system. In spite of the efforts made, the time was not then, and evidently is not yet, ripe for a thorough cleansing of our public life.

In the late eighteenth century there could have been no more corrupt political methods of appointment than those in vogue in England. Within a half century it changed, and today there is no other such unpolitical and incorruptible body of public servants as those who comprise what is called the "Civil Service" in England, none of whom is in the slightest degree influenced either in his loyal service or in tenure of office by politics. No Englishman has been able to tell me how it came about, and no explanation is to be found in history. One thing is certain, that nothing very much can be accomplished by legislation which does not agree with the public opinion of the time, and it was evident that our efforts to improve our political service by reforming the civil service by legislation did not meet public opinion, though it loomed large in politics in the three decades from the early 70's.

THE CAMPAIGN OF 1876

Reform, however, could scarcely be a sharp party issue. Like the pensions scandals, both parties had to hedge and give lip service to reasonable ideals while sticking in practice to what influenced votes for their machines. It was thus in a time of confused issues and of extreme economic distress that the democracy of the nation was to be put to a unique and severe test in the election of 1876.

There were four parties in the field, though two were unimportant. The first to hold their convention were the Prohibitionists, and their platform is not without interest as showing the inveterate habit of reform or third parties to sweep into their fold every possible sort of reformer and crank, with the consequence that such parties are likely to enter the campaign burdened with a multiplicity of controversial issues, creating as many opponents as followers. In this case, the Prohibitionist platform demanded the total prohibition of the manufacture, selling, or transportation of all "alcoholic beverages" in all parts of the United States under the control of Congress; woman suffrage; the reduction by law of postal, telegraph, and railroad rates; the suppression of speculation in stocks and in "every form of property"; the abolition of polygamy and prostitution; an enforced strict observance of Sunday; the use of the Bible in public schools; and the abolition of "executive and legislative patronage."

On May 18, the day after the Prohibitionists met, a new party, the Independent Nationals, or Greenbackers, met in Indianapolis, and adopted a brief platform demanding paper money and protesting against any further issue by the government of bonds payable in gold, "by which we would be made, for a long period, hewers of wood and drawers of water for foreigners."

The real contest, of course, was between the Republicans and Democrats, and the prospect was extremely black for the former. The foulness of the administration scandals and the depth to which the economic depression had now gone were, in combination, an almost impossible load for any party to carry.

When the Republican Convention met in Cincinnati on June 14, there was no question of renominating Grant for a third term, and the favorite candidate appeared to be James G. Blaine of Maine. The Republicans had become split into two factions, the "Stalwarts," who had stood by Grant and all his works, and the "Half-Breeds," who had been opposed to him. Among the latter the most eminent was Blaine, who regarded himself as one of the saviors of the party. Although exonerated from specific charges, he also had been smirched somewhat by one of the railroad scandals of the day, and although, then and later, nothing was ever definitely fastened upon him, the fact remained that with only a small government salary Blaine became wealthy and persistently declined to explain how.

He had made a powerful and bitter enemy of Senator Roscoe Conkling, the boss of New York, who was said to possess the "finest torso" in American public life, and whom Blaine had pilloried for his vanity in describing his "turkey-cock strut." Conkling was personally honest but was a machine politician of the ordinary sort, his aides in New York politics being Chester A. Arthur and the young Thomas C. Platt, the future boss.

Both Blaine and Conkling desired the nomination, but when on the sixth ballot it became evident that none of the leading candidates could secure the requisite two-thirds vote, the convention suddenly swung around and nominated Rutherford B. Hayes, Governor, for his third term, of Ohio. Hayes was a perfectly colorless candidate, who had a fortune acquired with entire honesty, whose personal rectitude was above question, and who had had a good record as an officer in the Union army and had made a good governor.

Two weeks later, the Democrats nominated Governor Samuel J. Tilden of New York, a lawyer and reformer who had been one of those chiefly responsible for the overthrow of Boss Tweed and of the "Canal Ring" at Albany.

The platform of neither party was a notable document. The Democrats denounced the high tariff, and the Republicans rather mildly endorsed the doctrine of protection; both stood for sound money and the resumption of specie payments; each threw mud in considerable quantities at the other. With two perfectly honest men as candidates, both without magnetism or sharp flavor, with no very clear-cut issues, the campaign was dull and uninteresting until the close. Then the nation suddenly awoke, in fear and anger, to find itself facing one of the most serious crises in its history.

When the election returns were in on the evening of November 7, it seemed clear that Tilden had been elected by 185 electoral votes to 184, having carried all the doubtful Northern States. Hayes considered himself defeated. Apart, however, from a minor irregularity in the electoral vote of Oregon, there were three Southern States,—South Carolina, Florida, and Louisiana,—which had had disputed elections and had sent in two sets of returns. The popular majority of Tilden over Hayes was 250,000 of all votes and 1,250,000 of the white vote, but the chairman of the Republican National Committee, Zachary Chandler, at once claimed the Southern votes and insisted that Hayes had won.

There was no provision in our Constitution covering such a situation, and no legislation provided for settlement of such a dispute. The Senate at the moment was Republican, and the House Democratic. There was much public excitement, and threats of violence, but the people behaved with remarkable moderation, and waited quietly. As the weeks went by, however, and the methods of our election were laid bare and the danger of reaching the 4th of March with no President became clear, disgust and anxiety permeated all quarters.

Finally, in January, Congress passed an Act providing for a commission of fifteen members, including five Democrats and five Republican members of the two

Houses, two Democrats and two Republican judges of the Supreme Court, and a fifteenth to be chosen by these fourteen. The commission when organized had eight Republicans and seven Democrats, and it was not until March 2, almost on the eve of inauguration, that the commission, having decided every disputed point on strictly party lines, and having given every questionable vote to Hayes, declared him elected President by 185 to 184.

Throughout the trying months both candidates had behaved in the most exemplary way, each placing the good of the nation in its crisis above his personal ambition. There was no appeal to public or partisan passion, and the people were asked to await the outcome with calmness and to accept the result of the verdict. Both candidates exhibited patriotism of a high order, and the country was extremely fortunate in that there was practically nothing to choose between them in conduct or in qualities for the office of chief executive.

The investigations of the commission revealed so much fraud, intimidation of negroes, and other crimes, by both parties (in which the candidates had had no part), that it was a rather chastened America which received the verdict. Unfortunately, the Hayes-Tilden campaign was no dirtier than many others in our history. The only difference was that in this case crime and fraud were dragged into the light of day for all citizens to see.

The deeper one goes into the filthy mess of 1876, the

more impossible it is, as the circles of fraud widen and widen, to determine which candidate was really elected, but, on the whole, historians, including a number of those strongly attached to the Republican Party, incline to believe that Tilden was defrauded of his election. In any case, not from personal ambition but the good of the country there was nothing for Hayes to do but to accept at once the findings of the commission, and it is to the credit of the people at large that after precisely a century of the experiment of democratic government on a scale never before attempted, they had sufficient self-control and understanding of the basis on which a self-governing nation must carry on that the "stolen election," as it was considered by the majority, should have been quietly and peaceably acquiesced in for the good of the country.

Unhappily, the Republicans marred their victory, when the power was theirs, by slandering the ill and suffering Tilden, who had given such an exhibition of honor and patriotism, and by bringing suit against him for a fraudulent return on his income tax in 1862, an untrue charge that they could not prove, but with which they harried him until it was clear on account of his declining health that he was definitely no longer a political opponent. The American people have many things to be proud of, but the conduct of our politics is emphatically not one of them.

CHAPTER VI

THE NATION AT DEAD CENTRE

THE new President was distinctly not a great man, nor was Mrs. Hayes a "great lady." They were markedly what are called "folks," but were to win the esteem and respect of the people by the perfect rectitude and courage of the President and the simplicity and modesty of the wife. Because of her refusal to serve wine at the White House, society might nickname her "Lemonade Lucy," but she won the hearts of the ordinary people, who were interested in the doings of the Hayes children and the unaffected hospitality to old friends with whom the White House was often overflowing. The President, however, did not win the hearts of the politicians.

The nation, as Professor Muzzey has well said, had reached a "dead centre." It had, for the most part, pulled out of the issues and passions of the Civil War period, and had not yet fully sensed those that were approaching in the new economic period. Political parties are not marked by high courage, and neither of the major ones had yet taken definite stands on issues which were still rather inchoate and the popularity of which was uncertain. But if the parties were not divided by issues, they were both of them keen on the spoils of office, and success at the polls. Hayes had not been a popular choice among the politicians of his own party, and his way was not to be made easier from the fact that two of the most powerful of these, Blaine and Conkling, who also hated each other with a bitter hatred, had each wished the high post for himself.

SOME OF THE PROBLEMS BEFORE PRESIDENT HAYES

Moreover, the problems which confronted the new President were all, as we say, "full of dynamite" from the standpoint of the practical politician. These were, in the main, the final reinstatement in the national life of the now reconstructed Southern States, the reform demanded by the people in the civil service, the resumption of specie payments, the whole problem of the disastrous business depression, and the threatened overturn of the balance of powers demanded by the nature of our government due to the efforts of Congress to build up the power of the legislature at the expense of the Executive.

The political danger to be run in trying to carry out a programme of reform and rehabilitation might well have daunted a President who was sure of his overwhelming popularity with the people at large, which might offset the attacks of politicians, but Hayes was an obscure man. He had been nominated for that very reason, and had no public following to give him confidence. The unflinching courage with which he persisted in what he believed to be the right course throughout his term is the more notable on that account.

AN UNWELCOME GUEST

MISS FISK M'KINSEY DECLARES SHE HAS NOTHING TO WEAR

—AND ABSOLUTELY WEARS NOTHING

—AND SUFFERS THE CONSEQUENCES.

C. S. REINHART

ZERO WEATHER AND PREVAILING STYLES AT GRANT'S
SECOND INAUGURAL BALL

Featured by *Harper's Weekly* in the issue of March 22, 1873.

He had already shown physical courage, for during the tense weeks while the disputed election hung in doubt, not only had many threats been made against his life but one actual attempt had been made to assassinate him by an unknown assailant who fired a pistol at him through the window one night while he was dining.

Unusual precautions had to be taken on his trip to Washington to assume office, but the courage which he was to be called on to show during the next four years was of a different and a higher sort.

Trouble started at once with the announcement of his appointments to the Cabinet. Although he had to yield to the demand of Oliver P. Morton, the boss of Indiana, in the appointment of Richard W. Thompson as Secretary of the Navy,—the only thoroughly bad selection,— the rest of the Cabinet officials made a strong group. Among the notable members were John Sherman in the Treasury, William M. Evarts in the Department of State, and Carl Schurz in that of the Interior. As part of his plan for giving back to the South its proper place in the government, Hayes had wished to place a Southerner in the Cabinet, and had even considered the rebel general, Joseph E. Johnston. As it became clear that this would be going too fast for public opinion, the President compromised, and gave the Postmaster-Generalship to David M. Key of Tennessee. Although less prominent than Johnston, Key had fought on the Confederate side and, what was even worse in the eyes of the politicians, he was a Democrat.

Good as the Cabinet was for the country, it immediately made trouble for Hayes. Blaine, who had gone to the Senate, combined his resentment against the President for having defeated him for the nomination with the pique he felt because Hayes had declined to include a Maine man in the Cabinet, and he violently denounced the man whom his party had just elected. Conkling of New York considered he had a right to dictate New

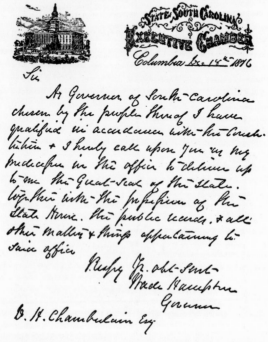

IN THE STATE ELECTION OF 1876 IN SOUTH CAROLINA, BOTH HAMPTON AND CHAMBERLAIN CLAIMED TO HAVE BEEN ELECTED GOVERNOR
Above is Wade Hampton's letter calling upon Chamberlain to surrender the office.

York appointments. He disliked Evarts from his State, and had wished a post for his underling, Tom Platt, so he, like Blaine, was also at once in opposition. So likewise was the powerful Cameron of Pennsylvania, who wanted a job for his son, and most of the practical politicians were bitterly opposed to Schurz as a civil service reformer and to Key as a Southerner and a Democrat. For some days the Senate withheld confirmation of

CHAMBERLAIN'S REPLY TO WADE HAMPTON'S LETTER

Hayes's appointments of his advisers, but it being evident that this senatorial obstruction was not popular in the country, they at last grudgingly confirmed all the nominees.

By the time Hayes reached the White House, all the Southern States but South Carolina and Louisiana had got rid of carpet-bag governments, and had been re-

263

stored to white, which now meant Democratic, rule, but Republican governments were still upheld by the army in the two named. In each of them it is as impossible to tell which party had won the local election as whether Hayes or Tilden had been elected in them as President. Those who had been elected to local office by each party proceeded to organize State governments, and for a while there was complete confusion.

It was perfectly obvious, however, that except for the presence of the troops under control of Congress, the people, or at least the whites, would declare for the Democrats. In South Carolina the Republican governor was a Massachusetts carpet-bagger named Chamberlain, and the Democratic was the distinguished South Carolinian, Wade Hampton. The State, like Louisiana, had been counted Republican by the commission which declared Hayes to have been elected President, and when Hampton's title to office was taken into court a negro Republican judge decided adversely to him. In Congress, men like Blaine demanded that the Republican governments must be considered legal and maintained by force or Hayes's own title to the Presidency would be put in question again.

Hayes, however, realized that the time had passed for continuing to govern any part of the South by troops in the interest of a party. He hoped, also, too optimistically, that with freedom from restraint a two-party system might be restored in that section, and that many whites as well as almost all blacks might join the Republican ranks. That could not be. Bitterness against the Republicans for the long agony which they had forced on the South, racial feeling which their course had fostered, and the fact that they had made the Republican Party in the South almost wholly the party of the negroes, had created the solid South of the Democratic whites.

HAYES DOES NOT PLAY POLITICS

Nevertheless, Hayes's policy was the right and wise one, but he was not playing politics. He did, indeed, have to find berths for a rather unconscionably large proportion of the local politicians, black and white, who had brought about the recent Republican decision in the two States and in Florida, but that once done, the South was clear of Federal troops and could organize itself in its own way.

That way would clearly be to rid itself by various means of the dominance of the negro vote, and practically to nullify the Fifteenth Amendment. On this there are a number of things to be said. Had Lincoln's plans for a sympathetic reinstatement of the South in our national life not been thwarted by such men as Stevens, Sumner, and others in Johnson's term, the way might have been opened for the Southern whites to have adopted the two-party system. Had they also been allowed to work out the negro problem by themselves, they might have included the negro in such a system, in the course of time. But the Republican politicians and the fanatic pro-negro reformers having caused the political lines to be drawn on racial ones, the only result could be to drive the whites out of the Republican Party, and greatly to accentuate the serious racial problem.

If any one objects to the nullification for more than fifty years of an amendment to the Constitution, he has to answer the question as to what else could have been done which was better under the circumstances? Even the wildest of Abolitionists would hardly have desired to live long himself under negro domination and government. What that might be under the lead of unscrupulous Northern politicians had been shown clearly enough in the carpet-bag era. The amendment had been forced unfairly on States in which the negro element ran from 40 to more than 50 per cent of the total by States in which the negro element was negligible, socially and politically.

Hayes not only withdrew the troops from the South but made several trips to that section, the first President since the war to do so. Unfortunately, however, he did not reap any benefit from his policy of reconciliation. The dislike and mistrust now felt for him by Northern Republican politicians were understandable. On the other hand, in the Democratic South he was looked upon as having been unjustly seated in the Presidency in place of Tilden, and as a Republican he could gain no adherents in that section. In addition, although he had withdrawn the troops, he opposed the repeal of the law which gave Federal deputy marshals and supervisors the power to regulate elections and to appeal to the courts in case of fraud, and of the law which empowered the President to use troops in election contests. He seems at once to have feared the encroachment of the legislature on the Executive, from the way the bills were passed; to have wished to conciliate the South and to do nothing which might appear officially to withdraw protection from the free vote of the negro. The consequence was that he pleased no one.

In less than two months Hayes had lost the support of the leaders of his own party, and the bitterness of the contested election prevented him from gaining any support from even the most independent of Democrats. His next move after settling the Southern question alienated him yet further from his own party.

THE SPOILS QUESTION

From the day of Andrew Jackson, the spoils system had become more and more strongly entrenched in our national life. In fact, the whole political machinery of both parties had come to rest upon using Federal as well as State offices to secure votes, and the practical politician, usually a man of stunted morality, not only accepted the system as a matter of course but did not see how his own power or that of his party could be maintained on any other.

As the system had developed, it had had two results. One was greatly to strengthen the power of the Senate and the party managers at the cost of that of the President, who in the Constitution had been given the right of making appointments. Gradually it had become customary to consider the Federal appointments in any State as a sort of perquisite of the senator from that State, and the President was expected to choose his nominees from among the list of names agreed upon by the senator and the State boss, if the latter two were not, as they often were, one and the same person. Under this system, the names offered were likely to be those of men who were locally useful to the machine organization rather than those of men chosen solely for their fitness for the office. The other result of the system, besides that of buttressing the political machine by graft, was the wastefulness and inefficiency of the Federal service.

The condition of that service had become appalling in the eyes of honest citizens who wanted decent government, and men of very different types, such as Charles Sumner, Carl Schurz, George William Curtis, and others, who had been working for improvement, had secured the passage by Congress in 1871 of an Act providing for the setting up of a civil service commission to study the question. Grant, however, who was reported to have claimed, in spite of the stench of his administration, that our civil service was then "the best in the world," gave no aid, and in 1874 completely surrendered to Congress on the subject.

Hayes was the first President to grapple seriously with the evil, and he did so courageously, understanding fully the forces which he was bound to antagonize. Unfortunately the time was not yet ripe, and public opinion not yet sufficiently stirred, to allow the President to make any permanent change in the system. Nevertheless, as a result of the fight made by him, the question could not thereafter be allowed merely to slumber in innocuous and hypocritical paragraphs of party platforms.

The problem was not an easy one to solve. In a democracy there is no way known to us of carrying on government other than by means of parties. A party to be effective must be organized and lasting, which means that it must have a hierarchy of organizers of all grades from the national leaders down to the smallest of ward bosses. The motives which these can count upon in their followers to maintain allegiance to the organization will naturally depend upon the moral and intellectual level of those followers. If the general mass both of politicians and voters are motivated by desire of personal profit, the spoils of office, in one form or another, are bound to be highly important, if not indeed wholly essential, in holding the organization together. If organization is necessary, and it apparently is, then bad as is corruption in office, if reform is carried out so rapidly as to destroy the cohesion of the organization, we merely substitute for the evil of corruption that of a breakdown in party organization, with ensuing political chaos.

All such problems may be approached from three standpoints, that of the practical politician of the ordinary moral level, that of the impractical reformer, and that of the statesman. The politician wishes no reform whatever in a system which he understands how to use and believes to be essential. The crank reformer wishes to change everything so rapidly as to make him, perhaps, even more dangerous than the politician. The statesman wishes to make progress, and as rapidly as possible, but realizes that he cannot go faster than he can induce public opinion to support him. In any case he is likely to be damned by both the other types, by the reformer because of his alleged inconsistency and because he does not do enough, and by the politician because of his alleged lack of loyalty and because he does too much.

The practical exigencies of the situation were only too unhappily pressing at the very beginning of Hayes's term, and it must be confessed that the number of offices he bestowed upon the Southern politicians, including the officers of the returning boards in Florida and Louisiana who had made his election possible, had an exceedingly bad odor. On the other hand, he was genuinely devoted to reform, and in large part sacrificed himself upon its altar.

In the Department of the Interior, where the start was

made, he gave Schurz a free hand, and supported him in his sweeping removals when it was established beyond a doubt by investigation that the Indian Bureau was a gangrened mass of corruption. Although the negro had innumerable friends, friends like the Abolitionists who were willing to break up the country that his position might be improved, the woes of the Indian had never interested any one. Almost no voice had ever been raised on his behalf.

Screened by the spoils system of office and this lack of public interest in our wards, to whom we have many times broken our most solemn national oath, the Indian Bureau and agents waxed fat on graft at the expense of the redskin. Forced to depend upon the agents, he was given miserable blankets and rotting food, bought by the government at high prices, officials making huge profits on the transactions. His lands were trespassed upon, and he could get no remedy. The consequence was constant unrest and a succession of minor wars, both of which markedly diminished after Schurz had made, temporarily, a clean sweep of the incompetent and corrupt political appointees whom he found in office. But he did so at the expense of having war waged upon himself, for the politicians never forgave him for his efforts and eventually drove him from politics.

Hayes himself led the attack on one of the most notorious strongholds of the spoils system,—the New York Custom House. Although this service was under the

Treasury Department in Washington, the New York boss, Senator Conkling, had come to look upon it as his personal satrapy, and its personnel as mere pawns in the local political game. When in May, 1871, Hayes told the Secretary of the Treasury that "party leaders should have no more influence in appointments than other equally respectable citizens," the gage of battle was thrown down. The President went even further and declared that no Federal office-holder should be subjected to assessments on his salary for political purposes, nor be permitted to take part in political organizations or campaigns. To men like Conkling it seemed as though the President was not only threatening their personal power but that his policy would ruin the whole Republican organization.

When an investigating commission headed by John Jay reported on conditions in the custom house, it was found that 200 of Senator Conkling's local henchmen were on the pay roll without doing any work whatever for the government; that all salaries were levied upon in campaigns; that technical positions were held by ignorant politicians; that imports were undervalued; and that there was in general gross fraud and inefficiency. At the head of the organization, as collector of the port, was Chester A. Arthur, who up to that time had been merely a spoilsman politician and a friend of Conkling. The naval officer of the port was A. B. Cornell, who was also chairman of the State and National Republican Committees. Similar conditions were found to exist in custom houses elsewhere, but the President at once declared war on Conkling and his gang as representing the worst centre of infection.

Arthur, Cornell, Conkling, and Platt were the four who controlled New York politics, and when the first two were asked to resign by the President, they declined. Conkling, Republican boss though he was, did not hesitate to say that Hayes had never been elected and that Tilden should have been put in the White House. In September, at the State Convention, he prevented the passage of a resolution upholding the "lawful title" of Hayes to the office, so that the Republicans in the greatest State in formal convention declined to recognize the legality of their own President.

It is not necessary to recite in detail the long struggle of Hayes to have Arthur and Cornell replaced by men capable of giving an honest and business administration in one of the most important departments of the government. Although the Senate blocked every effort he made, the President would not admit defeat. When Conkling won one of the strategical moves, Hayes wrote in his diary, "The end is not yet. I am right and shall not give up the contest." In July, 1878, when Congress was not in session, he removed Arthur and Cornell, but it was not until early in February, 1879, that the President won and the Senate at last confirmed his new appointees.

Conkling was completely defeated, but neither the

party nor the people supported Hayes. So strong among the bosses and the rank and file of the Republican voters was the opposition to reform that in the elections of 1878 even such Republican States as Pennsylvania went Democratic, as did the President's own State of Ohio; and in the election of 1880 the party nominated Chester A. Arthur for the Vice-Presidency. But although the Republican leaders like Conkling and Blaine would have liked to read the President out of the party, and Conkling even attempted to have his title to office invalidated by a reopening of the election question, he had done more than any of them for the rehabilitation of that party in the eyes of honest and independent voters. If it had not been for his fight for good government it is unlikely that the party would have won in the next Presidential campaign.

Reform had to wait, but the New York Civil Service Reform League was founded in 1877, to be followed by a national league four years later, and Hayes undoubtedly deserves the credit for being the first President to fight to cleanse our politics of the gigantic evils of the spoils system. In this, as in his effort to free and reinstate the South, he belonged to the coming era rather than, as Grant had, to the one which was passing.

EFFECTS OF BUSINESS DEPRESSION

Throughout almost his entire term the country was deeply concerned with the business depression noted in

the preceding chapter, and with the more technical problem of the currency. If the most spectacular financial
episodes of the panic had occurred in Grant's régime,
it was to be the duty of Hayes to suppress the physical
violence which was so to alarm the nation in 1877.

There had been local violence in the anthracite coal

*Second. And, among other things, said rules shall provide and declare, as
nearly as the conditions of good administration will warrant, as follows:
First, for open, competitive examinations for testing the fitness of applicants
for the public service now classified or to be classified hereunder. Such examinations shall be practical in their character, and so far as may be shall
relate to those matters which will fairly test the relative capacity and fitness
of the persons examined to discharge the duties of the service into which they
seek to be appointed.*

*Fifth, that no person in the public service is for that reason under any
obligations to contribute to any political funds or to render any political service, and that he will not be removed or otherwise prejudiced for refusing to
do so.*

*Sixth, that no person in said service has any right to use his official author-
ity or influence to coerce the political action of any person or body*

SECTION FROM THE CIVIL SERVICE REFORM ACT OF DECEMBER 4, 1882
From the original Act in the Department of State, Washington.

region of Pennsylvania from 1862 onward, due to the
activities of the notorious "Molly Maguires," members
of a secret Irish society known as the Ancient Order of
Hibernians, originally organized in Ireland to resist the
unjust demands of landlords. Although in our own day
the coal miners are mainly southeast Europeans, in this
earlier period they were Irish, which accounts for the
fact that the "Molly Maguires" were all of that race. If
they were also all Roman Catholics, it is only fair to say

that that church was itself wholly opposed to the movement. In the fight with the operators for better conditions, the weapon of the Mollies was cold-blooded murder, either of owners or gang bosses, and the amount
of their activity rose and fell in inverse relation to the
strength of legitimate trade-union activity. The reign of
terror which they maintained was at last broken in 1876
by the work of an Irish Catholic detective, James Mc-
Parlan, but in 1877 a far more serious situation was
brought on by organized labor.

Railroad earnings had dropped 50 per cent since the
beginning of the panic, partly from diminished business
and partly by cut-throat competition for such business
as remained, until it was said in the first six months of
1877 that there was not a single road making a cent of
profit on through freight. Wages had already been cut
more than once since 1873 when in July, 1877, the leading companies announced another 10 per cent reduction.
As a result, serious strikes, starting on the Baltimore &
Ohio, and running thence, as *The Commercial and Financial Chronicle* said, "like a wave of fire along all our
principal lines," immediately ensued. The militia proving
insufficient to cope with the rioters, Federal aid was in-
voked, and Hayes despatched regular troops to a number
of points.

Serious as the rioting was at such places as Baltimore
and Martinsburg, the worst situation of all was confronted at Pittsburgh, where many lives were lost in

pitched battle and the property damage was not less than $5,000,000. This amount was doubled by the rioters in other places, in not a few of which the militia fraternized with the strikers and proved wholly unreliable. The great strikes of 1877 resulted in the employment for the first time of Federal troops to settle a labor dispute, and the effects were notable, both in the subsequent growing opposition to labor organizations in the courts, and in the greater solidarity to be noted thereafter in the labor class itself. The President had maintained order, but in spite of the obvious problems arising from the changed relations between employer and employed in the new economic order of great corporations, no effort was made to grapple with them. *Laissez-faire* and force were as yet the only doctrines with which the government could meet the new situation emerging.

CRISIS IN CURRENCY QUESTION

The problem of sound money, which Hayes also had to consider, offered a typical example of the way in which a great public question is usually confused by a mixture of ignorance, prejudice, and private interest, though the President himself was as correct in his attitude on this as on the problems of the South and of reform.

The extremely hard times through which the country was passing made the payment of debts by those who owed them peculiarly difficult and unpleasant. Such periods, as we noted in the preceding chapter, always arouse deep resentment on the part of the debtor class, and afford special opportunity to the demagogue and for the spread of financial heresies.

There were particular factors at work in the depression of 1873–79 which accentuated the condition, and the administration of Hayes, although it saw the end of one evil, saw also the introduction of another. It ended the paper money of the war but introduced the silver fallacy which led straight to the great sound-money panic and fight in the 1890's.

As the business depression widened and deepened, the cry for cheap money on the part of the ignorant or dishonest became louder. Our currency system at this time was peculiarly rigid and incapable of expanding and contracting with the real or fancied need of business. It is a fallacy to believe that business prostration can be cured by an easy-money policy, whether of expanded currency or extended credit, but a large part of the electorate believed that it could be so cured, and in any case demanded cheap money in which to pay their debts. Moreover, the currency system really was faulty in its over-rigidity, and was to remain so for another four decades.

Speaking generally, the currency consisted of gold, paper, and bank notes. The twenty years from 1870 to 1891 were years of stationary or declining production of gold in the entire world, just as the twenty years following 1891 were to be years of vast increases in supplies. Practically no increase in our currency could therefore be looked for in gold coinage or gold certificates backed by deposit of gold.

The administrations of Grant had seen the rise of the greenback movement, demanding that expansion should be achieved by the issue of mere fiat paper money, but that had been blocked by the action of the expiring Republican Congress in January, 1875, which had passed the Act providing for the gradual reduction in the number of greenbacks and their final redemption in gold to be effected January 1, 1879.

The third form of currency, bank notes, was also comparatively inelastic, as the notes had to be based on the deposit of government bonds, which were limited in amount and which were being retired rather rapidly.

Thus, those who demanded cheap money had to find some other form, especially after the Democratic House of Representatives had passed a bill in 1877 demanding the repeal of the Resumption Act, only to have it properly blocked in the Senate.

A combination of circumstances, including those just mentioned and the others to be noted, raised the ominous silver issue, which unfortunately—for political life is far healthier with two strong major parties—was to blight the Democratic Party as effectually as its stand on slavery and the South had done just before the Civil War.

The policy of bi-metallism, that is of trying to keep both gold and silver in circulation and interchangeable, had been attempted by the United States for seventy years, after the initiation of the experiment by Alexander Hamilton in 1792. The effort had finally proved a failure in our country as in others. Adopting the comparative commercial value of the two metals in his own day, Hamilton had thought that if a gold dollar and a silver dollar each contained the amount of gold and silver respectively which had the same commercial value at any moment, their parity could be maintained, and they would be interchangeable as coins, both remaining in circulation. As a grain of gold was worth in the market 15 times a grain of silver when he started, he fixed the ratio at 15 to 1, the silver dollar having in it 371.25 grains of pure silver and the gold dollar 24.75 grains of gold.

As long experience has proved, however, the two metals cannot possibly be kept at any fixed ratio commercially. Not only the amounts of each produced annually from the mines, but the demands for each all over the world for purposes other than coinage, vary so constantly and so greatly as to make each fluctuate in terms of the other as readily as, let us say, do the comparative prices of a bushel of wheat and a pound of coffee. Moreover, according to a well-established economic law, if there are two kinds of metal currency and the commercial value of the metal in one is more than that in the other, the one which is worth more will be hoarded by the public and the one of lesser value will circulate as "money."

This is precisely what happened to the gold and silver dollars of Hamilton. Even before they had got into circulation from the mint, the delicate ratio had been destroyed by commercial prices, and as the gold in a gold dollar was worth commercially a little more than the silver in the silver dollar, gold dollars disappeared from circulation. In 1834, an effort was made to readjust the balance, and the coinage ratio was changed to sixteen to one. As this, however, threw the balance out again slightly in the opposite direction, the gold dollars quickly came back into circulation and it was the commercially more valuable silver ones which in turn disappeared.

By 1873, the silver dollar had been out of circulation for so many years that when Congress was revising the coinage laws the silver dollar was dropped from the list of coins which were to be minted. There was no objection to this at the time, though the subject was thoroughly threshed out in debate. The coinage of silver was of interest to almost no one at the moment, and the currency would not have been increased, for it would have cost the government more to turn out silver dollars than gold ones, so those who demanded cheap money had nothing to gain, and the silver mine owners could get more for their silver by selling it in the open market than by having it coined into dollars.

The production of silver from the mines, however, unlike gold, was increasing with enormous rapidity, rising from 43,000,000 ounces in 1870 to 75,000,000 in 1880 and 167,000,000 by 1893. At the same time there was a much lowered demand. India, which had been almost a bottomless sink for the hoarding of the metal, ceased to absorb it, and some nations, notably Germany, which had become convinced of the bi-metallic fallacy, not only stopped coining silver but dumped large quantities on the market. The consequences of all these factors working together was that silver, which in 1873 had borne a ratio to gold of 15.92 to 1, dropped to one of 18.39 to 1.

The American mines were producing huge quantities, and if the mine owners could induce Congress to begin coining silver dollars again at the ratio of sixteen to one, they could make a large profit by taking their depreciated silver to the mint and receiving back dollars at that ratio when the commercial ratio was 15 per cent lower. If the government could be made to do this in unlimited quantities, the mine owners believed that they could dump all their surplus on the government at a good and fixed price, and some of them at least were incorrectly but honestly convinced that such a process, even if it were to continue indefinitely, would not affect the gold currency.

This error, however, was nothing but the greenback paper money fallacy in as bad, if somewhat more subtle, form. Not only would the gold dollars, as had been shown before, disappear from circulation and be hoarded, being worth more commercially than the silver ones, but if the government were forced to buy silver in unlimited quantities and issue dollars at a fixed ratio while the real value of the silver was steadily declining in the world markets, there would come a time when the government's ability to redeem these silver metal dollars would be just as small as its ability to redeem unlimited issues of mere paper money. It had not yet redeemed even the greenbacks of the war.

The mine owners suddenly began to talk about the failure to include silver in the currency revision bill as "The Crime of '73," and in November, 1877, the House of Representatives passed an Act, introduced more than a year earlier by the Democratic representative from Missouri, Richard P. Bland, providing for the free and unlimited coinage of silver. It passed the House by a vote of 165 to 34, but the Senate was more cautious, although Senator Allison of Iowa believed, as he said, that "legislation gives value to the precious metals"! The Republican Blaine, like his fellow Republican Senator Allison, also came out for free silver, whereas, on the other hand, the Democratic Senators Lamar and Bayard spoke strongly in favor of sound money, so little was the question as yet a party one.

Finally, in spite of a majority in the Senate in favor of free coinage of silver, the bill as passed by that body directed the Secretary of the Treasury to buy not less than $2,000,000 nor more than $4,000,000 of silver each and every month, and to have the amount bought coined into dollars. In the House, "Silver Dick" Bland, as the leader of the silver forces came to be called, denounced the compromise, and fulminated in demagogic fashion against the capitalists who were betraying the people by preventing the unlimited coinage of the cheaper metal. He declared that if they could not be forced to capitulate he was "in favor of issuing paper money enough to stuff down the throats of the bond-holders until they are sick," a remark loudly applauded by the House, regardless of party.

The pressure brought on Hayes to sign the bill, which had passed both Houses, was extraordinarily great, the number of people who really understood the problem and its dangers being small compared with the vast number who saw in the bill merely a panacea for the extreme financial distress under which they were suffering. In spite of the opinion of even three members of the Cabinet, including the Secretary of the Treasury, John Sherman, that the President ought not to veto the bill, Hayes had both the wisdom and courage to do so and to return it to Congress. With it he sent a message justly pointing out that to make a dollar which was worth only ninety cents legal tender for the payment of all debts, including the interest on the government bonds, was dishonest repudiation, and that in the last analysis a nation's credit depended on its honor. His action was of no avail, and on February 28, 1878, Congress in a burst of passion passed the bill over the Presidential veto.

Nevertheless, the courageous stand of Hayes may not have been wholly without effect. Had the unlimited free coinage which Bland desired been permitted by law instead of the moderate purchases directed by the Bland-Allison Bill, the effect upon the nation, just preparing to resume payment in gold, would have been immediately disastrous. There was a much smaller Congressional party in favor of such a measure than of the one finally enacted, and as it required at least a two-thirds vote to re-pass a measure over the President's veto, any measure agreed upon would have to be such as to command that requisite two thirds. As it was, though the honor of the country was sullied and a dangerous precedent had been created, complete disaster was avoided, and when, nineteen years later, the question came up for final settlement it was understood by a much greater element of the voters than in 1877.

Meanwhile, Sherman, who was not a Free Silverite and whose opposition to the veto had been based on political considerations only, was carefully preparing for the resumption of specie payments which had been set for January 1, 1879. He had accumulated a stock of about $140,000,000 in gold in the Treasury, and as January approached the greenbacks slowly rose to par. The day, however, was awaited by both the government and business men with deep anxiety. Would there be a run for gold on the Treasury and the banks in larger quantities than could be paid out even with all the preparations made? After five years of panic and economic ruin, the nation was beginning to glimpse better times ahead. Would the catastrophe of a failure to make redemption a success plunge it again into the misery from which it was just emerging?

The day came and passed with a calm that was almost ludicrous in view of the natural and intense anxiety with which it had been awaited. At the Treasury only $135,-000 of greenbacks were presented for payment in gold, whereas $400,000 in gold was presented for exchange into greenbacks! The credit of the government was evidently considered unassailable, and the country heaved a sigh of relief, though throughout it there rolled the ground-swell of discontent on the part of those who having borrowed money when paper was at a heavy discount were now called upon to repay their debts in a currency at par with gold.

The feud between Hayes and Congress kept up until the end, as did the effort of Congress to encroach on the powers of the Executive. Hayes had been unwisely insistent that the laws authorizing the use of Federal troops to keep order at the polls when needful should not be repealed. The Democratic Congress was as insistent that they should be. The only constitutional way of securing the repeal was either to have them declared unconstitutional by the Supreme Court, which was not tried, or to have Congress pass a bill repealing them over the President's veto, which Congress could not muster enough votes to do.

Congress therefore adopted the method of achieving its aim by tacking on to the end of appropriation bills clauses which were practical repeals of the Force Acts. Whether the President was wise or consistent in opposing repeal may be open to question but there is no question that his duty was to fight the unconstitutional method adopted by Congress. As the President pointed out, if the government could be brought to a stop by failure of appropriations unless the President should consent to any and all legislation on all subjects which Congress might embody in appropriation bills in the shape of "riders," then the Presidential veto became a farce, and the whole theory of our government and its division of powers fell to the ground.

If the Congressional theory was correct, then Congress might pass the entire legislation of an entire session as a "rider" to a single bill providing for the national expense, and adjourn leaving the President with the alternatives of approving everything which Congress might have suggested or vetoing the bill as a whole and stopping the functioning of the entire Federal service for lack of funds. Congress, both in the regular and special sessions necessitated by its actions, was obstinate, but at last, after five vetoes, in the course of which the entire Judiciary Department had been left without pay for months, Hayes won his point and scored the victory.

On the whole, few Presidents have left a better record, and Hayes's efforts to heal the wounds of the South, to bring about the reform of the civil service, to maintain the honor of the nation by a sound money policy, and his resistance to the unconstitutional usurpation of power by Congress, entitle him to a high place as an able, honest and courageous Chief Executive.

The very struggles, however, which have won him the respect of posterity made him anathema to the politicians of his own day and party. Nor did he possess those qualities which might have given him popular support against the politicians. He was not the military hero that Jackson and Grant had been; he had no personal magnetism, not even the odd quaintness of a Coolidge, to intrigue the public; nor had he that gift of dramatizing a situation which Roosevelt could employ so well. There was not the faintest chance for him of a renomination in 1880.

THE CAMPAIGN OF 1880

The campaign of that year was singularly uninteresting and equally unedifying. In the Republican Convention which assembled at Chicago on June 2 the leading candidates at first were Grant and Blaine, who were not on speaking terms with each other. It having been shown, after thirty-five ballots, that neither could be nominated, there was a sudden shift to General James A. Garfield of Ohio, and the Republican ticket became Garfield and Arthur, the nomination for Vice-President having been given to the discredited collector of the port of New York who had been removed from office by Hayes.

After the Greenback Party, which was not to gain a single electoral vote and whose influence had much declined, had nominated James B. Weaver, the Democrats met at Cincinnati on the 22d and nominated General Winfield S. Hancock.

There was little to choose between the platforms of the leading two parties, both of which hedged on the issues, although the Democrats flatly advocated free and unlimited coinage of silver, while the Republicans omitted any reference to that question. The Democratic platform, indeed, was thoroughly unsound as to currency and finance. In the Republican Convention a resolution endorsing civil service reform was passed only with difficulty after a debate which brought out the classic question from delegate Flanagan of Texas, who asked on the floor if the victors were not to have offices to give out "what are we up here for?"

The campaign was tame, and there was no difference in the methods of the two parties, which were those of the time—if not also of ours. The Republican campaign committees, Congressional and National, demanded in all about 7 per cent of their annual salaries from all Federal office-holders, and the Democrats levied where they could. Scandals, or what could be made to appear such, were raked up against each candidate, and Garfield's alleged connection with the Crédit Mobilier and a paving contract were given wide circulation. Toward the end of Hayes's administration the problem of Chinese labor in California had become acute, and in order to damage the Republican nominee in that State, a forged letter purporting to be signed by Garfield was circulated just late enough to do harm without opportunity for convincing refutation. At heavy expense, the vote of Indiana, which had been Democratic in 1876, was admitted by the Vice-President-elect, Arthur, to have been bought and paid for by the Republicans. In a total popular vote of 9,218,-251 Garfield won by a majority of only 9,464. A shift of 10,517 votes out of the total of 1,103,945 in New York, where Conkling and Platt reigned, would have given the election to Hancock in spite of Garfield's 214 electoral votes to his 155.

Although it is impossible to tell before he assumes office how a man will succeed as President, as we shall soon discover in this chapter, it is probable that Garfield was a better candidate for the office than Hancock, though both were men of sound personal character. Garfield, who had started life as a canal-boy, and was the last American President born in a log-cabin, had made a successful and characteristically American career for himself. He had worked his way through Williams College, been a teacher, then won a major-generalship by good work in the war, and from 1863 had been a member of Congress.

The new President did not announce his Cabinet appointments until after his inauguration on March 4, 1881, when it became evident that he had tried to reconcile the two groups in his party as well as the several sections of the country. Blaine of Maine was named Secretary of State, Senator William Windom of Minnesota, a sound-money Westerner, Secretary of the Treasury, Robert T. Lincoln, son of the war President, was put in the War Department, William H. Hunt, a Louisiana lawyer who had been loyal in the war, was given the Navy, and Wayne McVeagh of Pennsylvania became Attorney-General, while Thomas L. James, postmaster of New York, became Postmaster-General. It was the last appointment which was to prove the most important for the moment.

The "Stalwarts" of the party, notably Conkling, had been opposed to the nomination of Garfield and had only reluctantly supported him in the campaign. When, on March 23, the President sent in a list of nominations to the Senate, including appointments in New York as to which he had not consulted Conkling, the latter declared war. Unable to secure the rejection of the nomination of W. H. Robertson as Collector of the Port, a man whom Conkling especially disliked politically, the irate Senator resigned his seat, while his follower Platt simultaneously took the same step, thus winning the nickname of "Me Too," and they asked for vindication against the President's interference with local patronage by a reelection by the New York Legislature. To their discomfiture and the no little amusement of the nation, the legislature declined to re-elect either of them, and the President had won his first round.

Meanwhile, the Postmaster-General had been unearthing scandals of the most odoriferous sort in the letting of contracts on what were called "Star Routes," that is, routes on which the mails were carried by rider or stage. In spite of attempted intimidation by Congress, Garfield was pressing the investigation when, while waiting for a train in the Washington station, he was shot by a disappointed office-seeker, Charles J. Guiteau, on July 2. Although the wounded President lingered on for two and a half months, the shot proved fatal in the end, and he died at his summer home at Elberon, New Jersey, on September 29.

"Chet Arthur, President of the United States! Good God," some one remarked, and it was in that spirit of consternation the nation received the long-feared news.

It is impossible to say how much Garfield might have been able to accomplish had it not been for Guiteau's bullet, which made him a martyr in the eyes of the people. He appears to have been to some extent weak and vacillating in character, and Blaine had expected to be the power behind the throne. One of the results of the sudden change in the administration was the relegation of that statesman, who had taken a rather jingo attitude in foreign relations, to private life, as in the

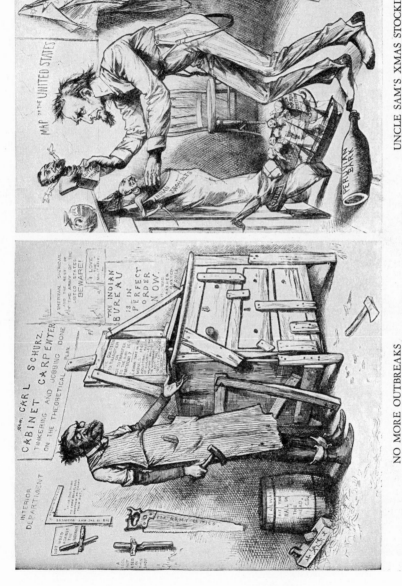

NO MORE OUTBREAKS

"I do not repel but invite inspection and observation on the part of military officers."—CARL SCHURZ.

From "Harper's Weekly," January 25, 1879.

UNCLE SAM'S XMAS STOCKING

"It doesn't promise very well at the start but maybe it will pan out better toward the bottom."

From "Leslie's Illustrated Weekly," December 31, 1881.

THE OPENING OF BROOKLYN BRIDGE, MAY 24, 1883

The celebration of the completion of the work begun in 1870 was attended by President Arthur and many distinguished visitors. Fireworks followed the speeches and parade.

From a colored lithograph in the J. Clarence Davies Collection, Museum of the City of New York.

reorganization of the Cabinet Arthur replaced him by F. T. Frelinghuysen of New Jersey.

ARTHUR AS PRESIDENT

The sobering effect of responsibility and high office has often been noted in public life, but seldom have they had such unexpected influence as upon the spoilsman politician who now became President. Even as late as February, within a fortnight of his inauguration as Vice-President, at a great public dinner in New York he had boasted cynically of the purchase of the vote of Indiana, as though it were an amusing joke.

From the moment, however, that he became President, there was an extraordinary change, a change that first amazed and then angered his old political gang. He declined to remove Garfield's appointee Robertson at the behest of Conkling and Platt, and in his first message to Congress came out squarely for civil service reform, as he did also for a repeal of the Bland-Allison Act, better treatment of the Indians, and a revision downward of the tariff. During his administration the Pendleton Act was passed, in 1883, which placed about 14,000 Federal offices in the civil service open to competitive examination, and empowered the Executive to extend the list. Arthur, who promptly signed the bill, worked loyally with the commission which it created, and when he left the White House about 16,000 offices had been rescued from the spoilsmen.

His political courage was also shown in his veto of a Chinese exclusion bill, because it was contrary to a treaty with China, an action which seriously damaged his popularity in California. The river and harbor bill, passed regularly by Congresses, presumably for the improvement of such bodies of water as might have real commercial importance, had become a national scandal. This "pork barrel," as it was called, had developed into a huge source of legalized graft for the strengthening of the popularity of congressmen in their home districts, and by 1882 amounted to nearly $19,000,000. In that year Arthur vetoed it on the ground of its "demoralizing effect," but an angry Congress at once re-passed it over the veto.

Although the legislature had passed what is called the President's "Snivel Service Reform" measure, it treated his demand for tariff revision much as it had his effort to cleanse the pork barrel. Duties had remained at practically the highest level attained as specifically emergency war measures, but the return of prosperity after the long depression had resulted in such an increase of imports that the annual surplus accumulating in the Treasury was becoming embarrassing, amounting for the year 1881-2 to approximately $100,000,000.

Such recurring surpluses evidently called for a reduction in taxation and revenue, but, as always happens, the beneficiaries of protection were loath to let their special privileges be reduced or lapse. In May, 1882,

Congress did authorize the appointment of a tariff commission, one of the many which have been supposed to study the question without prejudice.

The report of this commission recommended numerous changes which would have resulted in a total lowering of duties by about 25 per cent, but Washington was soon swarming with the lobbyists of the protected industries, and when Congress at last passed the Tariff Act of 1873 the report had been torn to shreds, and there were no marked changes, as a whole, from the high war tariff, the reduction in government income being secured by reductions in internal taxes.

Although Arthur had made a good President, he had alienated the old "Stalwart" group of Republican leaders, and his earlier record had made him somewhat suspect to the reform element in spite of their approval of what he had done while in office. Dignified in person, he had given the nation a dignified administration, but he had not caught the imagination of the people, and unfortunately reform is never popular. There was no demand from any important quarter for his renomination, and as Platt announced, "Blaine's turn has come."

There were signs that all might not be easy going for the Republicans in the campaign of 1884. The mid-term elections of 1882 had been marked by Democratic victories, including an overwhelming one in New York, and there was a growing feeling that the efforts of the greater State bosses to control national politics and conventions which had been so notable in 1880 had gone too far.

THE CAMPAIGN OF 1884

When the Republican Convention met at Chicago the result was almost a foregone conclusion. Arthur received a large complimentary vote but the heavy political guns were on the side of Blaine, who was nominated for the Presidency on the fourth ballot, and John A. Logan, long the boss of Illinois, was added for the second office. Both nominations were extremely disliked by the better elements in the party. Theodore Roosevelt, then a young man beginning public life, wrote to his new friend, Henry Cabot Lodge, that "It is impossible for me to say that I consider Blaine and Logan as fit nominees, or proper persons to fill the offices of President and Vice-President." Later, when he had taken the stump for Blaine, he told one audience that Blaine "was nominated against the wishes of the most intellectual and honorable men of the great seaboard cities," but that he had been honestly nominated and therefore it was necessary for the party to stand by him.

On the other hand there were many Republicans, with less strong stomachs than Roosevelt and Lodge, who could not bring themselves either to vote or to advise the American people to vote for candidates whom they considered totally unfit.

An unexpectedly large bolt from party regularity occurred, and those independent Republicans who felt that the attainment of decent government was worth one Republican rebuke organized committees and advised the Democrats that they would vote for their candidate if he were such as they could accept.

That party, in its convention at Chicago, which met on July 8, took only two ballots to nominate Grover Cleveland, reform Governor of New York, in spite of Tammany opposition. Cleveland, who was a self-made Buffalo lawyer, had risen with clean hands through the political offices of sheriff of the county and Mayor of Buffalo to the governorship of the State, though Roosevelt, hide-bound to party, referred to him only as "the Sheriff." The nomination was acceptable to the reform Republicans, and the fight for election promised to be the most hotly contested in many campaigns.

It proved to be one of the most disgraceful in our annals, the charges brought against both candidates being "worthy," as *The Nation* said, "of the stairways of a tenement-house." Private papers which reflected on Blaine's private life were bought and submitted to Cleveland for use in the campaign. When he read them, he immediately tore them up and threw them into the fire with the remark that the other side could "have a monopoly of the dirt." His followers, however, were less scrupulous, and every possible old calumny against Blaine was raked up and made the most of. On the other hand, Cleveland's public record being found above reproach, his life was searched for a smirch which might serve to deprive him of votes.

Although the war had been over nearly twenty years, the "bloody shirt" was still considered one of the drawing cards for the Republicans, so orators tried to prove Cleveland's lack of patriotism because he had not been in the army. The facts were that during the war his mother was a widow with four sons, and extremely poor. Two of the sons promptly enlisted and of the other two, Grover was the only one who was in a position to contribute to his mother's support. The Republicans, however, found a fact which they hoped to be a winner. Cleveland's private life during his maturity had been as blameless as his public, but it was discovered that some years earlier he had made a slip, and had had an illegitimate child, although he had made what amends he could by the subsequent support of both mother and son. When informed that the enemy had unearthed this and was going to use it, he telegraphed to his supporters "whatever you say, tell the truth," and the truth was told.

Both parties were trying to gain the Irish Catholic vote, which was important, especially in the pivotal State of New York, and as *The Irish World* was supporting Blaine it looked as though he might get the suffrage of this then alien-minded group, until the very last week of the campaign. He had just reached New York after a speaking tour in the West, and a dinner was tendered him at the old Fifth Avenue Hotel, at which, for some reason, the Reverend S. D. Burchard had been chosen to make an address. Blaine was tired and was paying little or no attention to what the clergyman was saying.

TWO INSULTS.
[World, Oct. 31.]

"RUM, ROMANISM AND REBELLION."

Religion, Without Regard to Sect, Rises in Indignation.

PROTESTANTS, HEBREWS AND CATHOLICS.

Sharp Denunciation of the Blaine Ecclesiastical Ovation.

The HERALD has received numerous communications denouncing as indecorous and injudicious the remarks made by Rev. Dr. Burchard at the Blaine ecclesiastical reception on Wednesday.

WILL LOSE BLAINE THOUSANDS OF VOTES.
[Star, Oct. 31.]

CLERGYMEN IN POLITICS.
[Graphic, Oct. 31.]

MIGHT HAVE SPARED THE CHURCH.
[Truth, Oct. 31.]

BLAINE KNOW NOTHINGISM REVIVED.
[Albany Argus, Oct. 31.]

THE BLAINE BANQUET LYING SLOGAN.
[Newburg Register, Oct. 30.]

DRAGGING RELIGION INTO POLITICS.
PHILADELPHIA, Pa., Oct. 30, 1884.

HE WAS REPORTED CORRECTLY.
PHILADELPHIA, Pa., Oct. 30, 1884.

THE NEW YORK HERALD OF NOVEMBER 1, 1884, REPRINTED SOME OF THE PROTESTS AROUSED BY BURCHARD'S SPEECH

He thus did not notice when the reverend gentleman, engaged in a sphere in which he obviously did not belong, declared that "we are Republicans, and don't propose to leave our party and identify ourselves with the party whose antecedents have been Rum, Romanism, and Rebellion."

The alliterative political catastrophe ran over the nation like fire. Blaine was ruined. The election was so close that for several days after it the result was in doubt, and depended on the electoral vote of New York, where it was finally conceded that Cleveland had won by the narrow margin of 1149 votes in a total of almost 1,200,-000. Considering the number of votes always bought on both sides in an election, which would certainly have amounted to many times 1100 in a State like New York, it may be impossible always in so close a contest to say which side had been "honestly" elected, but it seems certain that the Reverend Mr. Burchard's inept sally into politics turned enough votes from Blaine to dash the last hope of that candidate for the highest office in the land.

For the nation there can be no doubt of the benefit of having had the Republican rule of nearly a quarter of a century come to a temporary end. As we have said, in such a form of government as ours or England's it is highly advantageous to have two strong and virile parties, whichever one's own views may induce one to adhere to. It is almost equally bad for an opposition to wander too long in the wilderness without being sobered by the responsibility of office as it is for the party in power to remain there so long as to become corrupt and irresponsible through an overweening sense of its ability to retain control of office whatever it may do.

Unfortunately, although the Democrats had at last, for the first time since Buchanan, elected a President, they had done so under circumstances which would make his success almost impossible. Cleveland's election had been brought about only by the aid given by the discontented Republicans known as "Mugwumps"—a term now applied to any independent voter—but they, having rebuked their own party for the nomination of Blaine, could not be counted permanently in the Democratic camp. Moreover, though the Independents had decided the election, they were made up of many reformers and extremists, who would only be satisfied with much more than any practical statesman would be able to accomplish. Both parties, also, were still split on the question of sound money, a majority of the Democrats being against it. In the civil service, Presidents from Arthur on felt the need and duty of reform, but in this they were all, of either party, to have the professional politicians against them, most of the public lukewarm or opposed, and only a small group of the better element appreciative.

SOME OF CLEVELAND'S DIFFICULTIES

Cleveland at once encountered this condition. The Democrats had been out of office for twenty-four years. They were hungry for spoils. Practically all public offices were held by Republicans, and only 12 per cent were protected by the civil service. The resultant pressure on the President was colossal. For months the killing business of filling minor positions, "the d——d everlasting clatter for office," as Cleveland expressed it in a desperate personal letter to a friend, kept up. This disgraceful waste of the time and strength of our Presidents will continue until, as in England, we get all our postmasterships, custom-house positions, and innumerable other minor appointments which it is absurd to have depend on the party in power, out of politics, and on a permanent basis of non-partisan efficiency.

Cleveland did his best, but satisfied no one. When, after the most careful examination, and in the face of the threat that it would lose him 10,000 votes, he reappointed the Republican postmaster in New York City, a howl went up from the politicians and "political workers." They would not be satisfied with less than all the possible offices open to them, 88 per cent of the whole. On the other hand, the Mugwumps and reformers, men like Carl Schurz and Elliot F. Shepherd, were disgruntled at any signs of political appointment, and strong Republicans like Roosevelt, who understood the exigencies of the case well enough, emitted howls of glee whenever the President made an appointment that could be made to appear an abandonment of the reform principle.

One of the most interesting threads running through our history, though it has never received any special consideration other than episodic, is that of the conflict between the Executive and legislative powers, to which we have several times referred. Except for occasional dramatic episodes, like Wilson's contest with the Senate over the ratification of the Peace Treaty, it is assumed that the various departments work more or less in harmony. In fact, especially between legislature and Executive, there has been a constant struggle for power, chiefly due to the desire on the part of the Senate or Congress as a whole to encroach on the prerogatives of the President. We saw this as one of the crucial moments in the administration of Andrew Johnson, and it was due to Cleveland that in one point the balance was restored.

In his Cabinet, which included Thomas F. Bayard as Secretary of State, William C. Whitney in the Navy, and Daniel Manning in the Treasury, the President had decided to number two Southerners, L. Q. C. Lamar of Mississippi as Secretary of the Interior and Augustus H. Garland of Arkansas as Attorney-General. The Southern appointments aroused much resentment among the Republicans, both in the press and Senate, but were confirmed. In July, however, a few months after his inauguration, Cleveland suspended a Federal district attorney in Alabama and appointed another in his stead. When the Senate met in December, it demanded that the Attorney-General submit to it all the papers in the case, and passed a vote of censure on him when, on the President's advice, he declined to do so.

The Senate pointed to the Tenure-of-Office Act, which it had passed to entrap President Johnson and to enlarge its own power, but Cleveland was obdurate, and it was clear that in cases in which an official did not come under the civil service the executive head of the government could not be held accountable for his running of the governmental machinery if he lost all control of his subordinates. In this case the President was supported by the public and finally, in 1887, the Senate repealed the law which had violated the spirit of the Constitution, thus closing the last chapter in Johnson's impeachment case.

One of the great dangers in a democracy is the influence exerted upon legislators by what have come to be known as "pressure groups," and the purchase of the votes of such groups by passing legislation especially designed to win their favor. One of the most powerful of these groups for the past two generations has been that of the veterans of our several wars, who have been responsible for the huge scandals of our pension disbursements, which to a considerable extent have come to be nothing but a dole given to a favored class. The topic will be referred to again in our final chapter, but finds its place here because Cleveland was the first President who attempted to grapple with the growing evil, and thus added to his list of enemies the influential Grand Army of the Republic.

Since the Civil War both political parties had bid for "the soldier vote" by favoring pensions in their platforms, and in the first two years of Cleveland's administration 56,875 names had been added to the pension roll as against 41,467 in the last two years of Arthur's term, bringing the total by the end of 1887 to over 406,000, including 33,000 Mexican War survivors or their widows whom Cleveland had added. The President had no wish to deprive any ex-soldier or his dependents of a pension if his case merited one, but the amount of fraud and graft which had grown up about the system had already become staggering. An impetus to these had been given by the passage in 1879 of the Arrears-of-Pension Act, one of those measures which are always enacted in response to pressure as post-war years pass to extend the field of government bounty.

Under this Act, a pensioner could claim not only his pension for disability but also back pay from the time to which the disability could be traced. The number of claims presented monthly rose sixfold immediately after the passage of the Act, and a class of pension lawyers grew up who made their living by seeking out persons with real or fraudulent claims, and getting the pensions awarded for a share in the back pensions. In many cases Congress took the matter out of the hands of the Pension Bureau by passing special bills awarding the pensions to individuals, more than 2000 such bills being sent to Cleveland for his signature. On investigation a great proportion of the claims were shown to be wholly fraudulent, and the President vetoed as many of these as he had time to examine.

In 1887, Congress, under pressure, again attempted to widen the circle of those who could share in the plunder by passing the Dependent Pension Bill, under which any one who had served three months in the war (finished twenty-two years before) could demand $12 a month if he were disabled and dependent on himself for support even though he had never received any injury from his brief war service. In other words, if a man got drunk, fell off a wagon and disabled himself, he could claim $12 a month for life from the United States because, somewhere from twenty-two to twenty-six years before he had served for three months in the army or navy. This bill also Cleveland vetoed.

Any honest and loyal citizen, whether ex-service man or not, should have seen that such a veto was wholly justified, as were those of all the vetoed private bills, none of which were negatived by the President without an exposition of their fraudulent character. Although the Grand Army of the Republic formally upheld him, the resentment against him among the members of that body was so strong that he had to withdraw his acceptance of the invitation to appear at their meeting in September on account not only of threats of personal violence against him, which he did not fear, but of clear evidence that the office of President would be subjected to great indignity if he attended.

The feeling of the veterans, which had reached the "100 per cent" stage of post-war emotion, had been further stirred by a gracious act which the President had endeavored to perform toward the South, although himself, of course, a Northerner. The war had been over for nearly a generation. The South was reinstated, and

Cleveland thought it time that old resentments should be buried. In the attic of the War Department were a lot of Confederate regimental flags, and the President made

VIRGINIA FLAGS AT HOME AGAIN

Secretary of War Returns All That Can be Identified.

PLACED IN THE MUSEUM

Box Contains Sixty-two War Banners—Was Sent to Governor.

FROM *THE TIMES DISPATCH*, RICHMOND, OF MARCH 28, 1905
Courtesy of the Confederate Museum, Richmond.

the suggestion that these be restored to the States of the South. Although this was done with the approval of the entire country under Roosevelt in 1905, the time was not yet ripe for such action, and Cleveland was so bitterly assailed on all sides, especially by the Republican politicians and the Grand Army posts, that he had to withdraw the order. Honest as was his attitude on pensions and kindly as was his intention in the flags episode, both won him the hostility of a considerable section of the voters.

Another act won him enemies in other quarters. The public land and its usurpation had become no less a scandal than pensions, and Cleveland was the first President to be greatly interested in conservation. During his term he rescued 80,000,000 acres which had been occupied illegally, but this gained him the hostility of the railroads, cattle kings, and innumerable lesser fry who had been profiting at the expense of the nation.

The railroads, and with them a number of the big business interests affiliated with them in one way and another, were further outraged by the passage of the Interstate Commerce Act on February 4, 1887, one of the most important measures of Cleveland's first term, though it was not generally effective in practice until considerably later. It was, however, a landmark in the relations of business to government and in our ways of thought.

We have already noted the facility, as in the case of the Standard Oil Company, with which powerful and unscrupulous men could build up their own larger enterprises at the expense of the small and weak by secret agreements with the roads by which they got rebates, lower rates, and other favors. We have also noted the fight on the roads made by the Western legislatures in the interests of the farmers and other shippers. Many of the State laws which were aimed at curbing the abuses had been fought by the railroads through the courts, as well as by less legitimate means, but in 1876 one of the cases, which had been appealed to the Supreme Court, that of Munn vs. Illinois, had brought an epoch-making decision from that tribunal.

This decision affirmed that "property does become clothed with a public interest when used in a manner to make it of public consequence, and affect the community at large. When, therefore, one devotes his property to a use in which the public has an interest, he, in effect, grants to the public an interest in that use, and must submit to be controlled by the public for the common good."

Other decisions had followed, and finally, under Cleveland, the Interstate Commerce Act was passed which, among other things, prohibited special rates, rebates, and other unfair practices, such as discrimination between persons or places. It also made pooling illegal, required that schedules of rates must be made public, and instituted a commission to hear complaints, supervise the interstate roads, and assist in bringing suits against offending companies.

Although the Democratic Party was for cheap money and free silver, the President was sound on both points and continued throughout his term to urge upon Congress the repeal of the Bland-Allison Act which had forced the government to buy, before Cleveland was to leave office, a total of about $311,000,000 of silver from the silver mine owners, and to coin this huge sum into steadily depreciating silver dollars. These were worth only about seventy-five cents in 1888, were useless in foreign exchange, and disliked by the people. Cleveland clearly recognized that it would be only a question of time when this steady adulteration of our currency system at the minimum rate of $24,000,000 a year would seriously damage the national credit, cause the disappearance of hoarded gold, and threaten the very solvency of the government, but he could secure no action by Congress.

Nor was he any more successful with the tariff. Like his recent predecessors, he was faced with an annually mounting surplus of revenue over expenses, due to the prosperity of the country and the excessive duties collected under the war tariff. Such surpluses as $103,000,-000 in 1887 and $119,000,000 in 1888 could not be retained in the Treasury without curtailing seriously the amount of money in circulation. Nor could they be used to purchase the moderate amount of government bonds outstanding, both because there was a question as to the legality of such action and also because, as such bonds formed the basis of the national bank currency, the debt could not be retired without heavily curtailing the circulating medium. On the other hand, if the surpluses could neither be retained nor used to pay off our debt, they were a constant temptation to Congress to resort to all sorts of extravagant measures of expenditure.

Cleveland studied the problem from the other standpoint, that of reducing the unnecessary revenue and lightening the burden of taxation. The more he did so, the more he became convinced of the impolicy, from the point of view of the welfare of all citizens, of continuing to raise prices by protecting certain manufacturers, employing only about 15 per cent of the total number of persons engaged in industry. On December 6, 1887, he devoted, for the first time in our history, the whole of the annual message to one problem, the tariff. In his last message, 1888, he returned to it again, as he did to his other plans of reform, and complained of "the many millions more to be added to the cost of living of our people" under the tariff, and "to be taken from our consumers, which unreasonably swell the profits of a small but powerful minority," which "is not equality before the law."

Though a tariff revision bill was passed by the House at the very end of Cleveland's term it was blocked by Senator Nelson W. Aldrich and others in the Republican Senate, and the President was able to accomplish nothing more than focussing public attention upon the question. From then on, it was to become one of the leading political issues.

In some of the phrases of Cleveland's last message we begin to feel that we are entering upon the arena of the political struggles of the new age. The Civil War had cut a wide swath between the ante-bellum and post-bellum America, and now that struggle was fast fading into history. We glimpse the new period ahead when the

President declared to Congress that "Communism is a hateful thing and a menace to peace and organized government; but the communism of combined wealth and capital, the outgrowth of overweening cupidity and selfishness, which insidiously undermines the justice and integrity of free institutions, is not less dangerous than the communism of oppressed poverty and toil, which, exasperated by injustice and discontent, attacks with wild disorder the citadel of rule. He mocks the people who proposes that the government shall protect the rich and that they in turn will care for the laboring poor. Any intermediary between the people and their government or the least delegation of the care and protection the government owes to the humblest citizen in the land makes the boast of free institutions a glittering delusion and the pretended boon of American citizenship a shameless imposition."

The nation had passed across the dead centre, and was beginning to gain momentum in the direction of new and vital issues.

Our country is rich in the men and women who have risen to distinction as workers and leaders. Our country is rich in natural scenes of beauty and grandeur. Our country is rich in buildings which have expressed the courage, tenacity, and imagination of our people.

The final pages of each volume of this edition of James Truslow Adams's *History of the United States* present in attractive form some of these outstanding personalities, some of the most thrilling moments of our history, some of our most beautiful natural scenes, some of the most conspicuous representations of our architectural imagination—a veritable panorama of American life.

JOHN BROWN ARRAIGNED BEFORE THE COURT AT
CHARLESTOWN, WEST VIRGINIA

Painted by James E. Taylor. In the collection of the Library of Congress.

In 1859, John Brown with a party of nineteen, part white and part colored, seized the arsenal at Harper's Ferry, Virginia, and terrorized the town. His plan was to start an insurrection among the slaves. He was captured by a small Federal force commanded by Colonel Robert E. Lee, and speedily brought to trial. He was convicted of treason, criminal conspiracy, and murder in the first degree, and after a fair trial he was sentenced to be hanged on Friday the second of December, 1859.

Although he was hailed as a martyr by a small group in the North, the majority of sober opinion condemned and deplored his action, which further inflamed feeling in the South and widened the breach between the two sections.

GRANT AND LEE

Memorial portraits by C. D. Mosher of Chicago, printed in 1888 with the title "Two Heroes of the Late War. America Reunited Forever." From the Library of Congress.

The awfulness of the tragedy of the Civil War in our country is forcibly brought to our minds as we look upon the faces of Grant and Lee—two great Americans, different in their upbringing, different in individual traits, but alike in the qualities of sterling character. They were friends at West Point, each admired the other during the great conflict, and on the fateful morning at Appomattox each showed the other the finest qualities of American soldier and gentleman.

UNIFORMS AND BADGES TO DISTINGUISH RANK IN
THE UNION AND CONFEDERATE ARMIES

From the "Atlas to Accompany the Official Records of the Union and Confederate Armies."

Top Row—*Left to right:* Union Army—Lieutenant-General, Undress; Brigadier-General, Full Dress; Colonel of Infantry, Full Dress; Captain of Artillery, Full Dress; Major of Cavalry, Full Dress; Lieutenant-Colonel, Surgeon, Officer's Overcoat and Staff Trousers; Sergeant-Major, Artillery, Full Dress; Sergeant, Infantry, Full Dress; Private, Infantry, Fatigue Marching Order; Corporal, Cavalry, Full Dress; Private, Light Artillery, Full Dress; Greatcoat, for all mounted men.

Second Row—*Left to right:* Union Army—Epaulettes, from Second Lieutenant to Lieutenant-General; Shoulder Straps, from Second Lieutenant to Lieutenant-General; Buttons, of the Staff, Infantry, Artillery, Engineers, Ordnance, Topographical.

Third Row—*Left to right:* Confederate Army—General; Colonel, Infantry; Colonel, Engineers; Major, Cavalry; Surgeon-Major, Medical Department; Captain, Artillery; First Lieutenant, Infantry; Sergeant, Cavalry; Corporal, Artillery; Private, Infantry; Infantry, Overcoat; Cavalry, Overcoat.

Lower Row—*Left to right:* Confederate Army—Collar Badges, from Second Lieutenant to General; Sleeve Badges, General, Colonel, Captain, Lieutenant; Chevrons, Sergeant-Major, Quartermaster Sergeant, Ordnance Sergeant, First Sergeant, Sergeant, Corporal; Caps, General; Colonel, Cavalry; Captain, Infantry; Lieutenant; Buttons, General Officers, Engineers Officers, Artillery Officers, Infantry Officers, Riflemen Officers, Cavalry Officers, Enlisted men of Artillery.

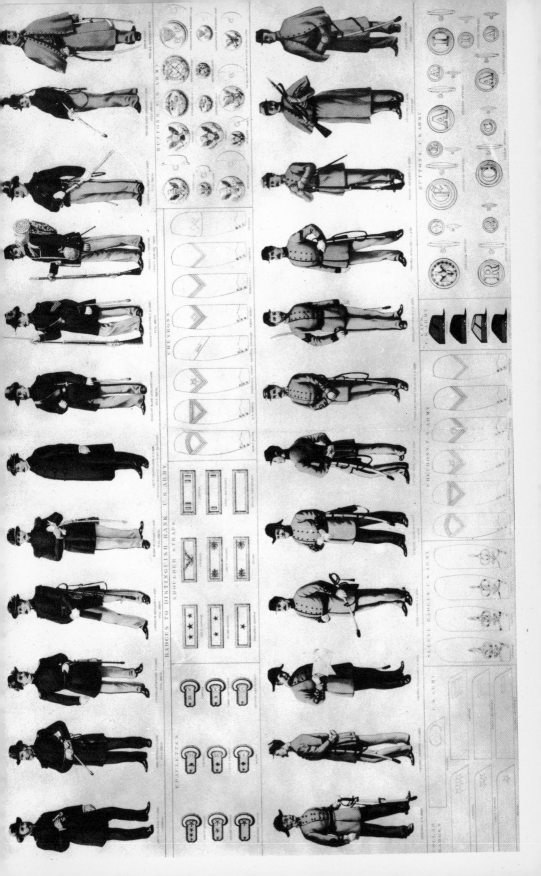

FARRAGUT AT THE BATTLE OF MOBILE BAY

*From a painting by William H. Overend in the Wadsworth Atheneum,
Hartford, Connecticut.*

While Grant was fighting Lee's army in Virginia, and Sherman was advancing through Georgia, Farragut was attacking the last great Confederate seaport, Mobile. The chief defenses of the city were Fort Morgan on Mobile Point; Fort Gaines; a Confederate flotilla in the harbor; and a network of torpedoes laid in the channel.

Sailing second in a line of battleships, Farragut in his flagship *Hartford*, under heavy fire from the Confederate *Tecumseh*, bore down upon Fort Morgan. To the warning "'Ware torpedoes!" Farragut, trying to pierce the screen of smoke from his post on the main rigging, answered "Damn the torpedoes!" The Federal fleet navigated the torpedo zone successfully and vanquished the iron-clad ram *Tennessee*. Fort Morgan, at the mercy of the converging fire from the Federal army and fleet, was forced to surrender.

GENERAL ULYSSES S. GRANT AND STAFF

From the collection in the War Department.

From left to right they are: Colonel Adam Badeau; General Cyrus B. Comstock; Colonel Frederick T. Dent; Colonel William L. Duff; General John A. Rawlins; Captain Henry C. Robinett; Colonel Ely S. Parker; and General Horace Porter. It is believed that the figure on the extreme right is Colonel Theodore S. Bowers.

ARMY SCENES DURING THE CIVIL WAR

From etchings by Edwin Forbes, 1876, in the J. Pierpont Morgan Collection in the Library of Congress.

Above: Confederate and Union soldiers trading for coffee and tobacco between the lines during a truce.

Below, left: On Picket—an infantryman seeking to protect his rifle from the rain. *Right:* Wash Day—drying clothes on a rifle barrel. In the background is a column on the march.

A BARBER'S SHOP AT RICHMOND

A painting by Eyre Crowe which was exhibited in London. The reproduction is from "The London Illustrated News" of March 9, 1861.

Rather far removed from the glistening white splendors of today that offer practically unlimited opportunities for attainment of feminine, as well as masculine beauty, the simplicities of this emporium of the sixties seem entirely adequate. It is also quite comfortable judging by the attitude of the customers.

THE SURRENDER AT APPOMATTOX

From a painting by B. West Clinedinst.

After four years of continuous warfare the Army of Northern Virginia was forced to yield to overwhelming numbers and resources, and on April 9, 1865, Lee surrendered to Grant at Appomattox Court House.

The meeting between the two generals took place in the sitting room of the McLean house, in the presence of Colonel Orville E. Babcock, Major-General E. O. C. Ord, Colonel Horace Porter, Colonel Charles Marshall, Brevet Major-General J. G. Barnard, Colonel T. S. Bowers, and Colonel E. S. Parler. The high qualities of both generals shone forth, the generosity of one matching the dignity of the other. Grant offered terms not only honorable but magnanimous. By exempting the surrender of side arms of officers he permitted Lee to retain his magnificent sword, a presentation from the State of Virginia. He also allowed the Confederates, privates as well as officers, who were mounted on their own horses to keep them. "They will need them for the spring plowing," he said. Lee replied, "This will have the best possible effect upon the men . . . and do much toward conciliating our people."

THE LINCOLN MEMORIAL, WASHINGTON, D. C.
SEEN FROM ACROSS THE LAGOON
IN CHERRY-BLOSSOM TIME

Unequalled for its sheer beauty of line, simplicity of design, and perfection of proportion, the Lincoln Memorial stands—America's tribute to one of her greatest leaders. Built of the finest white marble from Yule, Colorado, it occupies a site in Potomac Park selected to make it a part of a general scheme which embraces the Capitol and the Washington Monument. In the number and spacing of its Greek columns it expresses the symbolism of the thirteen original States and the present union of forty-eight. The architect, Henry Bacon, worked for ten years to complete and execute his design. The splendid figure of Lincoln, notable for its simple dignity, which occupies the centre of the building, is the creation of Daniel Chester French. It is a monumental work in marble, rising to a height of over thirty feet. The mural paintings on the north and south wall, containing forty human figures, are the work of Jules Guérin, who combined color and line to express Freedom, Fraternity, and Immortality. Unlike many masters, Mr. Guérin employed no young assistant painters, even for so simple a matter as filling in background and repeating motives, but painted every stroke himself.

THE MONSTERS

A group of the Legendary Gods of the Hopi Indians of Arizona, one of a series of paintings of the Tribal Dancers by Fred Kaboti, a Hopi, done under the auspices of the Museum of the American Indian, Heye Foundation, New York City. The painting depicts the masked figures of the Katchinas, legendary protectors of the race, who appear every February in a series of ceremonial dances handed down from the earliest times.

THE PROGRESS OF THE CENTURY

A Currier and Ives lithograph of 1876 eloquent of the pride of the nation in the discoveries and inventions of the century, among which were the Lightning Steam Press, the Electric Telegraph, the Locomotive, and the Steamboat.

GLORY TO GOD IN THE HIGHEST PEACE GOOD WILL TOWARD MEN

LIBERTY AND UNION NOW AND FOR EVER

ONE AND INSEPARABLE

ANDREW JOHNSON'S TAILOR SHOP AT
GREENVILLE, TENNESSEE

President Andrew Johnson was humbly born in a log hut in Raleigh, North Carolina. He had little education and was unable to write until taught by his young wife.

Starting as a tailor in this shop at Greenville, Tennessee, he became interested in politics and rose from one political position to another. He became a United States Senator, the only member of the Senate from a seceded State who remained loyal to the Union. He was twice military, as well as twice civil, governor of his State, and in 1864, by Lincoln's own wish, Johnson ran on the Presidential ticket and was elected Vice-President. He succeeded to the Presidency on Lincoln's death.

THE BURNING OF CHICAGO

A Currier and Ives lithograph in the Library of Congress.

The popular version of the cause of the fire is that Mrs. O'Leary's cow while being milked kicked over a lamp in her barn at 137 DeKoven Street. It is true that the fire started in that barn, and a kerosene lamp was found in the ruins, but, since Mrs. O'Leary milked her cow at 5.30, and the fire started about 8.45, the story is open to question.

The description accompanying the lithograph reads: "This terrible Conflagration commenced on Sunday evening, Oct. 8th, 1871, and continued until stopped by the rain on Tuesday morning, Oct. 10th, consuming the whole of the Business portion of the City, all the Public Buildings, Hotels, Newspaper Offices and Rail Road Depots, and extending over an area of Five square Miles. It is estimated that upward of 500 lives were lost, 150,000 people were rendered homeless, and property to the amount of 200,000,000 of dollars was destroyed."

PULLMAN'S EARLY SLEEPING CAR

In 1858, George Pullman, who had suffered the discomforts of the "Bunk" cars (an ordinary day coach divided into four compartments fitted with bunks against the sides), built his first sleeping cars for the Chicago & Alton Railroad. He remodelled two old coaches, built into them ten sleeping sections and two washrooms. Like the more ornate ones that followed, they were furnished in cherry and upholstered in plush. They were lighted by oil lamps, heated with box stoves, and mounted on four-wheel trucks, and Mr. Pullman managed to produce them at a cost of not more than $1000 each. The upper berths were of the swinging type ever since built into American sleepers.

The picture shows one of the oldest sleeping cars, built on the style of the Erie Canal packet, with three tiers of bunks on one side of the car only. This preceded Pullman's No. 9 (his first modern car).

LIFE OF A FIREMAN

ONE OF A SET OF SIX LARGE FOLIO LITHOGRAPHS PUBLISHED BY CURRIER AND
IVES IN 1866, FEATURING FIRE SCENES IN NEW YORK CITY

*By courtesy of The Mabel Brady Garvan Institute of American Arts and Crafts,
Yale University.*

The artists' description from their catalogue of celebrated Fire Pictures, reads: Plate 6.—The Metropolitan System. In the foreground is one of the modern style steam fire engines, drawn by a pair of stalwart horses which are rushing through the streets at full gallop to the scene of conflagration. A hook and ladder truck is just turning the corner, also drawn by horses. It is a night scene, and the fire effect is grand and thrilling, and the whole scene spirited, stirring and life-like.

Size sheet, 26 x 36 inches. Price, $3.

THE NIGHT HERDER ON WATCH DURING
THE ROUND-UP

From the painting by N. C. Wyeth.

"Rounding-up" means to hunt and to bring together thousands of cattle scattered over a large part of the country known as the free range. For convenience in hunting them, the free range is divided into a number of imaginary sections. Into these sections the "boss" of an outfit sends a score or more of punchers, divided into squads of twos and threes, each squad covering a given section. This is called "Riding the circle."

N. C. Wyeth in Scribner's Magazine, March 16, 1906.

A SAMPLER DISCOVERED IN INDEPENDENCE, MISSOURI, AND BELIEVED TO BE OVER 300 YEARS OLD

The sampler, perhaps the oldest in America, had been serving the humble purpose of a table runner under a reading lamp in Independence, Missouri, until it recently came into the possession of Mrs. Ardelia Palmer. Tradition claims that this sampler was given to Robert Beale, Queen Elizabeth's Secretary of Privy Council, by Mary Queen of Scots when she divided her last few jewels, money, and mementoes just before her execution. In 1850 the sampler, then in the possession of Mrs. John G. McCurdy (Elizabeth Beale), was used as a "sample" or example of beautiful stitches in sewing and embroidery for the little girls who attended the Dame School kept by her at Independence. At one end the sampler consists of beautiful and elaborate embroidery showing acorns with blue silk husks, green leaves, and a design of conventionalized pinks, while the other is of very beautiful lace in several patterns. The central portion is embroidered in a small design the same color as the linen. It is signed by the initials "M. F." which it is believed may be those of Mary Fleming, one of the maids of honor to Mary Queen of Scots.

THE FIRST COURT HOUSE IN JACKSON COUNTY

The little log court house of Independence, Missouri, believed to be the oldest court house west of the Mississippi, was built in 1828 at a cost of approximately $150. Today it is used as the headquarters of the Community Welfare League. Independence is known as the "Queen City of the Trails," as it was here that the Santa Fé Trail, the Oregon Trail, and the California Trail started.

FIRST COURT HOUSE OF JACKSON COUNTY
BUILT 1847

COMMUNITY HOUSE

GRINTER
PHOTO
Jan/18

SUMMER IN THE COUNTRY

This Currier and Ives lithograph of 1866 was based on a drawing by Mrs. Frances F. Palmer, who was associated with the firm of lithographers, and used to make many trips into the country, sketching scenes which were used as background for the lithographs. The subject speaks eloquently of the beauties and joys of the country life of the day. The house, with its elaborate decorative detail, is a good example of a type of architecture prevailing at the time.

THE WOODEN INDIAN

Photographs by courtesy of Mr. John L. Morrison.

The Wooden Indian was a figure in the life of the world for over 300 years. From his first appearance in the apothecary's shop, where tobacco was dispensed on prescription, till he took up his stand throughout the country at the cigar-store entrance, he was a national figure. In all probability the first wooden Indians in this country were made by ship-carvers, several of these statues appearing as figureheads on ships.

Among the famous carvers of figureheads who turned to the making of wooden Indians were William Rush, foremost sculptor of Philadelphia in Revolutionary days, Samuel Mac-Intire, Julius Melchers, graduate of the Beaux Arts, Paris, and Herman Meitzer. The sculptors originated designs or copied book illustrations or prints. It is interesting that despite the numbers of these figures made there has never been a duplication. Though usually carved from a single stick of clear pine, extra blocks were sometimes glued on. Prices ranged from $20 for small Indians to $700 which was commanded by Melcher for one of his Detroit braves. There were four classes of design: chiefs; squaws or Pocahontases; blackamoors or Pompeys; and white men;—these last included Sir Walter Raleigh, Uncle Sam, Lord Dundreary, forty-niners, policemen, Highlanders, and a score of others.

At the right is a typical example, still the property of a cigar-store in New York City.

At the left is a Cleveland Indian, a quite fine specimen of carving, now in a museum. This figure was buried for years and dug up when excavations were being made.

THE ARCTIC WHALER

An etching by George Gale.

"The typical spouter that cruised the seven seas in search of whales," writes the artist, "was just the opposite of the clipper, being rugged and stanch in build to stand the terrific wrenching and lifting strain of cutting in a whale. As time was no object, and cargo capacity was the main consideration, they were built bluff, deep, and square-sterned, for they cruised in lonely seas, far from repair-shops or shipyards, and so were obliged to carry all the tools necessary to do such repair work themselves, for they were away from their home port three, four, even five years in a single voyage."

GRAND CANYON, ARIZONA

LOOKING DOWN THE CANYON FROM BETWEEN MOJAVE
AND PIMA POINTS. THE COLORADO RIVER IS SEEN
AT THE BOTTOM OF THE CANYON

What one sees standing at the rim of the Grand Canyon is something long to be remembered. This sight is probably not surpassed in the whole world. It is not merely the thought that this is a most interesting configuration of the earth surface which thrills one, while it inspires, not only with its change in colors and its quiet solemnity, but with the overpowering thought that the work of nature has a permanence and continuity which no work of man ever possesses.

MAMMOTH CAVE

Photograph from the National Park Service, Washington.

To explore the entrance of a great cavern such as the Mammoth Cave in Kentucky brings an experience which is long remembered. One worms one's self through narrow crevices, along slippery and rocky passages and comes out into a tremendous natural theatre, which, when lighted by the electric flash-light or a colored light, shows as sparkling and brilliant as the most priceless jewels.

YELLOWSTONE CANYON, WYOMING

I doubt whether there is another such kaleidoscope in nature. There is apparently every gray from purest white to dull black, every yellow from lemon to deep orange, every red, pink, and brown. These tints dye the rocks and sands in splashes and long transverse streaks which merge into a single joyous exclamation in vivid color whose red and yellow accents have something of the Oriental. Greens and blues are missing from the dyes, but are otherwise supplied. The canyon is edged with lodge-pole forests, and growths of lighter greens invade the sandy slants, at times nearly to the frothing river; and the river is a chain of emeralds and pearls. Blue completes the color gamut from the inverted bowl of sky.

No sketch of the canyon is complete without the story of the great robbery. I am not referring to the several hold-ups of the old stage-coach days, but to a robbery which occurred long before the coming of man—the theft of the waters of Yellowstone Lake; for this splendid river, these noble falls, this incomparable canyon, are the ill-gotten products of the first of Yellowstone's hold-ups.

Robert Sterling Yard.

NATURAL BRIDGE

Photograph by courtesy of the Norfolk and Western Railway.

America has many quaint and beautiful natural bridges. The Natural Bridge in Virginia is one of them. As one approaches this beautiful spot, one has the sense of being in the presence of the homely beauty of primitive American country. It is pleasant to walk up the path from which you get the first view of the famous Natural Bridge. It has taken untold centuries perhaps for the little stream to wear its way through rocks and leave behind a record which is as distinct as if it were carved by hand upon a surface of stone.

NIAGARA FALLS

Although the Falls of Niagara are not the highest falls in the world, they are the most accessible to many people and the best known. Here is presented a scene, which occurs not infrequently in the wintertime when the passage of this tremendous volume of water is halted, as it were, in mid-air and one has the good fortune to see mystic and grotesque figures which are beautiful in the sunlight and in the moonlight.

REDWOODS, CALIFORNIA

From a photograph by courtesy of the Redwood Empire Association.

The foresight of some patriotic Americans has made it possible for us to have in some of our forest reservations many of these stately giants of nature. Perhaps there is nothing more restful or inspiring in all the world than a drive through the California redwoods where one's eyes are in the present and one's thoughts are in the past recalling the many centuries which have nourished these same gigantic trees which are monuments to the forces of mother nature.

"The headwaters of the Tuolumne and Merced rivers, two of the most song-ful streams in the world; innumerable lakes and waterfalls and smooth, silky lawns; noblest forests, the loftiest granite domes, the deepest ice-sculptured can-yons, the brightest crystalline pavements, and snowy mountains soaring into the sky 12,000 and 13,000 feet, arrayed in open ranks and spiry, pinnacled groups partially separated by tremendous canyons and amphitheatres; gardens on their sunny brows, avalanches thundering down their long, white slopes, cataracts roaring gray and foaming in the crooked, rugged gorges, and glaciers in their shadowy recesses working in silence, slowly completing their sculp-tures: new-born lakes at their feet, blue and green, free or encumbered with drifting icebergs like miniature Arctic Oceans, shining, sparkling calm as stars."

So John Muir, our beloved naturalist, has described this land of enchantment.

There was considerable amusement among the group of the Concord School of Philosophy when young Louisa May Alcott began to write stories for girls, but it didn't take long for the world to recognize that *Little Women* and other stories by the same author created a new kind of writing for America. There is not a day that the traveller in Concord doesn't ask to be shown the apple-tree where Louisa thought and wrote out the stories that have so captivated young readers for more than half a century. It would be difficult to estimate the influence of her stories on the generation which grew up in the period after the Civil War.

And near that house there is another interesting place where Nathaniel Hawthorne (*upper left*), mystic and novelist, wrote some of his most fascinating stories. *The Scarlet Letter* will doubtless long remain a true American classic, something which plumbs the depths of New England Puritanism and is at the same time a translation into our own language of the same old struggle so immortally depicted by Dante in his *Divine Comedy.*

We have always liked the writer who is able to give character to the homely scenes in the country about us. Whittier (*upper right*) was not, like Hawthorne or Emerson, a profound seer, but he knew what it was to live the restricted life of New England in the middle of the nineteenth century. He knew its deprivations as well as its joys, its harsh manifestations of winter as well as the beauty and charm of its summer scenes. One of the few poems which we in America could ill afford to lose would be his most popular poem—*Snowbound.*

Some years ago a distinguished American was told that the most popular poet in England and America was Longfellow and he was. Urbane, kindly, affectionate, catholic in his literary tastes, writing in words which could be understood by children in the schools, Longfellow will probably be remembered as long as our American poetry is read.

America takes pride in its men and women of letters. There are not so many as in England. Our literature is not so old as that of England, but there are variety, humor, satire, adventure, idealism, and realism, all reflecting honestly and vividly the life of our country as well as the sincere endeavor of men and women who believe in their craft.

Lowell (*upper left*) was a product of a most enlightened New England, supplemented by the best that Europe could give in learning and travel. He became our first leading man of letters and critic.

Whitman (*upper right*) was more original, perhaps, than Lowell and certainly was more eccentric. Today he stands higher in the judgment of most critics. In his verse there is originality and in his expressions of democracy a sincerity that seem to assure Whitman of a place among the American immortals.

James Whitcomb Riley (*lower right*) was peculiarly a product of the Hoosier State. Just as Lowell in *The Biglow Papers,* so Riley in his dialect verse has given a prominence to something in our history that has gone. It is pleasant to remember the boys in the Brandywine, the old town-wag, "Old Aunt Mary," "Little Orphant Annie," and a host of other characters so familiar to us in the last century—all caught by the fancy and wit and humor of Riley.

There are many persons who think that Mark Twain (*lower left*) is our greatest American writer. Certainly no writer has shown the American quality more conspicuously and perhaps will be long remembered as distinctly American as that individual who took as his *nom de plume* the famous two words from his Mississippi pilot days, Mark Twain.

To Robert Frost (*upper left*) New England is not only rocks and hills and streams, but a quality of character which has contributed much to the fibre of this country. It would be difficult to find on one page of four Americans a more diversified group in temperament and achievement than the four whose likenesses appear on the opposite page.

Booth Tarkington (*lower left*) is a novelist who has portrayed the life of the immortal boy in Penrod. He has depicted with rare humor the life of the Middle West, its conflicts, its business, and in all his work he has shown a sincerity and a faithfulness to his ideal which marks him not only as a novelist, but as a gentleman.

Willa Cather (*lower right*) came out of the West. For a time she taught college students literature and then she turned to the writing of novels. There is no name today in American fiction that stands higher than hers. She has written at least one book, which we think and hope may be long remembered in the annals of American fiction—*My Antonia*.

Sinclair Lewis (*upper right*) is also an American novelist. He came from a little town in Minnesota. He went to Yale. He was known in the University as a radical. He had red hair and was called "Red." It soon became evident that his nickname was doubly suitable. In *Babbitt* Sinclair Lewis has created a character that will be long remembered. He has used a phrase which was common in every town in America and has given it a new name, *Main Street*. There is no satirist who is altogether popular who does not perhaps exaggerate, but certainly Sinclair Lewis is a force in American fiction, and not merely because he is the only American up to the present time who has received the Nobel Prize in literature.